WOMEN
EDUCATION
AND EMPLOYMENT

WOMEN
EDUCATION
AND EMPLOYMENT

A Bibliography of Periodical Citations, Pamphlets, Newspapers and Government Documents, 1970-1980

RENEE FEINBERG

With a Subject Index
by Sanford Berman

Library Professional Publications 1982

First published in 1982 as a Library Professional Publication,
an imprint of The Shoe String Press, Inc.
Hamden, Connecticut 06514

Printed in the United States of America

Library of Congress Cataloging in Publication Data

    Feinberg, Renee.
Women, education, and employment.

Includes indexes.
1. Education of women–United States –Bibliography.
2. Women–Employment–United States –Bibliography.
I. Title.
Z5815.U5F44   016.376'973   82-7816
ISBN 0-208-01967-7   AACR2

For Sheelah

CONTENTS

II. WOMEN: EMPLOYMENT

FOREWORD

Equality Between Women and Men:
Myth or Reality?

Will equality between the sexes become a reality before the close of the eighties? The impetus for equality for minorities and women rose out of the Civil Rights Movement of the sixties. By the seventies, many states had organized commissions to investigate sexism in the schools and to present recommendations for change. It was generally recognized that sexism had become as entrenched in education as it had in the overall social customs of the country. Task force after task force examined text books, curricula, syllabi, guidance and counseling procedures, and teacher training programs. Everywhere sexist practices reinforced society's attitudes that the contributions and experiences of women were less significant than those of men.

An inevitable consequence of traditional attitudes toward women and women's roles is their role in the marketplace. Having less advanced training in fewer careers places a woman in a disadvantageous position when she presents herself as a participant in the labor force. Without significant investment in education and training she is less capable of commanding a high return for her services.

The failure to provide career options for women to the same degree as they are provided for men limits their lifelong potential to earn an income that will enable them to live comfortably. Today's full-time women workers earn, on average, approximately sixty percent of what men earn.

Women need to work at jobs that command a good income. Labor market statistics reveal that more women with young children between the ages of three and eleven are returning to work. The 5.8 million working mothers with preschool children in 1978 had 6.9 million children under age six. More women are divorced or separated and returning to work in order to support

themselves. Nearly two-thirds of all women in the labor force in
1978 were single, widowed, divorced or separated. More women
are heads of households and must work in order to provide for
their families. Among all families, about one out of seven was
headed by a woman by 1978, and thirty-nine percent of black
families were headed by women.

These statistics reveal a commitment to the work force that
stems out of a need to maintain income as sole earned or as dual
earner. Women are in the labor market because they must provide
for themselves and their families.

This is not a recent phenomenon. It is a myth that a woman's
work brings in the extras for the family. Her work provides bread
on the table and rent for the shelter. It is frequently the wife's
earnings which raise a family out of poverty. In husband-wife
families in 1978, 6.1 percent were poor when the wife did not work;
2.7 percent when she was in the labor force.

A significant body of research, which this valuable bibliography includes, provides evidence for the need to make significant
changes in education and employment priorities if women are to
enter the labor market on equal terms with men. The bibliography
is a resource for surveying policies, programs and practices in
order to achieve equality. The bibliography's rich resources create
a foundation for continued study and research on the way in which
women's work lives are affected by their education.

The impetus of the Women's Movement, which began in the
sixties and gained significant momentum in the seventies, appears
to be severely threatened in the eighties. Will the end of this decade
witness a regression to a traditional view of women's roles and the
prevalence of jobs identified by gender, or will the eighties witness
changes that will guarantee equality for all women? Equality, as a
reality, can occur only if it maintains a high place among the
nation's priorities.

1982

DR. GERTRUDE BERGER
Director
Brooklyn College Institute
in Women's Studies

PREFACE

Women's desire for educational achievement and future employment has profound affects on the choices they make and on their role in society. The young woman's leaning in the direction of more education and more meaningful work entails personal choices, for it often means the postponement of marriage and childrearing.

The revolutionary impact of the Women's Movement has so affected life in America that its tenets are generally accepted in theory. Language, both oral and written, employment opportunities and hiring practices, educational programs and academic disciplines now reflect the belief that women must be fully integrated into society, that not to do so is fundamentally wasteful of human resources and destructive of the potential of a free society.

But in fact, are women integrated into the mainstream? Are women entering the labor force to a greater degree? Is there job promotion, salary advancement? Are women employed in management? Are they making policy? Are they in the board rooms?

Are employment opportunities and advancement increasing because more women are entering college or returning to college? Are women able to find the day care that will enable them to leave home? What is the connection between the presumed increase in job opportunities and the educational environment? How are women counseled? Who is staying home and why? Is there job protection for the houseworker? How safe are the factories for women of childbearing years? Can the perception that women have made great strides in the academies as well as in the labor market actually be verified?

These are questions which are examined within the scope of this book. This bibliography lists more than two-thousand citations from English language publications emphasizing the themes of women, work and education, 1970-1980, in the United

States. Citations included have been limited to journal articles, pamphlets, government documents, newspaper items and the ERIC document literature. Monographs and dissertations have not been included.

The indexing services searched to compile this bibliography include: *Readers' Guide to Periodical Literature, PAIS, Index to Legal Periodicals, Psychological Abstracts, Women Studies Abstracts, Business Periodicals Index, Social Science Index, Vertical File Index, American Statistical Index, Congressional Information Service Index, Monthly Catalog, RIE (Resources in Education— ERIC), CIJE (Current Index to Journals in Education—ERIC), New York Times Index,* and *Wall Street Journal Index.* In the case of the *New York Times,* searching was done by computer and titles were imposed and appear in parentheses.

When this bibliography was begun in 1976, it was intended to address the question of how women's education and training influenced their position in the labor force. As it developed, it was expanded to include all issues related to women, education, and employment.

There were well over eight-thousand citations in the original compilation. Upon review, many of the titles were found to be repetitive, uninformative, difficult to complete using the resources of a large undergraduate library, polemical or irrelevant. These were discarded as were those citations to literature which are difficult to access, such as citations from insurance and banking bulletins, local law journals, and women's journals of limited circulation. Unfortunately, many of the references to the alternative literature which blossomed in the seventies were also eliminated for this reason.

Personal interviews were not included unless they touched on large issues such as sex discrimination suits against major companies. Superficial or one-page articles from popular journals were generally omitted. Also excluded were studies on the status of women on a particular campus, and general descriptions of women's studies programs. Finally, none of the criteria for inclusion were regarded as being hard and fast, as certain references were retained if they were intriguing or represented a unique point of view.

The arrangement of this bibliography is in subject categories as shown on the topical outline, and then alphabetic by main entry. Each entry is as bibliographically complete as possible or as deemed necessary for access in a representative undergraduate library. In cases where journals changed names during the decade, the name of the journal at the time of the citation is used.

The following sample citations illustrate the format used:

Periodical article:

Lee, Patrick and Nancy B. Gropper. "Sex role culture and educational practice." HARVARD EDUCATIONAL REVIEW, 44 (3), 1974, pp. 369–410.

Primary author: Lee, Patrick C. and
Secondary author: Nancy B. Gropper.
Article title: "Sex role culture and educational practice."
Journal title: HARVARD EDUCATIONAL REVIEW.
Volume number: 44
Issue number: (3)
Date: 1974
Pages: 369-410.

ERIC document:

Fox, Lynn H. "The mathematically precocious: male or female?" 1974. ERIC, 13 pp. ED 090 473.

Author: Fox, Lynn H.
Document title: "The mathematically precocious: male or female?"
Date: 1974.
Pages: 13
ERIC Document number: 090 473.

Pamphlet:

Association of American Colleges. *Sex discrimination provisions concerning students and employers contained in the Higher Education Act of 1972.* Je. 1972. 5 pp. (Available from AAC, 1818 R Street, NW, Washington, DC 20009.)

Author: Association of American Colleges.
Pamphlet title: Sex discrimination provisions concerning students and employers contained in the Higher Education Act of 1972.
Date: Je. 1972.
Pages: 5
Availability: (Available from AAC, 1818 R Street, NW, Washington, DC 20009.)

Government document:

U.S. Women's Bureau. *Careers for women in the 70's.* Washington, DC: GPO, 1973.

Author: U.S. Women's Bureau.
Title: Careers for women in the 70's.
Government Printing Office: Washington, DC: GPO.
Date: 1973.

Working as a reference librarian, I prepared this bibliography to assist those who, like me, work with undergraduate students who are always in a hurry to find a few articles on a current topic of social interest. As this bibliography sweeps across major fields of study, it has an interdisciplinary appeal to undergraduates who are guided by the table of contents. Each numbered entry is accessed through the subject index provided by Sanford Berman, and the author index by Cheryl Reeves further enhances its usefulness.

All in all, I believe this bibliography on women, work and education, 1970-1980, is a relevant and practical first step in bibliographic control of information on these themes. If it encourages students to reconsider the condition of women in light of the information cited here, it will serve its purpose, a purpose realized because friends lent encouragement and support. Since 1976, work on this book has been a part of holidays with good friends Donna Polhamus, Ken Bobrow and Carole Cochran, evenings with Pat Schuman and Kathleen Weibel, and workdays with Ellen Bolger who has been so generous with her support and clerical assistance. Special thanks are due to Cheryl Reeves who became my alter ego, and to my colleagues at Brooklyn College Library. And to my daughter Sheelah, extra special words of appreciation for playing without me those many weekends.

February 1982

RENEE FEINBERG

INTRODUCTORY NOTE TO USERS

The interest in women and women-related issues as a topic of research and study has grown steadily in the past decade. This bibliography is intended to help researchers and students at all levels to find information in newspaper and journal articles, government documents, and reports on women, education and employment. While it does not list *all* sources, it does provide access to at least some which will cover all the significant subjects of interest within these broad topics.

This bibliography may be used several ways depending upon the purpose a user has in mind. For instance, a student seeking a topic for a paper might use the topical outline for ideas. The citations under that topic might then serve as the basis for the paper or for further research. A researcher with an already identified topic related to women, work, and/or education might use this bibliography as a starting point for collecting references or as a means of expanding a list of references.

Because the bibliography has been limited in ways described in the preface, there are several other sources which might be consulted. Other bibliographics might supplement the information presented here. *Women's Education in the United States: A Guide to Information Sources* by Wilkins provides briefly annotated entries of books, ERIC reports, journal articles and government documents for the period 1968 to 1978. (See References Cited at end of Note for more details.)

Some bibliographies concentrate on more specific areas of women's education. *Women's Higher and Continuing Education* by Westervelt and Fixter covers citations in the period just before that emphasized in this bibliography. Costick, Hereth, and Cirksena compiled two annotated bibliographies on non-sexist career counseling for women. For those doing more extensive research, a listing of doctoral dissertations on women's education is provided by Franklin Parker and Betty June Parker.

Phelps, Farmer, and Backer include 240 abstracts of selected research studies and documents in *New Career Options for Women.* References on working women in the U.S. up through 1973 are found in Bickner's *Women at Work.* Two bibliographies by Soltow *et al.* emphasize the involvement of women in the American labor movement: *Women in American Labor History 1825-1935* and *American Women and the Labor Movement 1825-1974* which expands the earlier publication. Astin, Suniewick and Dweck cover primarily journal articles with some monographs, dissertations and government documents in *Women: A Bibliography on their Education and Careers.*

In addition to these bibliographies on work, education, and women, some more general bibliographies on the Women's Movement and Women's Studies include education and employment among other topics. Krichmar's *Women's Movement in the Seventies* includes international coverage not included in this bibliography. *Women's Studies: A Recommended Core Bibliography* compiled by Stineman covers only books, a form which also is excluded here. International coverage and inclusion of United Nations documents and law cases are features which make *The Sexual Barrier* by Hughes of interest for certain types of research.

Besides using other bibliographies, researchers may want to try the various indexing and abstracting services which might point out sources of information since 1980 or before 1970, or provide additional citations not included here. Each index may be arranged in a different way so it is important to study the directions and examples which are generally found in the front of the index.

It is also important to note that the subject headings used in an index may change over time as new terms come into general use or as new topics of research emerge. For instance, in the *Readers' Guide to Periodical Literature,* the term "sexual harassment" as a subject heading did not appear until 1979.

The indexes listed in the Preface (p. 16), which were used to compile this bibliography, are the most important ones to be consulted for articles and other material that have appeared since 1980. *ERIC* is the main source for educational literature since 1966. Many of the terms relevant to women were used from the inception of *ERIC.* However, "women's studies" and "sex discrimination" did not appear until 1972. "Sex role" and "sex stereotypes" were added in 1974, "affirmative action" first appeared in 1975, and "sex fairness" was added in 1978.

Subject headings in *Readers' Guide* from 1970 to 1980 illustrate an ongoing controversy about the use of subject headings and how they reflect societal attitudes. For example, up until 1974 *Readers' Guide* used the terms "women as lawyers" and "women as teachers," giving the impression that women in these fields were "playing" at being lawyers or teachers. The terms used now are "women lawyers" and "women teachers."

In *Psychological Abstracts* the term "human female" does not appear until the 1974 *Thesaurus of Psychological Index Terms.* Before that there was no term with which to find citations about women. Such subject headings as "working women" and "feminism" were not used until 1977.

To find citations in earlier literature, it may be necessary to look under more general headings, such as "education," "occupation," or "employment." In any case, in searching indexing and abstracting services which have been published over a period of years, it is important to keep track of the subject headings used, and to pay careful attention to any new terms added and old terms deleted over time.

This bibliography can serve as a starting point in studying many aspects of women, work, and education. The sources mentioned above can supplement and expand the effort to investigate these very important topics.

CHERYL REEVES

References

Astin, Helen S., Nancy Suniewick, and Susan Dweck. *Women: A Bibliography on Their Education and Careers.* New York: Behavioral Publications, 1974.

Bickner, Nei Liang. *Women at Work: An Annotated Bibliography.* Los Angeles: University of California, Manpower Research Center, Institute of Industrial Relations, 1974.

Costick, Rita, Fran Hereth, and Kathy Cirksena. *Non-sexist Career Counseling for Women: Annotated Selected References and Resources. Part 1. Part 2.* San Francisco: Far West

Laboratory for Educational Research and Development, 1978.

Hughes, Marija Matich. *The Sexual Barrier: Legal, Medical, Economic and Social Aspects of Sex Discrimination.* Washington, DC: Hughes Press, 1977.

Krichmar, Albert. *The Women's Movement in the Seventies: An International English Language Bibliography.* Metuchen, NJ: Scarecrow Press, 1977.

Parker, Franklin and Betty June Parker. *Women's Education, A World View: Annotated Bibliography of Doctoral Dissertations.* Westport, CT: Greenwood Press, 1979.

Phelps, Ann T., Helen S. Farmer, and Thomas E. Backer. *New Career Options for Women: A Selected Annotated Bibliography.* New York: Human Sciences Press, 1977.

Soltow, Martha Jane, Carolyn Forche, and Murray Massre. *Women in American Labor History 1825-1935.* East Lansing, MI: Michigan State University, School of Labor and Industrial Relations, Library, 1972.

Soltow, Martha Jane and Mary K. Wery. *American Women and the Labor Movement 1825-1974: An Annotated Bibliography.* Methuchen, NJ: Scarecrow Press, 1976.

Stineman, Esther. *Women's Studies: A Recommended Core Bibliography.* Littleton, CO: Libraries Unlimited, Inc., 1979.

Westervelt, Esther Manning and Deborah Fixter. *Women's Higher and Continuing Education: An Annotated Bibliography.* New York: College Entrance Examination Board, 1971.

Wilkins, Kay S. *Women's Education in the United States: A Guide to Information Sources.* Detroit: Gale Research Co. 1979.

I. WOMEN: EDUCATION AND TRAINING

A. EDUCATIONAL STATUS OF WOMEN

1. Preschool, Elementary, and Secondary Education

1. Etaugh, C. and P. Hall. "Is preschool education more highly valued for boys than girls?" SEX ROLES, Je. 1980, pp. 91-100.
2. Federbush, Marcia. "Let them aspire! A plea and proposal for equality of opportunity for males and females in the Ann Arbor Public Schools." Fourth Edition. 1973. ERIC, 92 pp. ED 092 416.
3. Grady, Elaine, John J. Dempsey, and Alice Wilson. "Pregnant adolescents: Educational opportunities." NASSP BULLETIN, 56, Ap. 1972, pp. 55-63.
4. Harrison, Charles H. "Schoolgirl pregnancy: Old problem; new solutions." 1972. ERIC, 65 pp. ED 066 692.

2. Undergraduate

a. General

5. Bennett, S. M. and others. "Factors in programming college experiences for women." JOURNAL OF THE NATIONAL ASSOCIATION of WOMEN DEANS, ADMINISTRATORS, AND COUNSELORS, 44, Wint. 1981, pp. 29-36.
6. Diamond, J. H. "New responsibility for business education." JOURNAL OF BUSINESS EDUCATION, 53, Oct. 1977, pp. 7-8.
7. Ferber, M. A. and W. W. McMahon, "Women's expected earnings and their investment in higher education." JOURNAL OF HUMAN RESOURCES, 14, Summ. 1979, pp. 405-20.

8. Gibbons, S. "Women in media courses continue to grow steadily." JOURNALISM EDUCATION, 34, Oct. 1979, pp. 17-8.

9. Howe, F. "Three missions of higher education for women: Vocation, freedom, knowledge." LIBERAL EDUCATION, 66, Fall 1980, pp. 285-97.

10. Manning, S. "Building a college where women matter." PLANNING HIGHER EDUCATION, 8, Wint. 1979, pp. 1-3.

11. Moore, Kathryn M. and Helen C. Veres. "A study of two-year college women in central New York State: Characteristics, career determinants and perceptions." 1975. ERIC, 93 pp. ED 103 069.

12. Oltman, Ruth M. "The evolving role of the women's liberation movement in higher education." 1971. ERIC, 9 pp. ED 092 416.

13. Peng, Samuel S. and Jay Jaffe. "Women who enter male-dominated fields of study in higher education." AMERICAN EDUCATIONAL RESEARCH JOURNAL, 16, Summ. 1979, pp. 285-94.

14. "Proportion of degrees awarded to women, 1971-1977." CHRONICLE OF HIGHER EDUCATION, Sept. 1979, pp. 12.

15. Richardson, Betty. "The happy hooker in the classroom: Female rights and professional responsibilities." BULLETIN OF THE MIDWESTERN MODERN LANGUAGE AS-SOCIATION, 6, Spr. 1973, pp. 111-20.

16. Sadker, Myra. "Needed - a more supportive environment for college women." 1970. ERIC, 12 pp. ED 067 585.

17. Sandler, Bernice. "What women really want on the campuses." CHRONICLE OF HIGHER EDUCATION, 24 Ap. 1972, pp. 8.

18. Sandler, Bernice. "Women in higher education: A progress report (status of women faculty, students and staff; United States)." AAUP JOURNAL, 67, Nov. 1973, pp. 17-20.

19. Sandler, Bernice. "Women in higher education; what constitutes equity?" VITAL SPEECHES, 38, 15 Je. 1972, pp. 32.

20. TenElshof, Annete. "Purpose and focus of a campus commission on the status of women." JOURNAL OF NATIONAL ASSOCIATION WOMEN DEANS AND COUNSELORS, 36, Wint. 1973, pp. 84-8.

21. "Women teachers give colleges low marks." US NEWS & WORLD REPORT, 9 Je. 1980, pp. 72-3.
22. Women's Equity Action League Educational and Legal Defense Fund. "Facts about women in higher education." 1972. ERIC, 14 pp. ED 163 885.
23. Zell, Laverne C. and Eric A. Weld, Jr. "Women's participation in higher education: A case study of degrees conferred by field of study by nine colleges and universities in the Cleveland metropolitan area, 1973-1974." 1974. ERIC, 67 pp. ED 112 013.

b. Admissions, Enrollment, and Financial Aid

24. Bengelsdorf, Winnie. "Women's stake in low tuition." 1974. ERIC, 20 PP. ED 096 0933.
25. Bob, Sharon. "The myth of equality: Financial support for males and females." JOURNAL OF COLLEGE STUDENT PERSONNEL, 18, My. 1977, pp. 235-8.
26. Clifford, M. M. and E. Walster. "Effect of sex on college admission, work evaluation and job interviews." JOURNAL OF EXPERIMENTAL EDUCATION, 41, Wint. 1972, pp. 1-5.
27. Dipboye, Robert L. and Jack W. Wiley. "Reactions of college recruiters to interviewee sex and self-presentation style." JOURNAL OF VOCATIONAL BEHAVIOR, 10, Feb. 1977, pp. 1-12.
28. Garlock, Jerry C. "An analysis of female enrollment and persistence in five selected industry and technology courses." 1975. ERIC, 6 pp. ED 111 447.
29. Magarrell, Jack. "Women account for 93 percent of enrollment gain." CHRONICLE OF HIGHER EDUCATION, 9 Ja. 1978, pp. 1+.
30. Mayo, J. A. "Sex role stereotyping and personality traits in admissions personnel." COLLEGE AND UNIVERSITY, 53, Wint. 1978, pp. 183-94.
31. Sandler, Bernice. "Sex discrimination, admissions in higher education and the law." COLLEGE AND UNIVERSITY, 50, Spr. 1975, pp. 197-212.
32. "Study of the advantages and disadvantages of student loans to women." 1974. ERIC, 118 pp. ED 111 298.
33. Thomas, Gail L., Karl L. Alexander and Bruce K. Eckland. "Access to higher education: The importance of race, sex,

social class and academic credentials." SCHOOL REVIEW, 87, Feb. 1979, pp. 133-56.

34. "Total college enrollment climbed 3.3% in 1977, women account for 93% gain." WALL STREET JOURNAL, 12 Jan. 1978, pp. 1, col. 5.

c. *Specific Schools*

35. American Association of University Professors, Grand Forks, North Dakota. "The status of women at the University of North Dakota, 1971-72." 1972. ERIC, 13 pp. ED 078 797.

36. "A compilation of data on faculty women and women enrolled at Michigan State University." 1970. ERIC, 56 pp. ED 056 630.

37. Schoen, Kathryn T. and others. "Report of the ad hoc committee to review the status of women at the Ohio State University, Phases I and II." 1971. ERIC, 360 pp. ED 062 959.

38. Smiley, Virginia. "The Chicago Women's Liberation School." CHANGE, 6, Ap. 1974, pp. 18-20.

39. "The status of women at the City University of New York: A report to the Chancellor." 1972. ERIC, 242 pp. ED 081 347.

d. *Women's Colleges*

40. "The case of women's colleges. National report." INTELLECT, 102, Mr. 1974, pp. 334-6.

41. Littleton, Betty. "The special validity of women's colleges." CHRONICLE OF HIGHER EDUCATION, 24 Nov. 1975, pp. 24.

42. Lydon, Susan. "Case against coeducation, or, I guess Vassar wasn't so bad after all." MS, 2, Sept. 1973, pp. 52+.

43. McGrath, Noreen. "Coeducation may place women at a disadvantage, study finds." CHRONICLE OF HIGHER EDUCATION, 8 Ja. 1979, pp. 20.

44. O'Brien, Gael M. "Women's colleges record enrollment increases." CHRONICLE OF HIGHER EDUCATION, 9 Feb. 1976, pp. 10.

45. "Separate and unequal. (Shortcomings and benefits of all women's colleges and departments of woman's studies)." HUMAN BEHAVIOR, 6, Dec. 1977, pp. 63+.

46. Tidball, M. Elizabeth. "Women's colleges and women achievers revisited." SIGNS, 5, Spr. 1980, pp. 504-17.

3. Graduate Study and Professional Schools

a. General

47. Allwood, Cynthia L. "Women in fellowship and training programs." 1972. ERIC, 37 pp. ED 081 371.
48. "As job doors open, more women enroll in graduate school." COMMERCE AMERICA, 14 Feb. 1977, pp. 12+.
49. Chalmers, E. L. "Achieving equity for women in higher education graduate enrollment and faculty status." JOURNAL OF HIGHER EDUCATION, 43, Oct. 1972, pp. 517-24.
50. Fields, Cheryl M. "More women in graduate school." CHRONICLE OF HIGHER EDUCATION, 22 Jl. 1974, pp. 1+.
51. "Graduate study is attracting more women." CHRONICLE OF HIGHER EDUCATION, 26 Nov. 1979, pp. 9.
52. "The higher, the fewer. Report and recommendations: Committee to study the status of women in graduate education and later careers." Submitted to The Executive Board of the Graduate School, Univ. of Michigan, Ann Arbor, Michigan, March 1974. 1974. ERIC, 74 pp. ED 092 024.
53. Logan, S. H. "Testing for sex bias in graduate school admissions." COLLEGE AND UNIVERSITY, 55, Wint. 1980, pp. 156-70.
54. New York State Education Department. "Women in Post-secondary Education in New York State. Students, Faculty, and Administrators. An information paper." 1976. ERIC, 52 pp. ED 138 176.
55. Present, P. E. and D. H. Nelson. "Changing aspirations of women toward government careers and related graduate education." JOURNAL OF THE NATIONAL ASSOCIATION OF WOMEN DEANS, ADMINISTRATORS & COUNSELORS, 41, Wint. 1978, pp. 77-80.
56. Solmon, Lewis C. "Men and women graduate students: the question of equal opportunity. Final report." 1975. ERIC, 212 pp. ED 107 186.
57. Tanney, Mary Faith. "Professional training and women." COUNSELING PSYCHOLOGIST, 4(3), 1974, pp. 77-8.
58. Tenopyr, Mary L. "Attrition of women in graduate school—myths versus reality." 1977. ERIC, 10 pp. ED 152 190.
59. Trivett, David A. "Graduate education in the 70's." 1977.

ERIC, 65 pp. ED 145 763.

60. "Women are flocking to the nation's graduate schools of public administration." WALL STREET JOURNAL, 17 Jan. 1978, pp. 1, col. 5.

b. Doctorates

61. Centra, John A. and Nancy M. Kuykendall. "Women, men and the doctorates." 1974. ERIC, 218 pp. ED 104 179.
62. Kistiakowsky, Vera. "Women doctoral scientist in the United States." 1976. ERIC, 113 pp. ED 159 953.
63. McCarthy, J. L. "Doctorates granted to women and minority group members." SCIENCE, 12 Sept. 1975, pp. 856-9.
64. "99 leading institutions in proportion of Ph. D.'s granted to women, 1973-76." CHRONICLE OF HIGHER EDUCATION, 27 Feb. 1978, pp. 5.
65. Scully, M. G. "Women earn record number of doctoral degrees." CHRONICLE OF HIGHER EDUCATION, 4 Sept. 1979, pp. 16.
66. Sells, Lucy W. "Sex and discipline differences in doctoral attrition." 1973. ERIC, 5 pp. ED 077 475.

c. Medical Schools

67. "Career patterns of unaccepted applicants to medical school: A case study in reactions to a blocked career pathway." 1974. ERIC, 214 pp. ED 106 448.
68. Dube, W. F. "Woman students in U.S. medical schools: Past and present trends." JOURNAL OF MEDICAL EDUCATION, 48, Feb. 1973, pp. 186-9.
69. Gross, Wendy and Elaine Crovitz. "A comparison of medical students' attitudes toward women and women medical students." JOURNAL OF MEDICAL EDUCATION, 50, Ap. 1975, pp. 392-4.
70. Hilberman, Elaine and others. "Support groups for women in medical school: A first year program." JOURNAL OF MEDICAL EDUCATION, 50, Sept. 1975, pp. 867-75.
71. Johnson, Davis G. and William E. Sedlacek. "Retention by sex and race of 1968-1972 U.S. medical school entrants." JOURNAL OF MEDICAL EDUCATION, 50, Oct. 1975, pp. 925-33.
72. Kutner, Nancy G. and Donna R. Brogan. "A comparison of the practice orientations of women and men students at two

medical schools." JOURNAL OF THE AMERICAN MEDI-
CAL WOMEN'S ASSOCIATION, 35, Mr. 1980, pp. 80-6.
73. Walsh, M. R. "Rediscovery of the need for a feminist medical
education." HARVARD EDUCATIONAL REVIEW, 49,
Nov. 1979, pp. 447-66.

4. General Analysis

74. Barabas, Jean. "Women: Their educational and career roles.
An annotated bibliography of selected ERIC references."
1972. ERIC, 77 pp. ED 067 423.
75. Brickley, L. T. and others, eds. "Women and education;
symposium." HARVARD EDUCATIONAL REVIEW, 49,
Nov. 1979, pp. 413-526.
76. Brown-Turner, A. and others. "Knocking down the barriers to
education and employment for women." COMMUNITY &
JUNIOR COLLEGE JOURNAL, 51, Mr. 1981, pp. 4-6.
77. Butchart, R. E. "Issues and trends in American education:
Understanding the retreat from integration and affirmative
action: Implications of some historical parallels." PEABODY
JOURNAL OF EDUCATION, 57, Oct. 1979, pp. 1-9.
78. Butler, Matilda. "Education: The critical filter. A statistical
report on the status of girls and women in elementary and
secondary education." Volume 1. 1979. ERIC, 49 pp. ED 185
704.
79. Council on the Economic Status of Women of St. Paul,
Minnesota. "Women and education." 1979. ERIC, 31 pp. ED
188 345.
80. Davis, Nancy J. and Larry L. Bumpass. "The continuation of
education after marriage among women in the United States:
1970." DEMOGRAPHY, 13, My. 1976, pp. 161-74.
81. "Educational attainment by age, sex, and race, for the United
States: 1970 census of population, supplementary report."
1973. ERIC, 10 pp. ED 081 886.
82. Ekstrom, Ruth B. "Concerns of women in educational
research and development at three stages of professional
development: Student years, early postdoctoral years, and
intermediate professional years." Research memorandum.
1978. ERIC, 48 pp. ED 161 317.
83. Elbert, Sarah. "The changing education of American women."
CURRENT HISTORY, 70, My. 1976, pp. 220-3+.
84. Gaffga, Ruth H. "Employment of women and their education."

ADULT LEADERSHIP, 25(1), 1976, pp. 13–144.

85. Graham, Patricia Albjerg. "Whither equality of educational opportunity?" DAEDALUS, 109, Summ. 1980, pp. 115–32.

86. Hipple, J. L. and A. J. Hill. "Meeting the special needs of women in educational settings." JOURNAL OF THE NATIONAL ASSOCIATION OF WOMEN DEANS AND COUNSELORS, 36, Summ. 1973, pp. 170–72.

87. "How women and minorities rank in U.S. education." INTER-RACIAL BOOKS FOR CHILDREN, 8, 1977, p. 25+.

88. Kimmel, Marcia S. "Educational influences on career opportunities for women." 1974. ERIC, 13 pp. ED 099 323.

89. Lieberman, M. "Education and the feminist movement; symposium." PHI DELTA KAPPAN, 55, Oct. 1973, pp. 98–137; Reply. R. J. Simpson, 55, Ja. 1974, pp. 345–6.

90. Lopata, Helena Znaniecki. "Effect of schooling on social contacts of urban women." AMERICAN JOURNAL OF SOCIOLOGY, 79, Nov. 1973, pp. 604–19.

91. Lord, Sharon B. and Carolyn Patton-Crowder. "Appalachian women: A learning/teaching guide." 1979. ERIC, 188 pp. ED 186 206.

92. McLauchlan, M. "Women's education: A social revolution." ACCOUNTANT, 180, 25 Ja. 1979, pp. 97–8.

93. Minuchin, Patricia. "The schooling of tomorrow's women." SCHOOL REVIEW, 80, Feb. 1972, pp. 199–208.

94. Parker, Franklin. "Women at work and in school: The new revolution." INTELLECT, 106, Feb. 1977, pp. 310–2.

95. "Preliminary report of the Education Committee to the Illinois Commission on the Status of Women." 1973. ERIC, 38 pp. ED 081 361.

96. Pricebonham, S. "Women - bibliography on their education and careers." FAMILY COORDINATOR, 25(1), 1976, pp. 91–2.

97. Scott, Ann. "Educating American women for leisure class." EDUCATIONAL LEADERSHIP, Oct. 1971, pp. 28–31.

98. "Toward educational equity: A report of findings from outreach activities of the National Advisory Council on Women's Educational Programs during 1976." 1977. ERIC, 32 pp. ED 143 587.

99. U.S. Department of Health, Education and Welfare. *Programs for educational equity: Schools and affirmative action.* Washington, DC: GPO, 1975.

100. Wilcox, Kathleen and Pia Moriarity. "Schooling and work: Social constraints on equal educational opportunity." SOCIAL PROBLEMS, 24, Dec. 1976, pp. 204–13.
101. Wilson, Kenneth M. "Today's women students: New outlooks and new challenges." JOURNAL OF COLLEGE STUDENT PERSONNEL, 16, Sept. 1975, pp. 376–81.
102. Wirtenberg, Jeana T. and Charles Nakamura. "Education: Barrier or boon to changing occupational roles of women." JOURNAL OF SOCIAL ISSUES, 32(3), 1976, pp. 165–180.
103. "Women and education: Symposium." EDUCATIONAL LEADERSHIP, 31, Nov. 1973, pp. 99–101+.
104. "Women—Their access to education and employment." LITERACY DISCUSSION, 6, 1976, pp. 35–40.
105. Zuersher, Dorothy J. "Wanted: A more realistic educational preparation for women." EDUCATIONAL LEADERSHIP, 33, Nov. 1975, pp. 118–22.

B. EDUCATIONAL ACHIEVEMENT

1. General

106. Alper, T. G. "Relationship between role orientation and achievement motivation in college women; Wellesley role-orientation scale." JOURNAL OF PERSONALITY, 41, Mr. 1973, pp. 9–31.
107. Bielby, Denise Del Vento and William T. Bielby. *Career continuity of female college students: Capitalizing on educational investments.* 1976. 34 pp. (Available from the Institute for Research on Poverty, Univ. of Wisconsin, Madison, WI 53706.)
108. Campbell, Patricia B. "Feminine intellectual decline during adolescence." 1974. ERIC, 13 pp. ED 091 620.
109. Epstein, C. F. "Structuring success for women: Guidelines for gatekeepers." JOURNAL OF THE NATIONAL ASSOCIATION FOR WOMEN DEANS, ADMINISTRATORS, AND COUNSELORS, 37, Fall 1973, pp. 34–42.
110. Epstein, C. F. and A. L. Bronzaft. "Female modesty in aspiration level." JOURNAL OF COUNSELING PSYCHOLOGY, 21, Ja. 1974, pp. 57–60.
111. Farmer, Helen S. "Environmental, background, and psychological variables related to optimizing achievement and

career motivation for high school girls." JOURNAL OF
VOCATIONAL BEHAVIOR, 17, Ag. 1980, pp. 58–70.

112. Feather, N. T. "Coeducation, values, and satisfaction with
school." JOURNAL OF EDUCATIONAL PSYCHOLOGY,
66, Feb. 1974, pp. 9–15.

113. Ghadially, Rehana. "Career-oriented and noncareer-oriented
college women." JOURNAL OF SOCIAL WORK, 38, Ap.
1977, pp. 45–50.

114. Gould, Jane S. and Abby Pagano. "Sex discrimination and
achievement." JOURNAL OF THE NATIONAL ASSOCI-
ATION OF WOMEN DEANS AND COUNSELORS, 35,
Wint. 1972, pp. 74–82.

115. Heilbrun, A. B., Jr. and others. "Developmental and
situational correlates of achievement behavior in college
females." JOURNAL OF PERSONALITY, 42, Sept. 1974,
pp. 420–36.

116. Lynn, David B. "Determinants of intellectual growth in
women." SCHOOL REVIEW, 80, Feb. 1972, pp. 241–60.

117. McCanne, L. P. F. and others. "Impact of academic
environment and student services on the academic progress
of women." JOURNAL OF COLLEGE STUDENT PER-
SONNEL, 21, Ja. 1980, pp. 74–80.

118. Moss, Jacque D. and Frederick G. Brown. "Sex bias and
academic performance: An empirical study." JOURNAL
OF EDUCATIONAL MANAGEMENT, 16, Aug. 1979,
pp. 197–202.

119. Mott, C. J. "Achievement of women in self-paced earth
science course." COMMUNITY COLLEGE FRONTIERS,
6, Wint. 1978, pp. 4–5.

120. Nichols, Irene A. and Carole B. Shauffer. "Self concept as a
predictor of performance in college women." 1975. ERIC,
33 pp. ED 124–865.

121. Nowicki, Stephen. "Predicting academic achievement of
females from a locus of control orientation: Some problems
and some solutions." 1973. ERIC, 13 pp. ED 087 542.

122. Pomerants, Michael and Charles B. Schultz. "The reliability
and validity of two objective measures of achievement
motivation for adolescent females." EDUCATIONAL AND
PSYCHOLOGICAL MEASUREMENT, 35, Summ. 1975,
pp. 379–86.

123. Rey, Lucy D. "Predicting women's educational aspirations:

The influences of school, family, and sex role attitude variables." SOCIOLOGICAL FOCUS, 7(3), 1974, pp. 99–110.

124. Stent, Angela. "The women's bid for a Rhodes." CHANGE, 6, Je. 1974, pp. 13–6.

125. Vroegh, Karen. "Sex of teacher and academic achievement: A review of research." ELEMENTARY SCHOOL JOURNAL, 76, Ap. 1976, pp. 389–405.

126. Zanna, Mark P. "Intellectual competition and the female student. Final report." 1973. ERIC, 51 pp. ED 072 389.

2. Sex Differences

127. Alexander, Karl L. and Bruce K. Eckland. "Sex differences in the educational attainment process." AMERICAN SOCIOLOGICAL REVIEW, 30, Oct. 1974, pp. 668–82.

128. Bailey, R. C., O. Zinser and R. Edgar. "Perceived intelligence, motivation, and achievement in male and female college students." JOURNAL OF GENETIC PSYCHOLOGY, 127, Sept. 1975, pp. 125–9.

129. Berryman, Charles. "The influences of sex, race, and prior reading ability on newspaper reading skill improvement in the elementary school." 1975. ERIC, 9 pp. ED 096 670.

130. Brook, J. S. and others. "Aspiration levels of and for children: Age, sex, race, and socioeconomic correlates." JOURNAL OF GENETIC PSYCHOLOGY, 124, Mr. 1974, pp. 3–16.

131. Caplan, P. J. and M. Kinsbourne, "Sex differences in response to school failure." JOURNAL OF LEARNING DISABILITIES, 7, Ap. 1974, pp. 232–35.

132. Dwyer, C. A. "Influence of children's sex role standards on reading and arithmetic achievement." JOURNAL OF EDUCATIONAL PSYCHOLOGY, 66, Dec. 1974, pp. 811–16.

133. Etaugh, C. and S. Rose. "Adolescents' sex bias in the evaluation of performance." DEVELOPMENTAL PSYCHOLOGY, 11, Sept. 1975, pp. 663–4.

134. Feldhusen, J. and others. "Prediction of achievement with measures of learning, social behavior, sex and intelligence." PSYCHOLOGY IN THE SCHOOLS, 11, Ja. 1974, pp. 59–65.

135. Finn, J. D. "Sex differences in educational outcomes: A

cross-national study." SEX ROLES, 6, Feb. 1980, pp. 9–26.

136. Finn, Jeremy D. "Sex differences in educational attainment: A cross-national perspective." HARVARD EDUCATIONAL REVIEW, 49, Nov. 1979, pp. 477–503.

137. Fritz, Donald and Michael Szabo. "Sex, race, junior high curriculum, and the acquisition of process skills." 1974. ERIC, 9 pp. ED 091 206.

138. Gjesme, Torgrim. "Sex differences in the relationship between test anxiety and school performance." PSYCHOLOGICAL REPORTS, 30, Je. 1972, pp. 907–14.

139. Graves, D. H. "Sex differences in children's writing." ELEMENTARY ENGLISH, 50, Oct. 1973, pp. 1101–6.

140. Gross, A. L., Jane Faggen and Karen McCarthy. "The differential predictability of college performance of males and females." EDUCATIONAL AND PSYCHOLOGICAL MEASUREMENT, 34, Summ. 1974, pp. 363–5.

141. Joesting, J. "Influence of sex roles on creativity in women." GIFTED CHILD QUARTERLY, 19, Wint. 1975, pp. 336–9.

142. Johnson, Charles, Jr. and Jerry T. Jennings. "Sex differentials in school enrollment and educational attainment." EDUCATION, 92, Sept.-Oct. 1972, pp. 84–8.

143. Katz, Marsha G. "A sex difference in the distribution of oversufficient rewards." 1973. ERIC, 10 pp. ED 084 466.

144. Khan, S. B. "Sex differences in predictability of academic achievement." MEASUREMENT AND EVALUATION IN GUIDANCE, 6, Jl. 1973, pp. 88–92.

145. Laney, Billie Johnson. "A comparative study of expressive and comprehensive vocabulary development in male and female kindergarten children." 1970. ERIC, 126 pp. ED 056 031.

146. Lao, R. C. "Differential factors affecting male and female academic performance in high school." JOURNAL OF PSYCHOLOGY, 104, Ja. 1980, pp. 119–28.

147. Leinhardt, Gaea, Andrea Mar Seewald and Mary Engel. "Learning what's taught: Sex differences in instruction." JOURNAL OF EDUCATIONAL PSYCHOLOGY, 71, Ag. 1979, pp. 432–9.

148. Olive, Helen. "A note on sex differences in adolescents' divergent thinking." JOURNAL OF PSYCHOLOGY, 82, Sept. 1972, pp. 39–42.

149. Primavera, Louis H., William E. Simon and Anne M. Primavera. "The relationship between self-esteem and academic achievement: An investigation of sex differences." PSYCHOLOGY IN THE SCHOOLS, 11, Ap. 1974, pp. 213–6.
150. Samuels, S. Jay and James E. Turnure. "Attention and reading achievement in first-grade boys and girls." JOURNAL OF EDUCATIONAL PSYCHOLOGY, 66(1), 1972, pp. 29–32.
151. Webster, E. G. and others. "Sex comparison of factors related to success in Naval Hospital Corps School." PERSONAL PSYCHOLOGY, 31, Spr. 1978, pp. 95–106.
152. Zimet, Sara Goodman. "Sex differences in reading: The relationship of reader content to reading achievement." 1975. ERIC, 14 pp. ED 105 379.

3. Fear of Success and Underachievement

153. Anderson, Rosemarie. "Motive to avoid success: A profile." SEX ROLES, 4(2), 1978, pp. 239-48.
154. Durio, H. F. and C. A. Kildow. "Nonretention of capable women engineering students." RESEARCH IN HIGHER EDUCATION, 13, 1980, pp. 61-71.
155. Heilbrun, A. B., Jr. and others. "Male sex-gender identification: A source of achievement deficit in college females." JOURNAL OF PERSONALITY, 43, Dec. 1975, pp. 678–91.
156. Hutt, C. "Why do girls underachieve?" TRENDS IN EDUCATION, No. 4, Wint. 1979, pp. 24–8.
157. Illfelder, Joyce K. "Fear of success, sex role attitudes, and career salience and anxiety levels of college women." JOURNAL OF VOCATIONAL BEHAVIOR, 16, Feb. 1980, pp. 7–17.
158. King, Randall Howard. *The labor market consequences of dropping out of high school.* 1978. 114 pp. (Available from: Center for Human Resource Research, Ohio State Univ., Suite 585, 1375 Perry St., Columbus, OH 43201.)
159. Lavach, J. F. and H. B. Lanier. "Motive to avoid success in 7th, 8th, 9th, and 10th grade high-achieving girls." JOURNAL OF EDUCATIONAL RESEARCH, 68, Feb. 1978, pp. 216–8.

160. Mott, Frank L. and Lois B. Shaw. *Work and family in the school leaving years: A comparison of female high school graduates and dropouts.* 1978. 29 pp. (Available from: Center for Human Resource Research, Ohio State Univ., Suite 585, 1375 Perry St., Columbus, OH 43201.)

161. Puryear, Gwendolyn Randall and Martha Shuch Mednick. "Black militancy, affective attachment, and the fear of success in black college women." JOURNAL OF CONSULTING AND CLINICAL PSYCHOLOGY, 42(2), 1974, pp. 263-6.

162. Romer, N. "The motive to avoid success and its effects on performance in schoolage males and females." DEVELOPMENTAL PSYCHOLOGY, 11, Nov. 1975, pp. 689-99.

163. Wilson, Kenneth M. "Characteristics of over- and underachieving Freshmen women in two recent classes, eight liberal arts colleges (with college and specific summary)." 1973. ERIC, 23 pp. ED 081 797.

164. Winchel, Ronald, Diane Fenner and Phillip Shaver. "Impact of coeducation on 'fear of success' imagery expressed by male and female high school students." JOURNAL OF EDUCATIONAL PSYCHOLOGY, 66, Oct. 1974, pp. 726-30.

C. SEX-ROLE STEREOTYPING, SEXISM, AND DISCRIMINATION

1. Problems—General

a. Preschool, Elementary and Secondary

165. Arnold, L. "Sexism in the chemistry curriculum." CURRICULUM REVIEW, 16, Aug. 1977, pp. 180-3.

166. Bernstein, Jean. "The elementary school: Training ground for sex role stereotypes." PERSONNEL AND GUIDANCE JOURNAL, 41, 1972, pp. 97-101.

167. Biber, H., L. B. Miller and J. L. Dyer. "Feminization in preschool." DEVELOPMENTAL PSYCHOLOGY, 7, Jl. 1972, pp. 86+.

168. Bruce, Patricia. "Reactions of preadolescent girls to science tasks." JOURNAL OF PSYCHOLOGY, 86, 1974, pp. 303-8.

169. Cantor, G. N. "Sex and race effects in the conformity behavior of upper-elementary school-aged children." DEVELOP-MENTAL PSYCHOLOGY, 11, Sept. 1975, pp. 661–2.

170. Cegelka, P. T. "Sex role stereotyping in special education: A look at secondary work study programs." EXCEPTIONAL CHILDREN, 42, Mr. 1976, pp. 323–8.

171. Chasen, B. "Sex role stereotyping and prekindergarten teachers." ELEMENTARY SCHOOL JOURNAL, 74(4), 1974, pp. 220–35.

172. Citizens Advisory Council on the Status of Women. "Need for studies of sex discrimination in public schools, revised." 1972. ERIC, 14 pp. ED 091 272.

173. Crow, M. L. and K. Taebel. "Sex-role stereotyping is alive and well in sixth-graders." ELEMENTARY SCHOOL JOURNAL, 76, Mr. 1976, pp. 358–64.

174. Dempsey, Arthur D. "Sexual stereotyping of elementary school boys and girls by pre-service elementary school teachers." TEACHER EDUCATOR, 8, Wint. 1972-73, pp. 34–6.

175. Emery, E. Joan. "The effects of sexism upon the classification of children with learning disability." SCHOOL PSY-CHOLOGY DIGEST, 2(3), 1973, pp. 44–6.

176. Forslund, Morris A. and Ronald E. Hull. "Sex-role identification and achievement at preadolescence." ROCKY MOUNTAIN SOCIAL SCIENCE JOURNAL, 9, Ja. 1972, pp. 105–10.

177. Freeman, H., M. Schockett and E. Freeman. "The effects of gender and race on sex role preferences of fifth grade children." JOURNAL OF SOCIAL PSYCHOLOGY, No. 95, 1975, pp. 105–8.

178. Gillespie, Patricia H. and Albert H. Fink. "The influence of sexism on the education of handicapped children." EXCEP-TIONAL CHILDREN, 41, Nov. 1974, pp. 155–61.

179. Gold, A. R. and M. C. St. Ange. "Development of sex role stereotypes in black and white elementary school girls." DEVELOPMENTAL PSYCHOLOGY, 10, My. 1974, pp. 461+ .

180. Jacobs, Carol. "Sexism in the elementary school." TODAY'S EDUCATION, 61, Dec. 1972, pp. 20–2.

181. Jennings. S. A. "Effects of sex typing in children's stories on preference and recall." CHILD DEVELOPMENT, 46, Mr.

1975, pp. 220–3.

182. Lee, P. C. "Early classroom experience masculine or feminine?" PERSPECTIVE ON EDUCATION, 6, Fall 1973, pp. 10–5.

183. Levy, Betty. "The school's role in the sex-role stereotyping of girls: A feminist review of the literature." FEMINIST STUDIES, 1, Summ. 1972, pp. 5–23.

184. Lynch, Jerry. "Equal opportunity or lip service? Sex-role stereotyping in the schools." ELEMENTARY SCHOOL JOURNAL, 76, Oct. 1975, pp. 20–3.

185. McPherson, Carolyn. "Sex role stereotypes in the elementary school." MIDWEST EDUCATION REVIEW, 6, Wint. 1974, pp. 19–28.

186. Marantz, Sonia A. and Annick F. Mansfield. "Maternal employment and the development of sex-role stereotyping in five-to-eleven-year-old girls." CHILD DEVELOPMENT, 48, Je. 1977, pp. 668–73.

187. May, C. R. and M. E. Fakouri. "Taking a second look at young children's sex role choices." CONTEMPORARY EDUCATION, 45, Summ. 1974, pp. 270–3.

188. Michigan Women's Commission. *Sex discrimination in elementary reading program.* 1975. 58 pp. (Available from Michigan Women's Commission, 230 N. Washington, Lansing, MI 48933.)

189. Montemayor, Raymond. "Children's performance in a game and their attraction to it as a function of sex-typed labels." CHILD DEVELOPMENT, 45, Mr. 1974, pp. 152–6.

190. Mueller, Edward and Barbara Cooper. "The effect of preschool teacher's sex on children's cognitive growth and sexual identity." 1972. ERIC, 60 pp. ED 101 833.

191. Paley, Virginia. "Is the doll corner a sexist institution?" SCHOOL REVIEW, 81, Ag. 1973, pp. 569–76.

192. Peterson, C. and L. McDonald. "Children's occupational sex typing." JOURNAL OF GENETIC PSYCHOLOGY, 136, Mr. 1980, pp. 145–6.

193. Reed, Cheryl L. and others. "The relation of sex role stereotypes to the self-concepts of lower and middle class elementary school children." 1972. ERIC, 18 pp. ED 064 640.

194. Saario, Terry N., C. N. Jacklin and C. K. Tittle. "Sex role stereotyping in the public schools." HARVARD EDUCA-

TIONAL REVIEW, 43, Ag. 1973, pp. 386–416.

195. Sadker, Myra and David Sadker. "Sexual discrimination in the elementary school." NATIONAL ELEMENTARY PRINCIPAL, 52, Oct. 1972, pp. 41–5.

196. Schetlin, E. M. "Sexism, racism and the crucial K-12 years." JOURNAL OF THE NATIONAL ASSOCIATION FOR WOMEN DEANS, ADMINISTRATORS, AND COUN-SELORS, 40, Spr. 1977, pp. 102–3.

197. Serbin, L. A. and others. "A comparison of teacher response to the pre-academic and problem behavior of boys and girls." CHILD DEVELOPMENT, 44, Dec. 1973, pp. 796–804.

198. Simmons, D. "Sex role expectations of classroom teachers." EDUCATION, 100, Spr. 1980, pp. 249–53.

199. Singleton, Louis Cornacchia. "The effects of sex and race on children's sociometric choices for play and work." 1974. ERIC, 65 pp. ED 100 520.

200. Skarin, Kurt and Barbara E. Moely. "Sex differences in competition - cooperation behavior of eight-year-old chil-dren." 1974. ERIC, 11 pp. ED 096 015.

201. Smalley, Diane. "Are we lowering the self-esteem of girls?" SCHOOL AND COMMUNITY, 59, Ap. 1973, pp. 19+.

202. Tolor, A. and B. Tolor. "Children's figure drawings and changing attitudes toward sex roles." PSYCHOLOGICAL REPORTS, 34, Ap. 1974, pp. 343–9.

203. Williams, J. E., S. M. Bennett and D. L. Best. "Awareness and expression of sex stereotypes in young children." DEVELOPMENTAL PSYCHOLOGY, 11, Sept. 1975, pp. 635–42.

b. Post-Secondary

204. American Association of University Professors. "Sex discrimi-nation in Indiana's colleges and universities: A survey." 1972. ERIC, 12 pp. ED 080 066.

205. Astin, Helen S. and Alan E. Bayer. "Sex discrimination in academe." EDUCATIONAL RECORD, 53, Spr. 1972, pp. 101–18.

206. Cantrell, D. Dean. "Women: The perils of testing (stan-dardized tests biased against women)." GRADUATE WOMAN, 73, Jl.-Ag. 1979, pp. 55–6.

207. Christensen, K. C. and William E. Sedlacek. "Differential

faculty attitudes toward blacks, females, and students in general." JOURNAL OF THE NATIONAL AS-SOCIATION FOR WOMEN DEANS, ADMINISTRA-TORS, AND COUNSELORS, 37, Wint. 1974, pp. 78–83.

208. Dinerman, Beatrice. "Sex discrimination in academia." JOURNAL OF HIGHER EDUCATION, 42(4), 1971, pp. 253–64.

209. Hammond, E. H. "Sex discrimination in student personnel functions." NAASP JOURNAL, 11, Wint. 1974, pp. 27–32.

210. Kaplan, L. H. and J. Pao. "Problems facing women students in schools of medicine, law, and business." JOURNAL OF THE AMERICAN COLLEGE HEALTH ASSOCIATION, 26, Oct. 1978, pp. 76–8.

211. LaBay, Michael J. and Randolph N. Foster. "Sexual bias analysis in higher education: An appraisal of methodology useful to institutional researchers." 1973. ERIC, 26 pp. ED 077 996.

212. Onoda, Lawrence and Amalia Mendez. "Affirmative action survey of college counseling centers." JOURNAL OF COLLEGE STUDENT PERSONNEL, 18, Mr. 1977, pp. 104–44.

213. Sadker, Myra and others. "Teacher training texts: Sexist, too." INTERRACIAL BOOKS FOR CHILDREN BULLE-TIN, 10(7), 1979, pp. 4–9.

214. Schwartz, Mary C. "Sexism in the social work curriculum." JOURNAL OF EDUCATION FOR SOCIAL WORK, 9, 1973, pp. 65–70.

215. Scott, Ann. "The half-eaten apple: A look at sex discrimina-tion in the University." 1970. ERIC, 26 pp. ED 041 566.

216. "Sexism and bias: Symposium." JOURNAL OF THE NATIONAL ASSOCIATION FOR WOMEN DEANS, ADMINISTRATORS, AND COUNSELORS, 37, Wint. 1974, pp. 53–97.

217. Westervelt, Esther Manning. "Barriers to women's partici-pation in postsecondary education. A review of research and commentary as of 1973-74." 1975. ERIC, 76 pp. ED 111 256.

c. *General Analysis*

218. Bonk, K. and J. E. Gardner. "Sexism's universal curriculum." AMERICAN EDUCATION, 13, Jl. 1977, pp. 15–9.

219. Brody, C. M. "Do instructional materials reinforce sex stereotyping?" EDUCATIONAL LEADERSHIP, 31, Nov. 1973, pp. 119–22.

220. Brophy, Jere E. and Thomas L. Good. "Of course the schools are feminine but let's stop blaming women for it." PHI DELTA KAPPAN, 55, Sept. 1973, pp. 73–5.

221. Clement, Jacqueline Parker. "Sex bias in school leadership." 1975. ERIC, 65 pp. ED 109 777.

222. Etaugh, C. and V. Hughes. "Teachers' evaluations of sex-typed behavior in children: The role of teacher sex and school setting." DEVELOPMENTAL PSYCHOLOGY, 11, My. 1975, pp. 394–5.

223. Fishel, Andrew. "The politics of sex discrimination in education: A comparative analysis." 1975. ERIC, 29 pp. ED 108 079.

224. Fishel, Andrew and Janice Pottker. "School boards and sex bias in American education." CONTEMPORARY EDUCA-TION, 45, Wint. 1974, pp. 85–9.

225. Gibbons, A. R. and D. Eaton. "Exploring the nature and extent of sex bias." AMERICAN EDUCATION, 10, Ap. 1974. pp. 34–5.

226. Howe, Florence. "Sexism in education and the aspirations of women." CHANGING EDUCATION, Wint.-Spr. 1974, pp. 30–4.

227. Howe, Florence. "Sexism, racism, and the education of women." TODAY'S EDUCATION, 62, My. 1973, pp. 47–8.

228. Kagan, Jerome. "The emergence of sex differences." SCHOOL REVIEW, 80, Feb. 1972, pp. 217–27.

229. Lee, Patrick C. and Nancy B. Gropper. "Sex role culture and educational practice." HARVARD EDUCATIONAL RE-VIEW, 44(3), 1974, pp. 369–410.

230. McDowell, Margaret B. "Male and female chauvinism in the teaching of language and literature." 1972. ERIC, 8 pp. ED 077 031.

231. McLure, Gail T. "Sex discrimination in schools." TODAY'S EDUCATION, Nov. 1971, pp. 33–7.

232. McLure, Gail T. "Sex role stereotyping and evaluation: A systems approach." 1973. ERIC, 23 pp. ED 078 326.

233. McLure, John W. and Gail T. McLure. "Cinderella grows up: Sex stereotyping in the schools." EDUCATIONAL

LEADERSHIP, 30, Oct. 1972, pp. 31–3.

234. Meighan, R. and J. Doherty. "Education and sex roles: Symposium." EDUCATION REVIEW, 27, Je. 1975, pp. 163–248.

235. National Education Association. "Sex role stereotyping in the schools." 1973. ERIC, 71 pp. ED 091 623.

236. "Overcoming sex-role stereotypes: Symposium." CHILD-HOOD EDUCATION, 52, Feb. 1976, pp. 178–204.

237. Patrick, A. E. "Sex-role stereotyping and Catholic education." MOMENTUM, 3, Dec. 1972, pp. 6–13.

238. Racism and Sexism Resource Center for Educators, New York, New York. "Fact sheets on institutional sexism." 1976. ERIC, 16 pp. ED 157 845.

239. Ricks, Frances A. and Sandra W. Pyke. "Teacher perceptions and attitudes that foster or maintain sex differences." INTERCHANGE, 4(1), 1973, pp. 26–33.

240. Rothschild, Nina. "Sexism in the schools: A handbook for action." 1973. ERIC, 72 pp. ED 090 108.

241. Saario, Terry N. "School policies and sex bias." 1974. ERIC, 9 pp. ED 090 661.

242. Sadker, Myra and David Sadker. "Sexism in education: Reality and response." 1974. ERIC, 17 pp. ED 092 839.

243. Sadker, Myra and David Sadker. "Sexism in schools: An issue for the 70's." JOURNAL OF THE NATIONAL ASSOCIATION FOR WOMEN DEANS, ADMINISTRA-TORS, AND COUNSELORS, 37, Wint. 1974, pp. 69–74.

244. "Sexism in American schools? yes . . . but . . ." LEARNING, 1, Ap. 1973, pp. 60–1.

245. Stiles, Lindley J. and P. Martin Nystrand. "The politics of sex in education." EDUCATIONAL FORUM, 38(4), 1974, pp. 431–41.

246. Tittle, C. K. "Sex bias in educational measurement: Fact or fiction." MEASUREMENT AND EVALUATION IN GUIDANCE, 6, Ja. 1974, pp. 219–27.

247. Trenholm, Sarah and William R. Todd de Mancillas. "Student perceptions of sexism." QUARTERLY JOURNAL OF SPEECH, 64(3), 1978, pp. 267–83.

248. U.S. Congress. House. *Sex discrimination and sex stereotyping in vocational education.* Washington, DC: GPO, 1975.

249. Wise, Helen D., ed. "Special feature on equality: Racism, sexism, social classism." TODAY'S EDUCATION, Mr.-

Ap. 1974, pp. 75–82.

250. Zach, Lillian and Michelle Price. "The teacher's part in sex role reinforcement." (n.d.) ERIC, 11 pp. ED 070 513.

251. Zimet, Sara G. and Jules Loventhal, eds. "Recommendations for action: Report from the Colorado conference on stereotyping in education." 1974. ERIC, 29 pp. ED 092 472.

2. Textbooks and Curriculum Materials

252. Arlow, Phyllis and Merle Forschl. "Women in the high school curriculum: A review of high school U.S. history and English literature texts." WOMEN'S STUDIES NEWS-LETTER, 3, Summ.-Fall 1975, pp. 11–22.

253. Bernstein, Joanne. "Changing roles of females in books for young children." READING TEACHER, 27, Mr. 1974, pp. 545–9.

254. Bernstein, Joanne. "The image of female teachers as portrayed in fiction for young children: Up for discussion." SCHOOL LIBRARY JOURNAL, Ja. 1973, pp. 79–80.

255. Britton, Gwyneth E. "Danger: State adopted reading texts may be hazardous to our future (racism and sexism perpetuated in reading series)." 1974. ERIC, 36 pp. ED 096 611.

256. Britton, Gwyneth E. "Why Jane can't win (sex stereotyping and career role assignments in reading materials)." 1974. ERIC, 39 pp. ED 092 919.

257. Donlan, Dan. "The negative image of women in children's literature." ELEMENTARY ENGLISH, 49, Ap. 1972, pp. 604–11.

258. Easley, Ann. "Elements of sexism in a selected group of picture books recommended for kindergarten use." 1973. ERIC, 34 pp. ED 104 559.

259. Faggen-Steckler, Jane, Karen A. McCarthy and Carol K. Tittle. "A quantitative method for measuring sex 'bias' in standardized tests." JOURNAL OF EDUCATIONAL MEASUREMENT, 11, Fall 1974, pp. 151–61.

260. Frasher, Ramona and Annabelle Walker. "Sex roles in early reading textbooks." READING TEACHER, 25, My. 1972, pp. 741–9.

261. Graebner, Dianne Bennett. "A decade of sexism in readers." READING TEACHER, 26, Oct. 1972, pp. 52–8.

262. Grant, Anne. "Testing texts for racism and sexism." SCHOLASTIC TEACHER, Feb. 1973, pp. 16-7.

263. Hagar, Margaret E. and Sue Deffenbaugh. "Does Mama Bear always serve the porridge? Sex-role stereotyping in school reading materials." 1974. ERIC, 13 pp. ED 099 806.

264. Jacklin, Carol Nagy and Harriet N. Mischel. "As the twig is bent - sex role stereotyping in early readers." SCHOOL PSYCHOLOGY DIGEST, 2(3), 1973, pp. 30-8.

265. Jay, Winifred T. "Sex stereotyping in selected mathematics textbooks for grades two, four and six." 1973. ERIC, 168 pp. ED 087 627.

266. Jay, Winifred T. and Clarence W. Schminke. "Sex bias in elementary school mathematics texts." ARITHMETIC TEACHER, 22, Mr. 1975, pp. 242-6.

267. Kraft, Linda. "Lost herstory: The treatment of women in children's encyclopedia." SCHOOL LIBRARY JOURNAL, 20, Ja. 1973, pp. 26-35.

268. Kummerow, Kay Louise. "The relationship of age and sex of four, and six-year olds to the perceptions of sex roles as portrayed in children's literature." 1974. ERIC, 81 pp. ED 097 124.

269. Monre, V. "Feminine role in children's books." EDUCATIONAL POLICY, 52, Wint. 1973-74, pp. 93-4.

270. Nadesan, A. "Mother Goose: Sexist." ELEMENTARY ENGLISH, 51, Mr. 1974, pp. 375-8.

271. Nilsen, A. P. "Books a la mode: A reader's digest: Women in children's books." ELEMENTARY ENGLISH, 50, Oct. 1973, pp. 1029-33.

272. O'Donnell, R. W. "Sex bias in primary social studies textbooks." EDUCATIONAL LEADERSHIP, 31, Nov. 1973, pp. 137-41.

273. Oliver, L. "Women in aprons: The female stereotype in children's readers." ELEMENTARY SCHOOL JOURNAL, 74, Fall 1974, pp. 253-9.

274. Prida, Dolores and Susan Ribner. "A feminist view of the 100 books about Puerto Ricans." INTERRACIAL BOOKS FOR CHILDREN, 4(1) 1972, pp. 2+.

275. Rachlin, Susan Kessler and Glenda L. Vogt. "Sex roles as presented to children by coloring books." JOURNAL OF POPULAR CULTURE, 8, Wint. 1974, pp. 549-56.

276. Rinsky, L. A. "Equality of the sexes and children's literature."

ELEMENTARY ENGLISH, 50, Oct. 1973, pp. 1075+.

277. Rose, Karel. "Sleeping beauty awakes: Children's literature and sex role myths." 1973. ERIC, 9 pp. ED 089 322.

278. Rosenberg, M. "Evaluate your textbooks for racism, sexism." EDUCATIONAL LEADERSHIP, 31, Nov. 1973, pp. 107–9.

279. Schnell, Thomas R. and Judith Sweeney. "Sex role bias in basal readers." ELEMENTARY ENGLISH, 52, My. 1975, pp. 737–42.

280. "Sex equality in educational materials." AASA Executive Handbook Series, Vol. 4, No. 1. 1975, ERIC, 24 pp. ED 111 096.

281. "Sex stereotyping in instructional materials." 1973. ERIC, 8 pp. ED 090 550.

282. Shirreffs, Janet H. "Sex-role stereotyping in elementary school health education textbooks." JOURNAL OF SCHOOL HEALTH, 45, Nov. 1975, pp. 519–23.

283. Taylor, M. E. "Sex role stereotypes in children's readers." ELEMENTARY ENGLISH, 50, Oct. 1975, pp. 1045–7.

284. Trecker, Janice Law. "Women in world history texts: Females in male roles." INTERRACIAL BOOKS FOR CHILDREN, 5(4), 1974, pp. 3+.

285. Wilk, Susan L. "The sexual bias of textbook literature." ENGLISH JOURNAL, 62, Fall 1973, pp. 224–9.

286. Zwack, Jean M. "The stereotypic family in children's literature." READING TEACHER, 26, Ja. 1973, pp. 389–91.

3. Non-Sexist Education

a. Preschool and Elementary

287. Beimer, Linda. "Female studies: K-8 suggestions." SOCIAL SCIENCE RECORD, Spr. 1973, pp. 108–11.

288. "Little Miss Muffett fights back; recommended non-sexist books about girls for young readers." 1971. ERIC, 48 pp. ED 057 626.

289. MacEwan, Phyllis Taube. "Liberating young children from sex roles: Experiences in day care centers, play groups, and free schools." 1972. ERIC, 22 pp. ED 080 169.

290. "Materials for sex equality education for use by teachers, parents, and young people." 1974. ERIC, 44 pp. ED 099 894.

291. Price, Eleanor and Robert Rosemier. "Some cognitive and affective outcomes of same-sex versus coeducational grouping in first grade." JOURNAL OF EXPERIMENTAL EDUCATION, 40, Summ. 1972, pp. 70–7.

292. Schmid, Anne McEvoy. "Sexism in the elementary curriculum and how to overcome it: Let brother bake the cake." AMERICAN TEACHER, 57, Nov. 1972, pp. CE-4.

293. Sprung, Barbara. "Guide to non-sexist early childhood education." 1974. ERIC, 179 pp. ED 105 992.

294. Sprung, Barbara. "Non-sexist education: A new focus for early childhood programs." CHILDREN TODAY, Ja.-Feb. 1977, pp. 2–6.

295. Sprung, Barbara. "Opening the options for children: a nonsexist approach to early childhood education." YOUNG CHILDREN, 31, Nov. 1975, pp. 12–21.

b. Secondary

296. Farquhar, Norma and Carol Mohlmar. "Life competence: A non-sexist introduction to practical arts." SOCIAL EDUCATION, 37, Oct. 1973, pp. 516–9.

297. Fowler, L. J. "Sirens and seeresses: Women in literature and the high school curriculum." ENGLISH JOURNAL, 62, Nov. 1973, pp. 1123–6.

298. Green, Cynthia P. "The choice is yours: A women's studies curriculum for non-college bound high school girls." (n.d.) ERIC, 86 pp. ED 107 571.

299. Hawke, Sharryl. "Women's studies in the junior high school. Profiles of Promise. No. 42." 1975. ERIC, 55 pp. ED 104 770.

300. MacLeod, Jennifer S. and Sandra T. Silverman. "You won't do. What textbooks on U.S. Government teach high school girls, with 'Sexism in textbooks: An annotated source list of 150+ studies and remedies.' " 1973. ERIC, 118 pp. ED 091 255.

301. Magnusen, Etta and Jodi Wetzel. "Introducing high school students to the Women's Movement; a directed study project for undergraduates." 1973. ERIC, 17 pp. ED 096 233.

302. Pate, Betti. "Changing roles of women, social studies." 1973. ERIC, 62 pp. ED 079 277.

c. *Post-Secondary*

303. Astin, Helen S. and Allison Parelman. "Women's studies in American colleges and universities." INTERNATIONAL SOCIAL SCIENCE JOURNAL, 25(3), 1973, pp. 389–400.

304. Banner, Lois. *Women in the college curriculum: A preliminary report on the Princeton Project on Women in the College Curriculum.* 1977. (Available from Princeton Project on Women in the College Curriculum, Princeton Univ., Princeton, N.J. 08540.)

305. Doherty, Joan. "The college of education and the feminist movement." 1974. ERIC, 10 pp. ED 098 190.

306. Eaton, Cynthia and Carol Jacobs. "The action on sexism in education—Princeton: Changing the textbooks." AMERICAN EDUCATION, 9, Je. 1973, pp. 26-8.

307. Kjervik, D. K. "Influencing sex role opinions of undergraduate nursing students." JOURNAL OF NURSING EDUCATION, 18, Oct. 1979, pp. 43-9.

308. Loeffler, Marcia. "The feminists and their impact on the college community." COLLEGE STUDENT JOURNAL, 9(1), 1975, pp. 5-8.

309. "Molding of the nonsexist teacher: Symposium." JOURNAL OF TEACHER EDUCATION, 26, Wint. 1975, pp. 291-359.

310. "Women's studies stamp out sexist stereotypes." NATIONS SCHOOLS, 93, Ap. 1974, pp. 29-30.

d. *General Analysis*

311. Bard, Joseph. "Pennsylvania takes major steps to eliminate sexism." PENNSYLVANIA EDUCATION, 4, Oct. 1972, pp. 5+.

312. Collins, Julie A. "A reflective examination of the feminine role: Teaching strategies." HIGH SCHOOL JOURNAL, 28, Mr. 1973, pp. 259-73.

313. Cuffaro, Harriet K. "Reevaluating basic premises: Curricula free of sexism." YOUNG CHILDREN, 30, Sept. 1975, pp. 469-79.

314. Cutler, Marilyn H. "Ridding the schools of sexism: A mixed bag." AMERICAN SCHOOL BOARD JOURNAL, 160, Oct. 1973, pp. 41+.

315. "Eliminating sex discrimination in schools: A source book." 1975. ERIC, 154 pp. ED 109 810.

316. Flake-Hobson, Carol, Patsy Skeen and Bryan E. Robinson.

"Review of therories and research concerning sex role development and androgyny with suggestions for teachers." FAMILY RELATIONS, 29, Ap. 1980, pp. 155–62.

317. Gaite, A. J. H. "Sex stereotyping: Identifying and changing the role and influence of schools." 1974. ERIC, 11 pp. ED 092 828.

318. *Guidelines for equal treatment of the sexes in McGraw Hill Book Company publications.* 1974. (Available from McGraw-Hill, 1221 Avenue of the Americas, New York, N.Y. 10020.)

319. Harrison, Barbara. "Feminist experiment in education." NEW REPUBLIC, 11 Mr. 1972, pp. 13–7.

320. Kirschner, Betty Frankie. "Introducing students to women's place in society." AMERICAN JOURNAL OF SOCIOLOGY, 78, Ja. 1973, pp. 1051–4.

321. McClure, G. T. "Eliminate sex bias in the curriculum." EDUCATIONAL LEADERSHIP, 31, Nov. 1973, pp. 110–3.

322. New Jersey. Department of Education. Office of Equal Education Opportunity. *Resources for nonsexist, interethnic, multiracial education.* 1979, 47 pp. (Available from Department of Education P.O. Box 2019, Trenton, N.J. 08625).

323. Schwartz, L. L. "Can we stimulate creativity in women?" JOURNAL OF CREATIVE BEHAVIOR, 11(4), 1977, pp. 264–7.

324. "Sex equality in school." AASA Executive Handbook Series, Volume 5, No. 2. 1975. ERIC, 31 pp. ED 111 097.

325. "Today's changing roles: An approach to nonsexist teaching. Teaching resources with curriculum related activities: 1. Elementary, 2. Intermediate and Secondary." 1974. ERIC, 108 pp. ED 098 086.

326. Trecker, Janice Law. "Woman's place is in the curriculum." SATURDAY REVIEW, 16 Oct. 1971, pp. 83–86+.

327. Vetter, Louis and others. "Women in the work force: Follow-up study of curriculum materials." Research and Development Series No. 102. 1975. ERIC, 60 pp. ED 109 559.

328. "Women's studies and/or feminist education. Alice Henry, et al." OFF OUR BACKS, 10 Dec. 1977, pp. 7–10.

D. VOCATIONAL AND CAREER TRAINING

1. General

329. "AACJC (American Association of Community and Junior Colleges) study: Women in occupational education." COMMUNITY AND JUNIOR COLLEGE JOURNAL, 47, Ap. 1977, pp. 28–30.

330. Allen, Deena B. "Vocational education: Separate but not equal." 1975. ERIC, 11 pp. ED 116 026.

331. Bjorkquist, D. C. "Women & industrial education." SCHOOL SHOP, 32, Mr. 1973, pp. 58–62.

332. Boundy, Kathleen B. "Eliminating sex bias and discrimination in vocational education." INEQUALITY IN EDUCATION, 22, Jl. 1977, pp. 120–5.

333. Boyer, Elizabeth. "Women—are the technical occupational programs attracting them?" 1973. ERIC, 14 pp. ED 085 065.

334. Brandon, George L. "Research visibility. Educating women for the world of work." AMERICAN VOCATIONAL JOURNAL, 45, Dec. 1970, pp. 34–48.

335. Briggs, Norma. "Women apprentices: Removing the barriers." MANPOWER, 6, Dec. 1974, pp. 2–11.

336. Burzynski, H. G. "Promised land of paraprofessional careers: Technical education for women." AMERICAN VOCATIONAL JOURNAL, 45, Dec. 1970, pp. 21–3.

337. California. Legislature. Joint Committee on Legal Equality. *Career education and women: Edited transcript of hearing.* 1975. 116 pp. (Available from Joint Committee, State Capitol, Sacramento, CA 95814.)

338. "California opens 590 apprentice training programs to women." AIR CONDITIONING, HEATING, AND REFRIGERATION NEWS, 1 Mr. 1976, pp. 1+.

339. (Career education for high school women). NEW YORK TIMES, 16 Dec. 1973, pp. 14, col. 1.

340. Crovitz, Elaine. "Comparison of male and female physician's associate program applicants." JOURNAL OF MEDICAL EDUCATION, 50, Jl. 1975, pp. 672–6.

341. Davidson, S. H. and Margaret T. Shoenhair. "New view; vocational internship education for women." 1976. ERIC, 22 pp. ED 119 789.

342. Dorling, J. "Making a start on training for women." PERSONNEL MANAGEMENT, 7, Dec. 1975, pp. 18–21.

343. (Educating women for careers). NEW YORK TIMES, 13 My. 1972, p. 34, col. 1.

344. Eliason, Carol. "Women in community and junior colleges. Report of a study on access to occupational education." 1977. ERIC, 69 pp. ED 148 429.

345. Ellis Associates, Inc. "Expanding nontraditional opportunities in vocational education." 1977. ERIC, 205 pp. ED 145 136.

346. Feirer, J. L. "Why not women in industrial education?" INDUSTRIAL EDUCATION, 63, Ja. 1974, pp. 19+.

347. Greer, Holly S. and others, "Research to eliminate vocational education role stereotyping effectively." 1978. ERIC, 222 pp. ED 166 564.

348. Laws, Ruth M. "Striving for synergy in adult education as equal partners. A position paper for the Committee on Social Justice in celebration of International Women's Year to promote dialogue, discussion, and planning for elevation of the status of women through adult education." 1975. ERIC, 22 pp. ED 117 524.

349. Lehmann, P. "Cutting sex bias out of vocational education." WORKLIFE, 2, Feb. 1977, pp. 2–5.

350. Mapp, Patricia. "Women in apprenticeship—why not?" Final report, Wisconsin State Department of Industry, Labor, and Human Relations, Madison, Wisconsin. 1973. ERIC, 268 pp. ED 086 880.

351. Mitchell, E. "What about career education for girls?" EDUCATIONAL LEADERSHIP, 30, Dec. 1972, pp. 233–6.

352. Neill, S. B. "Job Corps charts a coed course." WORKLIFE MAGAZINE, 2, Feb. 1977, pp. 6–11.

353. O'Leary, Virginia E. "The Hawthorne effect in reverse: Trainee orientation for the hardcore unemployed woman." JOURNAL OF APPLIED PSYCHOLOGY, 56, Dec. 1972, pp. 491–4.

354. Rieder, C. H. "Work, women, and vocational education." AMERICAN EDUCATION, 13, Je. 1977, pp. 27–30.

355. Roberts, Martha C. and Elizabeth McDaid. "A training program for new paraprofessional child-care workers." PUBLIC WELFARE, 33, Spr. 1975, pp. 32–8.

356. Steele, Marilyn. "Women in vocational education." Project

baseline supplemental report. 1974. ERIC, 154 pp. ED 099 689.

357. Steiger, JoAnn. "Vocational preparation for women: A critical analysis." 1974. ERIC, 29 pp. ED 151 537.

358. Tarr-Whelan, Linda. "Educating women workers." LABOR LAW JOURNAL, 29, My. 1978, pp. 292–9.

359. Thomas, Hollie B. and others. "Impact of an educational program designed to assist women overcome the deterrents to entering non-traditional occupations." 1980. ERIC, 36 pp. ED 186 636.

360. Trecker, Janice Law. "Room at the bottom—girls' access to vocational training." SOCIAL EDUCATION, 38, Oct. 1974, pp. 533–7.

361. U.S. Office of Education. *Vocational education curriculum specialist study guide (teaching/learning modules).* Washington, DC: GPO, 1976.

362. U.S. Women's Bureau. *A women's guide to apprenticeship.* Washington, DC: GPO, 1978.

363. Wexler, H. "Coed practical arts (study by Jeana Wirtenberg of junior high schools in Los Angeles)." AMERICAN EDUCATION, 16, Ap. 1980, pp. 32–3.

364. (Women and career education). NEW YORK TIMES, 1 Oct. 1973, p. 24, col. 4.

2. Needs Assessment

365. Agin, A. A. and J. P. Prather. "Emerging women: Implications for the community college and the business-industrial community." ADULT LEADERSHIP, 25, Je. 1977, pp. 299–300+.

366. Daniel, Milly Hawk. "What are the jobs of the '80s? And are you being prepared for them?" MS, 8, Sept. 1979, pp. 44–5.

367. Lefkowitz, Mary. "Final report on the education and needs of women." 1970. ERIC, 10 pp. ED 081 329.

368. Mitchell, Grace N. "The new majority: The educational needs of present and future women students of the California Community Colleges." 1979. ERIC, 22 pp. ED 178 329.

369. Newman, Betsy. "Beyond the total women: Creative life planning to meet women's needs." PERSONNEL AND GUIDANCE JOURNAL, 57, Mr. 1979, pp. 359–61.

370. Roby, Pamela Ann. "Toward full equality: More job education for women." SCHOOL REVIEW, 84, Feb. 1976,

pp. 181–211.
371. Slark, Julie. "Women's needs assessment." 1980. ERIC, 66
     pp. ED 186 084.
372. Steiger, JoAnn M. and Sara Cooper. "The vocational
     preparation of women: Report and recommendation of the
     Secretary's Advisory Committee on the Rights and Respon-
     sibilities of Women." 1975. ERIC, 76 pp. ED 120 402.

3. Continuing Education

373. "Continuing education and supportive comprehensive services
     to school age mothers." Final evaluation report. 1972.
     ERIC, 79 pp. ED 085 632.
374. Konek, C. and TenElshof, A. "Providing a re-entry bridge for
     women: A need-centered continuing education program."
     ADULT LEADERSHIP, 25, Ap. 1977, pp. 239–41+.
375. Lee, C. O. and others. "A continuing education program for
     the mature women trained in a science: 1. the program."
     1978. ERIC, 39 pp. ED 167 356.
376. Markus, Hazel. "Continuing education for women: Factors
     influencing a return to school and the school experience."
     1973. ERIC, 37 pp. ED 078 296.
377. Mulligan, Kathryn L. "A question of opportunity: Women
     and continuing education." 1973. ERIC, 33 pp. ED 081 323.
378. Osborn, Ruth Helm and Mary Jo Strauss. "Development and
     administration of continuing education for women. 1964-
     1974." 1975. ERIC, 147 pp. ED 116 511.
379. Owens, Otis Holloway and Marilyn Emplaincourt. "Studies
     of the adult learner. Formal education at a standstill:
     Women's views." No. 4. 1977. ERIC, 87 pp. ED 134 122.
380. Richter, Melissa Lewis and Jane Banks Whipple. "A
     revolution in the education of women. Ten years of
     continuing education at Sarah Lawrence College." 1972.
     ERIC, 77 pp. ED 068 754.
381. Riddell, Janet and Sam Bingham. "Continuing education:
     The older wiser student." MS, 2, Sept. 1973, pp 54+.
382. U.S. Women's Bureau. *Continuing education programs and
     services for women.* Washington, DC: GPO, 1971.
383. Wells, Jean A. "Continuing education for women: Current
     development." 1974, ERIC, 17 pp. ED 099 622.
384. Wilms, Barbara "Getting at the women's market in higher
     ed." COLLEGE MANAGEMENT, 8, Ag. 1973, pp. 32–3.

4. Management Training

385. Alpander, G. C. and J. E. Gutmann. "Contents and techniques of management development programs for women." PERSONNEL JOURNAL, 55, Feb. 1976, pp. 76–9.

386. Anundsen, K. "Building teamwork and avoiding backlash: Keys to developing managerial women." MANAGEMENT REVIEW, 68, Feb. 1974, pp. 55–8.

387. Baron, A. S. "Communication skills for the women manager: A practice seminar." PERSONNEL JOURNAL, 59, Ja. 1980, pp. 55–8.

388. Baron, A. S. "Selection development and socialization of women into management." BUSINESS QUARTERLY, 42, Wint. 1977, pp. 61–7.

389. Burke, R. J. and T. Weir. "Readying the sexes for women in management." BUSINESS HORIZON, 20, Je. 1977, pp. 30–5.

390. Burrow, Martha G. *Developing women managers: What needs to be done?* 1978. 32 pp. (Available from AMACOM, 135 West 50th Street, New York, N.Y. 10020.)

391. Goldstein, P. J. and J. Sorensen. "Becoming the executive you'd like to be: A program for female middle managers." S.A.M. NEWS INTERNATIONAL, 42, Fall 1977, pp. 41–9.

392. Gomez-Mejia, L. R. and D. B. Balkin. "Can internal management training programs narrow the male-female gap in managerial skills?" PERSONNEL ADMINISTRATION, 25, My. 1980, pp. 77–83.

393. Herbert, Theodore T. and Edward B. Yost. "Women as effective managers—a strategic model for overcoming the barriers." HUMAN RESOURCE MANAGEMENT, 17, Spr. 1978, pp. 18–25.

394. Kozoll, Charles E. "The relevant, the honest, the possible: Management development for women." TRAINING AND DEVELOPMENT JOURNAL, 27, Feb. 1973, pp. 3–6.

395. Larwood, L. and others. "Training women for management: New problems, new solutions." ACADEMY OF MANAGEMENT REVIEW, 3, Jl. 1978, pp. 584–93.

396. Reha, R. K. "Preparing women for management roles." BUSINESS HORIZONS, 22, Ap. 1979, pp. 68–71.

397. Schwartz, E. B. and W. B. Waetjen. "Improving the self-concept of women managers." BUSINESS QUARTERLY, 41, Wint. 1976, pp. 20–7.
398. Stead, Bette Ann. "Educating women for administration." BUSINESS HORIZONS, 18, Ap. 1975, pp. 51–6.

E. VOCATIONAL COUNSELING

1. Vocational Interest and Career Choice

a. General

399. Almquist, Elizabeth M. and Shirley Angrist. "Career salience and atypicality of occupational choice among college women." JOURNAL OF MARRIAGE AND THE FAMILY, 32, My. 1970, pp. 242–8.
400. Astin, Helen, "Personal and environmental factors in career decisions of young women." Final report. 1970. ERIC, 95 pp. ED 038 731.
401. Bacon, Carolyn and Richard Lerner. "Effects of maternal employment status on the development of vocational-role perception in females." 126(2), 1975, pp. 187–94.
402. Berger, Gertrude and S. H. Blum. "Vocational desires of urban high school seniors: Study of sex differences." PSYCHOLOGY, 15, Nov. 1978, pp. 27–30.
403. Berger, Gertrude. "Females and social occupations: Forced or free choice." SCHOOL COUNSELOR, 25, Mr. 1978, pp. 250–4.
404. Berman, Yitzchak. "Occupational aspirations of 545 female high school seniors." JOURNAL OF VOCATIONAL BEHAVIOR, 2, Ap. 1972, pp. 173–7.
405. Bielby, Denise D. "Maternal employment and socioeconomic status as factors in daughters' career salience: Some substantive refinements." SEX ROLES, 4(2), 1978, pp. 249–65.
406. Blaska, Betty. "College women's career and marriage aspiration: A review of the literature." JOURNAL OF COLLEGE STUDENT PERSONNEL, 19, Jl. 1978, pp. 302–5.
407. Brito, Patricia K. and Carol L. Jusenius. "A note on young women's occupational expectations for age 35." VO-

CATIONAL GUIDANCE QUARTERLY, 27, Dec. 1978, pp. 165–75.

408. Bronzaft, Arline L. "College women want a career, marriage and children." PSYCHOLOGICAL REPORTS, 35, Dec. 1974, pp. 1031–4.

409. Burgette, Patricia Roop. "Perceptions of fifth and sixth grade females of vocational goals and expected life style." 1970. ERIC, 88 pp. ED 082 068.

410. Burlew, Ann Kathleen. "Career and educational choices among black females." JOURNAL OF BLACK PSYCHOLOGY, 3(2), 1977, pp. 88–106.

411. Burlin, Frances-Dee. "Occupational aspiration of adolescent females." 1974. ERIC, 11 pp. ED 124 838.

412. Cashen, V. M., M. L. Lewis and J. A. Lemmon. "Self concept and level of occupational aspiration of institutionalized vs. noninstutionalized female adolescents." PSYCHOLOGY, 16, Ag. 1979, pp. 29–32.

413. Curry, Evans W. and others. "Significant other influence and career decisions: Volume 11. Black and white female urban youth." Research and Development Series No. 138. 1978. ERIC, 191 pp. ED 159 333.

414. Dietrich, Marie C. "Work values evolution in a baccalaureate student nurse population." JOURNAL OF VOCATIONAL BEHAVIOR, 10, Feb. 1977, pp. 25–34.

415. Glogowski, Diane and Wayne Lanning. "The relationship among age category, curriculum selected, and work values for women in a community college." VOCATIONAL GUIDANCE QUARTERLY, 25, Dec. 1976, pp. 119–25.

416. Grosz, Richard D. and Catherine D. Joseph. "Vocational interests of black college women." 1973. ERIC, 17 pp. ED 075 731.

417. Hahn, C. "Me I want to be: Students' aspirations in the Seventies." SOCIAL EDUCATION, 38, Ap 1974, pp. 334–44.

418. Harmon, Lenore W. "The childhood and adolesent career plans of college women." JOURNAL OF VOCATIONAL BEHAVIOR, 1(1), 1971, pp. 45–56.

419. Herman, Michele H. and William E. Sedlacek. "Career orientation of high school and university women." JOURNAL OF THE NATIONAL ASSOCIATION OF WOMEN DEANS, ADMINISTRATORS, AND COUNSELORS,

Summ. 1974, pp. 161–6.

420. Homall, Geraldine M., Suzanne Juhasz, and Joseph Juhasz. "Differences in self-perception and vocational aspirations of college women." CALIFORNIA JOURNAL OF EDUCATIONAL RESEARCH, 26, Ja. 1975, pp. 6–10.

421. Jardine, Lauren L. and Stanley R. Wurster. "A study of attitudes of twelfth grade students toward high-success-oriented college/career goals of females." 1973. ERIC, 31 pp. ED 087 969.

422. Joesting, Joan and Robert Joesting. "The career outlook of women by women's studies students." COLLEGE STUDENT JOURNAL, 8, Feb.-Mr. 1974, pp. 46+.

423. Karman, Felice J. "Women: Personal and environmental factors in career choice." 1973. ERIC, 20 pp. ED 074 400.

424. Karman, Felice J. "Women: Personal and environmental factors in role identification and career choice." 1973. ERIC, 60 pp. ED 084 383.

425. Lamuel, Linda. "Career expressions of women." 1974. ERIC, 9 pp. ED 105 235.

426. Lee, Sylvia L. and others. "High school senior girls and the world of work: Occupational knowledge, attitudes, and plans." 1971. ERIC, 56 pp. ED 047 155.

427. Littig, Lawrence W. "A study of certain personality correlates of occupational aspiration of black and white college women." Final report. 1971. ERIC, 56 pp. ED 056 242.

428. Lyson, Thomas A. "Some plan to be farmers: Career orientations of women in American colleges of agriculture." INTERNATIONAL JOURNAL OF WOMEN'S STUDIES, 2, Ag. 1979, pp. 311–23.

429. McLaughlin, Gerald W. and others. "Socioeconomic-status and career aspirations and perceptions of women seniors in high school." VOCATIONAL GUIDANCE QUARTERLY, 25, Dec. 1972, pp. 155–62.

430. McLure, G. T. and E. Piel. "College-bound girls and science careers: Perceptions of barriers and facilitating factors." JOURNAL OF VOCATIONAL BEHAVIOR, 12, Ap. 1978, pp. 172–83.

431. Matheny, A. P., Jr., A. B. Dolan and J. Z. Krantz. "Cognitive aspects of interests, responsibilities and vocational goals in adolescence." ADOLESCENCE, 15, Summ. 1980, pp. 301–11.

432. Matthews, Esther E. "Personalizing occupational freedom for girls and women." 1970. ERIC, 48 pp. ED 075 734.
433. Mednick, Martha T. "Motivational and personality factors related to career goals of black college women." Final report. 1973. ERIC, 135 pp. ED 081 408.
434. Mowsesian, Richard. "Educational and career aspirations of high school females." JOURNAL OF THE NATIONAL ASSOCIATION OF WOMEN DEANS AND COUNSELORS, 35, Wint. 1972, pp. 65–73.
435. Oliver, Laurel W. "The relationship of parental attitudes and parent identification to career and home-making orientation in college women." JOURNAL OF VOCATIONAL BEHAVIOR, 7, Ag. 1975, pp. 1–12.
436. Patterson, Lois. "Girls career-expression of identity."VOCATIONAL GUIDANCE QUARTERLY, 21, Je. 1973, pp. 269–75.
437. Pettigrew, Nancy J. and Virlyn A. Boyd. "Career orientations of female students enrolling in agricultural curricula at Clemson University." 1976. ERIC, 12 pp. ED 120 423.
438. Picou, J. Steven and Evans W. Curry. "Structural, interpersonal and behavioral correlates of female adolescents' occupational choices." ADOLESCENCE, 8, Fall 1973, pp. 421–32.
439. Plost, Myrna and Martin J. Rosen. "Effect of career models on occupational preferences of adolescents." AUDIO VISUAL COMMUNICATION REVIEW, 22, Spr. 1974. pp. 41–50.
440. Ridgeway, C. "Parental identification and patterns of career orientation in college women." JOURNAL OF VOCATIONAL BEHAVIOR, 12, Fall 1978. pp. 1–11.
441. Schab, F. "What jobs do high school girls want?" INTEGRATED EDUCATION, 11, Nov. 1973, pp. 24–30.
442. Sherman, R. G. and J. H. Jones. "Career choice for women: The new determinants." JOURNAL OF COLLEGE STUDENT PERSONNEL, 17, Jl. 1976, pp. 289–94.
443. Slaney, R. B. "Investigation of racial differences on vocational variables among college women." JOURNAL OF VOCATIONAL BEHAVIOR, 16, Ap. 1980, pp. 197–207.
444. Smith, Eliot R. "Desiring and expecting to work among high school girls: Some determinants and consequences." JOURNAL OF VOCATIONAL BEHAVIOR, 17, Oct. 1980, pp. 218–30.

445. Stein, A. H. "Effects of maternal employment and educational attainment on sex-typed attributes of college females." SOCIAL BEHAVIOR AND PERSONALITY, 1(2), 1973, pp. 111–4.

446. Tangri, Sandra Schwartz. "Occupational aspirations and experiences of college women." 1971. ERIC, 7 pp. ED 060 470.

447. Tinsley, Diane J. and Patricia S. Faunce. "Enabling, facilitating, and precipitating factors associated with women's career orientation." JOURNAL OF VOCATIONAL BEHAVIOR, 17, Oct. 1980, pp. 183–94.

448. Touchton, Judith Gray and Thomas M. Magoon. "Occupational daydreams as predictors of vocational plans of college women." JOURNAL OF VOCATIONAL BEHAVIOR, 10, Ap. 1977, pp. 156–66.

449. Turner, Barbara F. "Socialization and career orientation among black and white college women." 1972. ERIC, 15 pp. ED 074 412.

450. Turner, Barbara F. and Castellano B. Turner. "Race, sex and perception of the occupational opportunity structure among college students." SOCIOLOGICAL QUARTERLY, 16, Summ. 1975, pp. 345–60.

451. Wallace, Jacquelyn L. and Thelma H. Leonard. "Factors affecting vocational and educational decision-making of high school girls." JOURNAL OF HOME ECONOMICS, 63(4), 1971, pp. 241–5.

452. Ware, Mark E. and Robert V. Apprich. "Variations in career cognition measures among groups of college women." MEASUREMENT AND EVALUATION IN GUIDANCE, 3, Oct. 1980, pp. 179–84.

453. White, K. M. and P. L. Ouellette. "Occupational preferences: Children's projections for self and opposite sex." JOURNAL OF GENETIC PSYCHOLOGY, 136, Mr. 1980, pp. 37–43.

454. Wilson, Marian L. "A study of the familial and career attitudes enrolled in typical and atypical programs." 1977. ERIC, 56 pp. ED 138 736.

455. Wolfson, Karen P. "Career development patterns of college women." JOURNAL OF COUNSELING PSYCHOLOGY, 23, Mr. 1976, pp. 119–25.

456. "Women still study for traditional jobs, says New York economist. (Views of Pearl Kamer)." PHI DELTA KAP-

PAN, 62, Oct. 1980, pp. 151+.

b. Sex Differences

457. Allison, E. and P. Allen. "Male-female professionals: A model of career choice." INDUSTRIAL RELATIONS, 17, Oct. 1978, pp. 333-7.

458. Cegelka, P. T., C. Omvig and D. C. Larimore. "Effects of aptitude and sex on vocational interests." MEASUREMENT AND EVALUATION IN GUIDANCE, 7, Jl. 1974, pp. 106-11.

459. Dawkins, Marvin P. "Education and occupational goals: Male versus female black high school seniors." URBAN EDUCATION, 15, Jl. 1980, pp. 231-42.

460. Fottler, Myron D. and Trevor Bain. "Sex differences in occupational aspirations." ACADEMY OF MANAGE-MENT, 23, Mr. 1980, pp. 144-9.

461. Fottler, Myron D. and Trevor Bain. "Managerial aspirations of high school seniors: A comparison of males and females." JOURNAL OF VOCATIONAL BEHAVIOR, 16, Feb. 1980, pp. 83-95.

462. Garrison, Howard H. "Gender differences in the career aspirations of recent cohorts of high school seniors." SOCIAL PROBLEMS, 27, Dec. 1979, pp. 170-85.

463. Goldman, Roy D. and others. "Sex differences in the relationship of attitude toward technology to choice of field of study." 1973. ERIC, 21 pp. Ed 083 508.

464. Hewitt, L. S. "Age and sex differences in the vocational aspirations of elementary school children." JOURNAL OF SOCIAL PSYCHOLOGY, 96, Ag. 1975, pp. 173-7.

465. Hoult, P. P. and M. C. Smith. "Age and sex differences in the number and variety of vocational choices, preferences and aspirations." JOURNAL OF OCCUPATIONAL PSY-CHOLOGY, 51, Je. 1978, pp. 119-25.

466. Karpicke, Susan. "Perceived and real sex differences in college students' career planning." JOURNAL OF COUN-SELING PSYCHOLOGY, 27, My. 1980, pp. 240-5.

467. Lunneborg, P. W. "Service vs. technical interest; biggest sex difference of all?" VOCATIONAL GUIDANCE QUAR-TERLY, 28, Dec. 1979, pp. 146-53.

468. Manhardt, Philip J. "Job orientation of male and female college graduates in business." PERSONNEL PSY-CHOLOGY, 25, Summ. 1972, pp. 361-8.

469. Neice, David E. and Richard W. W. Bradley. "Relationship of age, sex and educational groups to career decisiveness." JOURNAL OF VOCATIONAL BEHAVIOR, 14, Je. 1979, pp. 271–8.

470. New Educational Directions. "Sex as a determinant in vocational choice." Final report. 1977. ERIC, 33 pp. ED 145 135.

471. O'Bryant, S. L., M. E. Durrett and J. W. Pennebaker. "Developmental and sex differences in occupational preferences." JOURNAL OF SOCIAL PSYCHOLOGY, 106, Dec. 1978, pp. 267–72.

472. O'Bryant, S. L., M. E. Durrett and J. W. Pennebaker. "Sex differences in knowledge of occupational dimensions across four age levels." SEX ROLES, 6, Je. 1980, pp. 331–8.

473. Olive, Helen. "Sex differences in adolescent vocational preferences." VOCATIONAL GUIDANCE QUARTERLY, 21, Mr. 1973, pp. 199–201.

474. Polachek, S. W. "Sex differences in college major." INDUSTRIAL AND LABOR RELATIONS REVIEW, 31, Jl. 1978, pp. 498–508.

475. Rose, Harriett A. and Charles F. Elton. "Sex and occupational choice." JOURNAL OF COUNSELING PSYCHOLOGY, 18, Sept. 1971, pp. 456–61.

476. Scott, Craig S., Robert H. Fenske and E. James Maxey. "Change in vocational choice as a function of initial career choice, interests, abilities and sex." JOURNAL OF VOCATIONAL BEHAVIOR, 5, Oct. 1974. pp. 285–92.

477. Siegel, C. L. F. "Sex difference in the occupational choices of second graders." JOURNAL OF VOCATIONAL BEHAVIOR, 3, Ja. 1973, pp. 513–34.

478. Stake, Jayne E. and Ellen Levitz. "Career goals of college women and men and perceived achievement-related encouragement." PSYCHOLOGY OF WOMEN QUARTERLY, 4, Wint. 1979, pp. 151–9.

479. Thomas, Hollie B. "The effects of sex, occupational choice and career development responsibility on the career maturity of ninth-grade students." 1974. ERIC, 9 pp. ED 092 819.

480. Thomas, Hollie B. "The effects of social position, race, and sex on work values of ninth grade students." 1973. ERIC, 11 pp. ED 076 599.

481. Wagner, E. E. and T. O. Hoover. "Effect of sex, religion, and

ethnicity on occupational choice." JOURNAL OF AP-
PLIED PSYCHOLOGY, 59, Ap. 1974, pp. 247–8.

c. Sex-Role Expectations and Stereotypes

482. Almquist, Elizabeth M. "Sex stereotypes in occupational
choice—The case for college women." JOURNAL OF
VOCATIONAL BEHAVIOR, 5, Ag. 1974, pp. 13–22.
483. Ashby, Marylee Stull and Bruce C. Wittmaier. "Attitude
changes in children after exposure to stories about women
in traditional or non-traditional occupations." JOURNAL
OF EDUCATIONAL PSYCHOLOGY, 70, Dec. 1978, pp.
945–9.
484. Bartol, K. M. "Expectancy theory as a predictor of female
occupational choice and attitude toward business." ACA-
DEMIC MANAGEMENT JOURNAL, 19, Dec. 1976, pp.
669–75.
485. Basow, S. A. and K. G. Howe. "Sex bias and career
evaluations by college women." PERCEPTUAL AND
MOTOR SKILLS, 49, Dec. 1979, pp. 705–6.
486. Britton, G. E. "Sex sterotyping and career roles." JOURNAL
OF READING, 17, Nov. 1973, pp. 140–8.
487. California State University. Institute for Human Service
Management. "Research for women: Sex stereotyping, non-
traditional jobs, and vocational training." Final report.
1979. ERIC, 207 pp. ED 176 060.
488. Cook, L. and A. Rossett. "Sex role attitudes of deaf
adolescent women and their implications for vocational
choice." AMERICAN ANNALS OF THE DEAF, 120, Je.
1975, pp. 341–5.
489. Crawford, J. D. "Career development and career choice in
pioneer and traditional women." JOURNAL OF VOCA-
TIONAL BEHAVIOR, 12, Ap. 1978, pp. 129–39.
490. Ditkoff, G. S. "Stereotypes of adolescents toward the
working woman." ADOLESCENCE, 14, Summ. 1979, pp.
277–82.
491. Entwisle, Doris R. and Ellen Greenberger. "Adolescents'
views of women's work role." AMERICAN JOURNAL OF
ORTHOPSYCHIATRY, 42, Jl. 1972, pp. 648–56.
492. Entwisle, Doris R. and Ellen Greenberger. "A survey of
cognitive styles in Maryland ninth graders: Views of
women's roles." 1970. ERIC, 31 pp. ED 043 918.

493. Erickson, Linda G. and Margaret L. Nordin. "Sex-role ideologies and career salience of college women." 1974. ERIC, 22 pp. ED 095 449.

494. Gaskell, J. "Sex-role ideology and the aspirations of high school girls." INTERCHANGE, 8(3), 1977-78, pp. 43-53.

495. Goldman, R. D. "Sex differences in the relationship of attitude toward technology to choice of field of study." JOURNAL OF COUNSELING PSYCHOLOGY, 20, Sept. 1973, pp. 412-8.

496. Gottlieb, D. "Work and families: Great expectations for college seniors." JOURNAL OF HIGHER EDUCATION, 45, Oct. 1974, pp. 535-44.

497. Greenberg, Selma B. "Attitudes of elementary and secondary students toward increased social, economic, and political participation by women." JOURNAL OF EDUCATIONAL RESEARCH, 67, Dec. 1973, pp. 147-52.

498. Harris, S. R. "Sex typing in girls career choices: A challenge to counselors." VOCATIONAL GUIDANCE QUARTERLY, 23, Dec. 1974, pp. 128-33.

499. Heilman, M. E. "High school students' occupational interest as a function of projected sex ratios in male-dominated occupations." JOURNAL OF APPLIED PSYCHOLOGY, 64, Je. 1979, pp. 275-9.

500. Kalunian, P. and others. "Sex role stereotyping in career awareness." ELEMENTARY SCHOOL GUIDANCE AND COUNSELING, 8, Dec. 1973, pp. 135-9.

501. Klundt, Karen K. and Joy M. N. Query. *Occupational role expectations of women students.* 1976. 11 pp. (Available from Western Colorado State College, Gunnison, CO 81230).

502. Marshall, Sandra J. and Jan P. Wijting. "Relationships of achievement motivation and sex role identity to college women's career orientation." JOURNAL OF VOCATIONAL BEHAVIOR, 16, Je. 1980, pp. 299-311.

503. Orcutt, Mary Anna and W. Bruce Walsh. "Traditionality and congruence of career aspirations for college women." JOURNAL OF VOCATIONAL BEHAVIOR, 14, Feb. 1979, pp. 1-11.

504. Reiter, R. G. "Sex and the single field: Girls' and boys' occupational preferences." MEASUREMENT AND EVALUATION IN GUIDANCE, 8, Ap. 1975, pp. 51-4.

505. Richardson, Mary Sue. "Self-concepts and role concepts in the career orientation of college women." JOURNAL OF COUNSELING PSYCHOLOGY, 22(2), 1975, pp. 122-6.

506. Schlossburg, Nancy K. and Jane Goodman. "A woman's place: Children's sex stereotyping of occupations." JOURNAL OF VOCATIONAL GUIDANCE, 20, Je. 1972, pp. 266-70.

507. Sell, Jane Ann. "The relationship between black mothers' attitudes toward sex roles and their educational aspirations and expectations for their daughters." 1973. ERIC, 42 pp. ED 078 996.

508. Touliatos, J. and B. W. Lindholm. "Correlates of attitudes toward the female sex role and achievement, affiliation, and power motivation of college women." ADOLESCENCE, 12, Wint. 1977, pp. 461-70.

509. Valentine, D. and others. "Sex-role attitudes and the career choices of male and female graduate students." VOCATIONAL GUIDANCE QUARTERLY, 24, Sept. 1975, pp. 48-53.

510. Yanico, Barbara J. "Students' self-reported amount of information about 'masculine' and 'feminine' occupations." VOCATIONAL GUIDANCE QUARTERLY, 28, Je. 1980, pp. 344-51.

511. Yanico, Barbara J., Susan I. Hardin and Kent B. McLaughlin. "Androgyny and traditional versus nontraditional major choice among college freshmen." JOURNAL OF VOCATIONAL BEHAVIOR, 12, Je. 1978, pp. 261-9.

2. Vocational Interest Tests and Materials

512. Almquist, Elizabeth M. "Content analysis of the Strong Vocational Interest Blank for Women." JOURNAL OF VOCATIONAL BEHAVIOR, 5, Ag. 1974, pp. 13-22.

513. Carr, Ralph T. and others. "Project women: In a man's world of work: A guide for school counselors." 1972. ERIC, 25 pp. ED 074 216.

514. Casey, Timothy J. "The development of a leadership orientation scale on the SVIB for women." MEASUREMENT AND EVALUATION IN GUIDANCE, 8, Jl. 1975, pp. 96-100.

515. Clopton, James R. and Charles Neuringer. "An MMPI scale to measure scholastic personality in women." PERCEPTUAL AND MOTOR SKILLS, 37, Sept. 1973, pp. 963–6.

516. Cole, Nancy S. "On measuring the vocational interests of women." JOURNAL OF COUNSELING PSYCHOLOGY, 20, Mr. 1973, pp. 105–12.

517. Dewey, C. R. "Exploring interests: A non-sexist method; non-sexist vocational card sort." PERSONNEL AND GUIDANCE JOURNAL, 52, Ja. 1974, pp. 311–5.

518. Elton, Charles F. "A vocational interest test minus sex bias." JOURNAL OF VOCATIONAL BEHAVIOR, 7, Oct. 1975, pp. 207–14.

519. Gough, Harrison G. "Strong Vocational Interest Blank profiles of women in law, mathematics, medicine, and psychology." PSYCHOLOGICAL REPORTS, 37, Ag. 1975, pp. 127–34

520. Hanson, G. R., R. R. Lamb and E. English. "An analysis of Holland's Interest Types of Women: A comparison of the Strong-Holland and the ACT Vocational Interest Profile Scales for Women" JOURNAL OF VOCATIONAL BEHAVIOR, 4, Ap. 1974, pp. 259–69.

521. Heshusius-Gilsdorf, Louis T. and Dale L. Gilsdorf. "Girls are females, boys are males. A content analysis of career materials." PERSONNEL AND GUIDANCE JOURNAL, 54, Dec. 1976, pp. 206–11.

522. Hurwitz, Robin Elaine and Mary Alice White. "Effects of sex-linked vocational information on reported occupational choices of high school juniors." PSYCHOLOGY OF WOMEN QUARTERLY, 2, Wint. 1977, pp. 149–56.

523. Huth, Carol Monnik. "Measuring women's interests: How useful?" PERSONNEL AND GUIDANCE JOURNAL, 51, Ap. 1973, pp. 539–45.

524. Johnson, R. W. "Content analysis of the Strong Vocational Interest Blank for Women." JOURNAL OF VOCATIONAL BEHAVIOR, 5, Ag. 1974, pp. 125–32.

525. Lawler, Alice Cotter. "Career exploration with women using the non-sexist Vocational Card Sort and the Self Directed Search." MEASUREMENT AND EVALUATION IN GUIDANCE, 12, Jl. 1979, pp. 87+.

526. Moche, D. L. "Development of educational materials to

recruit women into scientific careers." AMERICAN JOUR-
NAL OF PHYSICS, 44(4), 1976, pp. 390–1.

527. Mott, Frank L. and Sylvia F. Moore. *The determinants and consequences of occupational information for young women.* 1976, 35 pp. (Available from Center for Human Resource Research, College of Administrative Science, Ohio State University, Columbus, OH 43210).

528. Munley, Patrick, Bruce R. Fretz and David H. Mills. "Female college students' scores on the men's and women's Strong Vocational Interest Blanks." JOURNAL OF COUN-SELING PSYCHOLOGY, 20, My. 1973, pp. 285–9.

529. National Institute of Education. Career Education Program. "Guidelines for the assessment of sex bias and sex fairness in career interest inventories." MEASUREMENT AND EVALUATION IN GUIDANCE, 8, Ap. 1975, pp. 7–11.

530. Prediger, Dale J. "Sex-role socialization and employment realities: Implications for vocational interest measures." JOURNAL OF VOCATIONAL BEHAVIOR, 7, Oct. 1975, pp. 239–51.

531. Spokane, Arnold R. "Occupational preference and the validity of the Strong-Campbell Interest Inventory for college women and men." JOURNAL OF COUNSELING PSYCHOLOGY, 26, Jl. 1979, pp. 312–8.

532. Tittle, C. K. and E. R. Denker. "Kuder Occupational Interest Survey profiles of reentry women." JOURNAL OF COUN-SELING PSYCHOLOGY, 24, Jl. 1977, pp. 293–300.

533. U.S. Center for Vocational and Technical Education. *Women in the work force: Development and field testing of curriculum materials.* Washington, D.C.: GPO, 1973.

534. Verheyden-Hilliard, Mary Ellen. "The use of interest inventories with the re-entering woman." 1974. ERIC, 47 pp. ED 095 369.

535. Vetter, Louise and others. "Career guidance materials: Implications for women's career devlopment." Research and Development Series No. 97 1974. ERIC, 90 pp. ED 106 542.

3. Counseling Methods and Services

a. Youth

536. Birk, Janice M. and Mary Faith Tanney. "Career exploration

for high school women: A model." 1973. ERIC, 27 pp. ED 079 662.

537. Ciborowski, P. J. "Career education seminar for high school females." SCHOOL COUNSELOR, 27, Mr. 1980, pp. 315–7.

538. Cramer, S. H. and others. "Evaluation of a treatment to expand the career perceptions of junior high school girls." SCHOOL COUNSELOR, 25, Nov. 1977, pp. 124–9.

539. McCune, Allen D. "Career education and vocational guidance in a small, rural school district. A counseling approach." 1980. ERIC, 40 pp. ED 183 340.

540. Majchrzak, Shirley. "Preparing young women for tomorrow: A handbook of career counseling strategies for intermediate and high school women." Monograph number 9. 1976. ERIC, 99 pp. ED 117 389.

541. Mitchell, Edna. "What about career education for girls?" EDUCATIONAL LEADERSHIP, 30, Dec. 1972, pp. 233–6.

542. Motsch, P. "Peer social modeling: A tool for assisting girls with career exploration." VOCATIONAL GUIDANCE QUARTERLY, 28, Mr. 1980, pp. 231–40.

543. "Project Women—in a man's world. A program to develop the career awareness of high school girls." 1972. ERIC, 25 pp. ED 098 454.

544. Richards, Diane S. and Joann Brooks. "Secondary students' views on occupational sex stereotyping and sex equity resources for vocational educators and counselors. A project report and bibliography." Information series no. 8. 1979. ERIC, 89 pp. ED 167 782.

545. Rohfeld, R. W. "High school women's assessment of career planning resources." VOCATIONAL GUIDANCE QUARTERLY, 26, Sept. 1977, pp. 79–84.

546. Sharpe, Ruth. "Counseling services for school-age pregnant girls." JOURNAL OF SCHOOL HEALTH, 65, My. 1975, pp. 284–5.

547. Steiger, JoAnn M. "Broadening the career horizons of young women against traditional single-sex enrollment patterns in vocational education." ILLINOIS CAREER EDUCATION JOURNAL, 32 (4), 1975, pp. 7–9.

548. Stevenson, Gloria. "Career planning for high school girls." OUTLOOK QUARTERLY, 17, Summ. 1973, pp. 22–5.

549. Tiedt, Iris M. "Realistic counseling for high school girls." SCHOOL COUNSELOR, 19, My. 1972, pp. 354–6.

550. Woodcock, P. R. and A. Herman. "Fostering career awareness in tenth-grade girls." SCHOOL COUNSELOR, 25, Mr. 1978, pp. 256–9.

b. *Adult*

551. Bartlett, Willis E. and Destry Oldsham. "Career adjustment counseling of 'young-old' women." VOCATIONAL GUIDANCE QUARTERLY, 27, Dec. 1978, pp. 156–64.

552. Boyd, Betty and Mary E. Griffith. "A critical professional need: The counselor for women." ADULT LEADERSHIP, 22, Nov. 1973, pp. 161–2.

553. Brenner, David and Patricia Ann Gazda-Grace. "Career decision making in women as a function of sex composition of career-planning groups." MEASUREMENT AND EVALUATION IN GUIDANCE, 12, Ap. 1979, pp. 8–13.

554. Britton, V. and P. B. Elmore. "Leadership and self-development workshop for women." JOURNAL OF COLLEGE STUDENT PERSONNEL, 18, Jl. 1977, pp. 318+.

555. "Counseling women: Symposium." JOURNAL OF THE NATIONAL ASSOCIATION FOR WOMEN DEANS, ADMINISTRATORS, AND COUNSELORS, 38, Fall 1974, pp. 3–11.

556. Eltzroth, Marjorie. "Vocational counseling for ghetto women with prostitution and domestic service backgrounds." VOCATIONAL GUIDANCE QUARTERLY, 22, Sept. 1973, pp. 32–81.

557. Getz, H. G. and J. H. Miles. "Women and peers as counselors: A look at client preferences." JOURNAL OF COLLEGE STUDENT PERSONNEL, 19, Ja. 1978, pp. 37–41.

558. Gray, J. D. "Counseling women who want both a profession and a family." PERSONNEL AND GUIDANCE JOURNAL, 59, Sept. 1980, pp. 43–8.

559. Harrison, Laurie R. "Career guidance for adults: Focus on women and ethnic minorities: A planning manual and catalog of programs." 1976. ERIC, 230 pp. ED 124 687.

560. Higginson, M V. and T. L. Quick. "Needed: Career counseling for women subordinates." SUPERVISORY MANAGEMENT, 30, Ag. 1975, pp. 2–10.

561. Hoffer, William. "Career conditioning for the new women."
     SCHOOL MANAGEMENT, 17, Mr. 1973, pp. 34–6.
562. Hohenshil, T. A. "Perspectives on career counseling for
     women: 1884-1974." VOCATIONAL GUIDANCE QUAR-
     TERLY, 23, Dec. 1974, pp. 100–3.
563. Jacobs, J. E. and J. M. Alberti, eds. "Realizing human
     potential: Alternatives for women; symposium." EDUCA-
     TIONAL HORIZON, 53, Spr. 1975, pp. 94–144.
564. Kahne, Hilda. "Women in the profession: Career considera-
     tions and job placement techniques." JOURNAL OF
     ECONOMIC ISSUES, 5, Sept. 1971, pp. 28–45.
565. Karelius-Schumacher, K. L. "Designing a counseling program
     for the mature woman student." JOURNAL OF THE
     NATIONAL ASSOCIATION FOR WOMEN DEANS,
     ADMINSTRATORS AND COUNSELORS, 41, Fall 1977,
     pp. 28–31.
566. Khan, J. and M. Price. "The evolution of Arrow, a
     life/career planning program for undergraduate women."
     IMPACT!, 3(2), 1974, pp. 52–7.
567. Kitabchi, G. and others. "Career/life planning for divorced
     women: An overview." VOCATIONAL GUIDANCE QUAR-
     TERLY, 28, Dec. 1979, pp. 137–45.
568. Koontz, E. D. "Counseling women for responsibilities."
     NATIONAL ASSOCIATION OF WOMEN DEANS,
     AND COUNSELORS JOURNAL, 34, Fall 1970, pp. 13–7.
569. Little, D. M. and A. J. Roach. "Videotape modeling of
     interest in non-traditional occupations for women." JOUR-
     NAL OF VOCATIONAL BEHAVIOR, 5, Ag. 1974, pp.
     133–8.
570. Morris, Jane. "Exploring nonconventional careers for
     women." SCHOOL COUNSELOR, 23, Nov. 1975, pp.
     127–32.
571. New York State. Department of Labor. Division of Research
     and Statistics. *Women jobseekers and the New York State
     Employment Service, July 1, 1971-June 30, 1974.* Albany:
     Department of Labor, 1975. 24 pp.
572. Norwood, Vera. "How women find jobs: A guide for
     workshop leaders." 1979. ERIC, 296 pp. ED 185 319.
573. Parrish, J. B. "Women, careers, and counseling: The new
     era." JOURNAL OF THE NATIONAL ASSOCIATION
     FOR WOMEN DEANS, ADMINISTRATORS, AND

COUNSELORS, 38, Fall 1974, pp. 11-9.
574. Pellegrino, Victoria. "First aid for the working woman. (Services which help women find and land meaningful, well-paid jobs)." NEW YORK, 7, Oct. 1974, pp. 98+.
575. Plotsky, Frances A. and R. Goad. "Encouraging women through a career conference: University of Texas, Austin." PERSONNEL AND GUIDANCE JOURNAL, 52, Mr. 1974, pp. 486-8.
576. Prediger, D. J. and R. J. Noeth. "Effectiveness of a brief counseling intervention in stimulating vocational exploration." JOURNAL OF VOCATIONAL BEHAVIOR, 14, Je. 1979, pp. 352-68.
577. Rice, J. K. "Vocational problem focus and client and counselor gender." VOCATIONAL GUIDANCE QUARTERLY, 26, Summ. 1977, pp. 69-75.
578. Richardson, Judy M. and Alice M. Thomas. "Evaluation of 'Women in Careers' program." 1978. ERIC, 107 pp. ED 170 481.
579. Roe, R. G. "Effect of the college placement process on occupational stereotypes." JOURNAL OF COUNSELING PSYCHOLOGY, 21, Mr. 1974, pp. 105+.
580. Rudnick, D. T. and E. J. Wallach. "Women in technology: A program to increase career awareness." PERSONNEL AND GUIDANCE JOURNAL, 58, Feb. 1980, pp. 445+.
581. Schlossberg, Nancy K. "A framework for counseling women." PERSONNEL AND GUIDANCE JOURNAL, 51, Oct. 1972, pp. 137-43.
582. Scott, Patricia Bell. "Preparing Black women for nontraditional professions: Some considerations for career counseling." JOURNAL OF THE NATIONAL ASSOCIATION FOR WOMEN DEANS, ADMINISTRATORS AND COUNSELORS, 40, Summ. 1977, pp. 135-9.
583 Sedaka, J. B. "Why not a women? Women in new careers program." AMERICAN EDUCATION, 15 Dec. 1975, pp. 11-5.
584. Shishkoff, M. M. "Counseling mature women for careers." NATIONAL ASSOCIATION OF WOMEN DEANS AND COUNSELORS JOURNAL, 36, Summ. 1973, pp. 173-7.
585. Smith, Walter S. and others. "Counseling women for nontraditional careers." 1977. ERIC, 68 pp. ED 150 533.
586. Stake, J. E. and J. Pearlman. "Assertiveness training as an

intervention technique for low performance self-esteem women." JOURNAL OF COUNSELING PSYCHOLOGY, 27, My. 1980, pp. 276–81.

587. Thomas, Leathia S. and Sandy Dickey. "Women and Girls Employment Enabling Service, Memphis, Tennessee." 1974. ERIC, 69 pp. ED 102 382.

588. U.S. Civil Service Commission. *Career counseling for women in the federal government: A handbook.* Washington, DC: GPO, 1975.

589. U.S. Women's Bureau. *Women in nontraditional jobs, a program model: Boston, nontraditional occupations program for women.* Washington, DC: GPO, 1978.

590. Vetter, Louise. "Career counseling for women." COUNSELING PSYCHOLOGIST, 4(1), 1973, pp. 54–67.

591. Voight, N. L. and others. "Community-based guidance: A Tupperware party approach to mid-life decision making." PERSONNEL AND GUIDANCE JOURNAL, 59, Oct. 1980, pp. 106–7.

592. Walker, Yvonne Kimmons and others. "Evaluation of the availability and effectiveness of MDTA Institutional Training and Employment Services for Women." Final report. 1974. ERIC, 79 pp. ED 095 278.

593. Worell, J. "New direction in counseling women." PERSONNEL AND GUIDANCE JOURNAL, 58, Mr. 1980, pp. 477–84.

4. Counselor Bias

594. Abramowitz, S. L. and others. "Comparative counselor inferences toward women with medical school aspirations." JOURNAL OF COLLEGE STUDENT PERSONNEL, 16, Mr. 1975, pp. 128–30.

595. Bingham, W. C. and E. W. House. "Counselors' attitude toward women and work." VOCATIONAL GUIDANCE QUARTERLY, 22, Summ. 1973, pp. 16–23.

596. Bingham, W. C. and E. W. House. "Counselors view women and work: Accuracy of information." VOCATIONAL GUIDANCE QUARTERLY, 21, Je. 1973, pp. 262–8.

597. Borgers, S. B. and others. "Does counselor response to occupational choice indicate sex stereotyping?" JOURNAL OF THE NATIONAL ASSOCIATION FOR WOMEN DEANS, ADMINISTRATORS, AND COUNSELORS,

41, Fall 1977, pp. 17–20.

598. Burlin, F. D. and R. Pearson. "Counselor-in-training response to a male and female client: An analogue study exploring sex-role sterotyping." COUNSELING EDUCATION AND SUPERVISION, 17, Mr. 1978, pp. 213–21.

599. Donahue, T. J. and J. W. Costar. "Counselor discrimination against young women in career selection." JOURNAL OF COUNSELING PSYCHOLOGY, 24, Nov. 1977, pp. 481–6.

600. Helwig, Andrew A. "Counselor bias and women." JOURNAL OF EMPLOYMENT COUNSELING, 13, Je. 1976, pp. 58–67.

601. Holland, J. L. "Some guidelines for reducing systematic biases in the delivery of vocational services." MEASURE-MENT AND EVALUATION GUIDANCE, 6, Ja. 1974, pp. 210–8.

602. Price, Gary E. and Sherry B. Borgers. "An evaluation of the sex stereotyping effect as related to counselor perceptions of courses appropriate for high school students." JOURNAL OF COUNSELING PSYCHOLOGY, 24, My. 1977, pp. 240–3.

603. Schlossberg, Nancy K. and John J. Pietrofesa. "Perspectives on counseling bias implications for counselor education." COUNSELING PSYCHOLOGIST, 4(1), 1973, pp. 44–54.

604. Schuck, Robert F. and others. "Attitudes of guidance counselors in Western Pennsylvania high schools toward medicine as a career choice for women." 1974. ERIC, 423 pp. ED 103 728.

605. Shapiro, Johanna. "Socialization of sex roles in the counseling setting: Differential counselor behavioral and attitudinal responses to typical and atypical female sex roles." 1975. ERIC, 49 pp. ED 106 727.

F. LEGAL ASPECTS AND REGULATIONS

1. Title IX

606. Association of American Colleges. Project on Status of Women. "Summary of issues being raised by women's group concerning the proposed regulations for Title IX of

the Education Amendments of 1972." WOMEN'S STUDIES NEWSLETTER, 2(4), Fall-Wint. 1975, pp. 13–7.

607. Fields, Cheryl M. "Anti-bias safeguards in Title IX don't apply to teachers, Judge rules." CHRONICLE OF HIGHER EDUCATION, 18 Ap. 1977, pp. 3+.

608. Fishel, Andrew and Janice Pottker. "Sex bias in secondary schools: The impact of Title IX." 1974. ERIC, 24 pp. ED 093 044.

609. Flygare, T. J. "HEW loses authority to regulate employment under Title IX." PHI DELTA KAPPAN, 61, Feb. 1980, pp. 418–9.

610. Graham, Peter J. "Title IX: Human rights in school sport." 1975. ERIC, 26 pp. ED 110 452.

611. Herzmark, Paula. "Title IX: Educational and implementation activities of state departments of education." 1976. ERIC, 11 pp. ED 123 802.

612. Hirata, I. "Title 9 and female athletes." JOURNAL OF THE AMERICAN COLLEGE HEALTH ASSOCIATION, 24, Dec. 1975, pp. 61–2.

613. "An interview on Title IX (of the Education Amendments of 1972) with Shirley Chisholm, Holly Knox, Leslie R. Wolfe, Cynthia G. Brown, and Mary Kaaren Jolly (impact on women's education)." HARVARD EDUCATIONAL REVIEW, 49, Nov. 1979, pp. 504–26.

614. National Advisory Council on Women's Educational Programs. *The Education Amendments of 1976: Impact on women and girls concerning Title IX and other amendments.* n.d. 3 pp. (Available from Suite 821, 1832 M Street N.W., Washington, DC 20036.)

615. "National Foundation for the Arts and Humanities found not enforcing Title IX." MEDIA REPORT TO WOMEN, 1 Je. 1978, pp 1+.

616. Northrop, Ann. "A new generation of athletes: Winning with Title IX." MS, 8, Sept. 1979, pp. 56–7.

617. Schnee, R. G. "Frying pan to fire—school advocacy or Title IX." PHI DELTA KAPPAN, 58, Ja. 1977, pp. 423–5.

618. Shelton, Dinah L. and Dorothy Berndt. "Sex discrimination in vocational education: Title IX and other remedies." CALIFORNIA LAW REVIEW, 62, Jl.-Sept. 1974, pp. 1121–68.

619. Silver, Paula F., Richard S. Podemski and Ann W. Engin.

"Attitudes toward sex role differentiation in education: Implications for Title IX implementation." JOURNAL OF RESEARCH AND DEVELOPMENT IN EDUCATION, 10, Wint. 1977, pp. 26–35.

620. Taylor, Emily and Donna Shavlik. "Institutional self-evaluation: The Title IX requirement." 1975. ERIC, 47 pp. ED 122 714.

621. Thurston, P. "Judicial dismemberment of Title IX." PHI DELTA KAPPAN, 60, Ap. 1979, pp. 594–5.

622. *Update on Title IX and sports no. 2: HEW proposed policy interpretation concerning Title IX and athletics.* Project on the Status and Education of Women, Jan. 1979, 4 pp. (Available from Association of American Colleges, 1818 R Street, N.W., Washington, DC 20009.)

623. Watkins, Beverly. "The university that said no to the guidelines (Brigham Young University Title IX)." CHRONICLE OF HIGHER EDUCATION, 3 Nov. 1975, pp. 5+.

624. U.S. Congress House. Committee on Education and Labor. Subcommittee on Postsecondary Education. *Sex discrimination regulations: Hearings June 17-26, 1975.* Washington, DC: GPO, 1975.

2. Legal Concerns

625. Allen, Robert L. "The Bakke case and affirmative action." BLACK SCHOLAR, 9, Sept. 1977, pp. 9–17.

626. Association of American Colleges. *Sex discrimination provisions concerning students and employers as contained in the Higher Education Act of 1972.* Je. 1972. 5 pp. (Available from AAC, 1818 R Street, N.W., Washington, DC 20009.)

627. Association of American Colleges. Project on the Status and Education of Women. "The Bakke Case: Implications for women in education." 1978. ERIC, 4 pp. ED 163 101.

628. Burstein, Paul. "Equal employment opportunity legislation and the income of women and nonwhites." AMERICAN SOCIOLOGICAL REVIEW, 44, Je. 1979, pp. 367–91.

629. "Case developments: An analysis of H.E.W. regulations concerning sex discrimination in education." WOMEN'S RIGHTS LAW REPORTER , 3, Dec. 1976, pp. 68–77.

630. "Digest of Federal Laws. Equal rights for women in education." Report no. 61. 1975. ERIC, 44 pp. ED 109 738.

631. (The effect of the Bakke Decision on women in sports). NEW YORK TIMES, 16 Oct. 1977, Sec. 4, pp. 2, col. 3.

632. Fields, Cheryl M. "Fifty-seven rights groups hit HEW on anti-bias enforcement." CHRONICLE OF HIGHER EDU- CATION, 22 Ja. 1976, pp. 7–8.

633. Fields, Cheryl M. "Government's guidelines on sex bias greeted with optimism and relief on many university campuses." CHRONICLE OF HIGHER EDUCATION, 24 Oct. 1972, pp. 1+.

634. Fields, Cheryl M. "Opening shots fired in legal challenge to special minority-admissions programs: Three dozen briefs filed with Supreme Court in support of University of California plan." CHRONICLE OF HIGHER EDUCA- TION, 5 Jl. 1977, pp. 7+.

635. Fields, Cheryl M. "U.S. publishes its anti-sex-bias guidelines for college but delays enforcement: Textbooks are not affected." CHRONICLE OF HIGHER EDUCATION, 24 Je. 1974, pp. 1–4.

636. Fields, Cheryl M. "Women's groups sue to compel HEW to probe charges of sex bias in sports." CHRONICLE OF HIGHER EDUCATION, 16 Jl. 1979, pp. 7+.

637. Fields, Cheryl M. "Women's sports groups campaign to preserve proposed anti-bias rules." CHRONICLE OF HIGHER EDUCATION, 23 Ap. 1979, pp. 19+.

638 Flygare, T. J. "HEW's new guidelines on sex discrimination in collegiate athletics." PHI DELTA KAPPAN, 60, Mr. 1979, pp. 529–30.

639. "HEW issues comprehensive regulations barring sex discrimi- nation in U.S. schools." CONGRESSIONAL QUARTER- LY WEEKLY REPORT, No. 33, 1975, pp. 1298–300.

640. Hoffman, C. "Women's Educational Equity Act." AMERI- CAN EDUCATION, 13, Dec. 1977, pp. 28–9.

641. "Nondiscrimination on basis of sex: Education programs and activities receiving or benefiting from federal financial assistance." 1975. ERIC, 19 pp. ED 108 275.

642. Olson, Claire. "The U.S. challenges discrimination against women." JUNIOR COLLEGE JOURNAL, 42, Je.-Jl. 1972, pp. 13–6.

643. Pearson, Jessica. "A handbook of state laws and policies affecting equal rights for women in education." 1975. ERIC, 134 pp. ED 109 808.

644. Pearson, William. "An overview of federal court decisions affecting equal rights for women in education." Report no. 70. 1975. ERIC, 193 pp. ED 109 807.

645. Project on the Status and Education of Women. *What constitutes equality for women in sport? Federal law put women in the running.* 1974. 21 pp. (Available from Association of American Colleges, 1818 R Street N.W. Washington, DC 20009.)

646. Sandler, Bernice. "Sex discrimination, educational institutions, and the law: A new issue on campus." JOURNAL OF LAW AND EDUCATION, 2, Oct. 1973, pp. 613–35.

647. "Sex bias in athletics, HEW outlines responsibilities of colleges." CHRONICLE OF HIGHER EDUCATION, 29 Sept. 1975, pp. 8–9.

648. Steinhilber, August W. "What the new anti-sex bias rules mean for schools." AMERICAN SCHOOL BOARD JOURNAL, No. 161, 1974, pp. 20–1.

649. Tinsley, Adrian and Elaine Reuben. "Academic women, sex discrimination, and the law: An action handbook." 1973. ERIC, 22 pp. ED 082 613.

650. Walsh, Ethel Bent. "The role of government in the attainment of equal opportunity for women in the universities." 1971. ERIC, 36 pp. ED 058 831.

651. U.S. Congress. House. Special Committee on Education Hearings. *Higher Education Amendments of 1971.* Washington, DC: GPO, 1971.

652. U.S. Congress. House. Subcommittee on Equal Opportunites Hearings. *Women's Educational Equity Act. Part 1.* Washington, DC: GPO, 1973.

653. U.S. Office of Education. *Women's Educational Equity Act Program. Annual Report FY 79.* Washington, DC: GPO, 1980.

G. OTHER EDUCATIONAL MATTERS

1. Special Problems

a. Math Achievement and Anxiety

654. Aiken, Lewis R., Jr. "Affective variables and sex differences in mathematical abilities." 1974. ERIC, 11 pp. ED 089 997.

655. Blum, L. and S. Givant. "Increasing the participation of

women in fields that use mathematics." AMERICAN MATHEMATICAL MONTHLY, 87, Dec. 1980, pp. 785–93.

656. Fennema, Elizabeth. "Mathematics learning and the sexes: A review." 1973. ERIC, 24 pp. ED 067 392.

657. Fox, Lynn H. "The mathematically precocious: Male or female?" 1974. ERIC, 13 pp. ED 090 473.

658. Haven, Elizabeth W. "Factors associated with the selection of advanced academic mathematics courses by girls in high school." 1972. ERIC, 75 pp. ED 062 173.

659. Hilton, T. L. and G. W. Berglund. "Sex differences in mathematics achievement: A longitudinal study." JOURNAL OF EDUCATIONAL RESEARCH, 67, Ja. 1974, pp. 231–7.

660. Kaminski, Donna M. and others. "Why females don't like mathematics: The effect of parental expectations." 1976. ERIC, 24 pp. ED 134 530.

661. Leder, Gilah C. "Sex differences in mathematics problem appeal as a function of problem context." JOURNAL OF EDUCATIONAL RESEARCH, 67, Ap. 1974, pp. 351–3.

662. Levine, Maita. "Identification of reasons why qualified women do not pursue mathematical careers." 1976. ERIC, 82 pp. ED 171 982.

663. Lyons, Linda. "The relationship of parental modeling, parental reinforcement, academic and career interests to the enrollment of high school females in accelerated mathematics programs." 1980. ERIC, 12 pp. ED 184 890.

664. Sells, L. W. "Mathematics: A critical filter." SCIENCE TEACHER, 45, Feb. 1978, pp. 28–9.

665. Sherman, Julia. "Predicting mathematics performance in high school girls and boys." JOURNAL OF EDUCATIONAL PSYCHOLOGY, 71, Ap. 1979, pp. 242–9.

666. Starr, Barbara Schaap. "Sex differences among personality correlates of mathematical ability in high school seniors." PSYCHOLOGY OF WOMEN QUARTERLY, 4, Wint. 1979, pp. 212–20.

667. Tobias, Sheila. "Beyond math anxiety, a world is waiting." GRADUATE WOMAN, 74, Ja.-Feb. 1980, pp. 10–11.

668. Tobias, Sheila and B. Donady. "Counseling the math anxious." JOURNAL OF THE NATIONAL ASSOCIATION OF WOMEN DEANS, ADMINISTRATORS AND

COUNSELORS, 41, Fall 1977, pp. 13–6.
669. "Why Susie can't add. (Girls should be counseled about importance of math to many careers)." HUMAN BEHAVIOR, 6, Ap. 1977, pp. 63+.

b. Sports and Physical Education

670. Atkinson, Karla. "In search of the freedom to grow: Report of the Physical Education/Athletics Task Force." 1973. ERIC, 24 pp. ED 126 059.
671. Brooks, C. "Buying and selling female high school sport talents." COACH WOMEN'S ATHLETICS, 7, Ja.-Feb. 1981, pp. 16+.
672. Campbell, M. A. and others. "Women in sport course." JOURNAL OF PHYSICAL EDUCATION, AND RECREATION, 51, Ja. 1980, pp. 71–3.
673. Dyne, Larry Von and Beverly T. Watkins. "Women's sport furor: NCAA and AIAW at odds over control." CHRONICLE OF HIGHER EDUCATION, 19 Ja. 1976, pp. 10+.
674. Fields, Cheryl M. "They don't trust the jocks: Women, citing NCAA's track record, are akeptical of its proposal to extend authority to their intercollegiate sports programs." CHRONICLE OF HIGHER EDUCATION, 12 My. 1975, pp. 3+.
675. Fisher, A. C. "Sports as an agent of masculine orientation." PHYSICAL EDUCATION, 29, Oct. 1972, pp. 120–2.
676. Griffin, Patricia S. "Perceptions of women's roles and female sports involvement among a selected sample of college students." 1972. ERIC, 16 pp. ED 080 513.
677. Hartman, Betty and Annie Clement. "The Ohio guide for girls' secondary physical education." JOURNAL OF HEALTH, PHYSICAL EDUCATION AND RECREATION, 44, Mr. 1973, pp. 20+.
678. "Hitting Stride: Women, long ignored as college athletes, move into 'big time.' " WALL STREET JOURNAL, 4 Je. 1975, pp. 1, col. 1.
679. Howe, Howard, II. "Sex, sports, and discrimination." CHRONICLE OF HIGHER EDUCATION, 18 Je. 1979, pp. 1+.
680. Hudson, Lynn. "Sports scholarships: Many are available for women, too." REAL WORLD, Nov. 1977, pp. 16+.
681. Johnson, T. P. "Girls on the boys' team: Equal protection in school athletics." NASSP BULLETIN, 58, Oct. 1974, pp. 55–65.

682. Kiester, Edwin, Jr. "A new phys ed program to serve all children." FAMILY HEALTH, Mr. 1974, pp. 19–20+.

683. King, Kathy. "Girls touch football, physical education." 1971. ERIC, 48 pp. ED 095 113.

684. Kingsley, J. L. and others. "Social acceptance of female athletes by college women." RESEARCH QUARTERLY, 48, Dec. 1977, pp. 727–33.

685. Mann, Constance. "The lack of girls' athletics." PHYSICAL EDUCATOR, 20, Mr. 1972, pp. 9–10.

686. Nolte, M. Chester. "With prodding from girls (and courts) public schools are backing away from sex bias in phys ed program." AMERICAN SCHOOL BOARD JOURNAL, 160, Sept. 1973, pp. 21–3.

687. Nyquist, Ewald B. "Win, women, and money: Collegiate athletes today and tomorrow." EDUCATIONAL RECORD, 60, Fall 1979, pp. 374–93.

688. Rindfleisch, Bev. "Filing for dollars: 1975 scholarship guide (for sports scholarships)." 2, Oct. 1975, pp. 26–7.

689. Rubin, Richard Alan. "Sex discrimination an interscholastic high school athletes." SYRACUSE LAW REVIEW, 25, Ap. 1974, pp. 535–74.

690. "Schoolgirl athletes are shaking things up." AMERICAN SCHOOL BOARD JOURNAL, 160, Sept. 1973, pp. 23–5.

691. "Trouble may be just ahead for your district if it discriminates against girls in athletics." Special report. AMERICAN SCHOOL BOARD JOURNAL, 160, Sept. 1973, pp. 19–25.

692. Turner, Mary Ann. "League constitution and bylaws for girls' interscholastic programs (suggested guide)." 1975. ERIC, 61 pp. ED 109 108.

2. Special Populations

a. Returning Women

693. Benham, Lee. "The returns to education for women." 1971. ERIC, 27 pp. ED 065 546.

694. Berman, M. R. and others. "Efficacy of supportive learning environments for returning women: An empirical evaluation." JOURNAL OF COUNSELING PSYCHOLOGY, 24, Jl. 1977, pp. 324+.

695. Bostaph, C. and M. Moore. "Career ambivalence and the returning adult women student." JOURNAL OF COLLEGE

PLACEMENT, 39, Summ. 1979, pp. 19+.

696. Cossey, Beatrice. "Concepts of the women's re-entry educational program. Continuing education programs for women: Educational growth and personal development, DeAnza Community College." n.d. ERIC, 20 pp. ED 092 805.

697. Cottle, T. J. "Overcoming an invisible handicap (returning to college at age 30)." PSYCHOLOGY TODAY, 13, Ja. 1980, pp. 89+.

698. De Wolf, Virginia and Patricia W. Lunneborg. "Descriptive information on over-35 undergraduate students." 1972. ERIC, 17 pp. ED 072 745.

699. Dunkle, Margaret C. *Field evaluation draft—Financial aid: Helping re-entry women pay college costs.* n.d. 14 pp. (Available from Women's Re-entry Projects, Project on the Status and Education of Women, Association of American Colleges, 1818 R Street, N. W., Washington, DC 20009.)

700. Eliason, Carol. "Neglected women: The educational needs of displaced homemakers, single mothers, and older women." 1978. ERIC, 63 pp. ED 163 138.

701. Fisher-Thompson, Jeanne. *Field evaluation draft—obtaining a degree: Alternative options for re-entry women.* 1980. 14 pp. (Available from Women's Re-entry Project, Project on the Status and Education of Women, Association of American Colleges, 1818 R Street, N.W., Washington, DC 20009.)

702. Kelman, Eugenia and Bonnie Staley. "The returning woman student: Needs of an important minority group on college campuses." Student development report. 1974. ERIC, 21 pp. ED 103 747.

703. McCrea, J. M. "New student body: Women returning to college." JOURNAL OF THE NATIONAL ASSOCIATION OF WOMEN DEANS, ADMINISTRATORS AND COUNSELORS, 43, Fall 1979, pp. 13-9.

704. Mohsenin, I. C. "Peer-sponsored conference: College re-entry strategy for adult women." EDUCATIONAL HORIZON, 58, Summ. 1980, pp. 193-6.

705. "Mrs. Suzy Coed: More older women return to college; most do very well; affluence, changed attitudes, encouragement by schools send them flocking back." WALL STREET JOURNAL, 12 Sept. 1972, pp. 1, col. 1.

706. Nichols, C. G. "A seminar in personality development for

mature women." NATIONAL ASSOCIATION FOR
WOMEN DEANS, ADMINISTRATORS AND COUN-
SELORS, 37, Spr. 1974, pp. 123–7.

707. Patterson, Janice B. "Occupational training for mature
women: A survey of the enrollment of women over age 35
in proprietary institutions in Cuyahoga County." 1975.
ERIC, 46 pp. ED 110 805.

708. Pearlman, Joan. "Back to school—back to work." NA-
TIONAL UNIVERSITY EXTENSION ASSOCIATION,
38 (18), 1974, pp. 14–7.

709. Plotsky, Frances and Susan Ohm. "A follow-up study of
returning students—A concentration on women." 1976.
ERIC, 56 pp. ED 171 976.

710. "Preparing for liberation (Counseling programs which offer
supportive services and academic info for women returning
to college)." HUMAN BEHAVIOR, 6, Ag. 1977, pp. 53+.

711. Reebling, J. E. "They are returning: But are they staying?"
JOURNAL OF COLLEGE STUDENT PERSONNEL, 21,
Nov. 1980, pp. 491–7.

712. Rice, J. K. "Self esteem, sex-role orientation, and perceived
spouse support for a return to school." ADULT EDU-
CATION, 29, Summ. 1979, pp. 215–33.

713. Richards, Lillian S. "Women's perception of their psychological and practical needs upon re-entry to a community
college: Implications for restructuring the learning environment." 1976. ERIC, 69 pp. ED 130 713.

714. Scott, R. and L. Holt. "New wave—college responds to
women returnees." PHI DELTA KAPPAN, 58, Dec. 1976,
pp. 338–9.

715. Setne, Verlis L. "An educational-vocational development
program for adult women." VOCATIONAL GUIDANCE
QUARTERLY, 25, Mr. 1977, pp. 232–7.

716. Taines, Beatrice. "Older women, new students." COM-
MUNITY AND JUNIOR COLLEGE JOURNAL, 44,
1973, pp. 17+.

717. Tittle, C. K. and E. R. Denker. "Re-entry women: A selective
review of the educational process, career choice, and
interest measurement." REVIEW OF EDUCATIONAL
RESEARCH, 47, Fall 1977, pp. 531–84.

718. Weinstein, Loribeth. *Field evaluation report—The counseling
needs of re-entry women.* 1980. 10 pp. (Available from

Women's Re-entry Project, Project on the Status and Education of Women, Association of American Colleges, 1818 R Street, N.W., Washington, DC. 20009.)

719. Weinstein, Loribeth. *Field evaluation report—Recruitment and admissions: Opening the door for re-entry women.* 1980. 13 pp. (Available from Women's Re-entry Project, Project on the Status and Education of Women, Association of American Colleges, 1818 R Street, N.W., Washington, DC 20009.)

720. Young, A. M. "Back to school at 35 or over." MONTHLY LABOR REVIEW, 102, Ag. 1979, pp. 53–62.

b. Rural Women

721. Dunne, F. "Women and work in rural America: A challenge to education." COMPACT, 14, Fall 1980, pp. 8–9.

722. Fratoe, Frank A. "Rural women and education." 1979. ERIC, 25 pp. ED 175 604.

723. Kelly, Paul and C. Ray Wingrove. "Educational and occupational choices for black and while, male and female students in a rural Georgia community." JOURNAL OF RESEARCH AND DEVELOPMENT IN EDUCATION, 9, Fall 1975, pp. 45–50.

724. Oldfield, B. and J. Wise. "Ms. farmers: An adult class for farm women." AGRICULTURAL EDUCATION MAGAZINE, 46, Ap. 1974, pp. 219–20.

725. Olivetti, L. James and Donald F. Smith. "Vocational guidance for rural women: glimpses of a pioneering effort." VOCATIONAL GUIDANCE QUARTERLY, 27, Mr. 1979, pp. 270–5.

726. "Study on the equality of access of girls and women to education in the context of rural development." 1972. ERIC, 69 pp. ED 076 446.

c. Gifted Women

727. Fox, Lynn H. and Lee J. Richmond. "Gifted females: Are we meeting their counseling needs?" PERSONNEL AND GUIDANCE JOURNAL, 57, Ja. 1979, pp. 256–60.

728. Rodenstein, J. and others. "Career development of gifted women." GIFTED CHILD QUARTERLY, 21, Fall 1977, pp. 340–7.

729. Schwartz, L. L. "Advocacy for the neglected gifted: Females."

GIFTED CHILD QUARTERLY, 24, Summ. 1980, pp. 113–7.

730. Shakeshaft, Charol and Pat Palmieri. "A divine discontent: Perspectives on gifted women." GIFTED CHILD QUARTERLY, 22, Wint. 1978, pp. 468–77.

731. Tidball, M. Elizabeth. "Research: The search for talented women." CHANGE, 6, My. 1974, pp. 51–64.

d. Minority Women

732. Buriel, R. and E. Saenz. "Psychocultural characteristics of college-bound and non-college-bound Chicanas." JOURNAL OF SOCIAL PSYCHOLOGY, 110, Ap. 1980, pp. 245–51.

733. Escobedo, T. H. "Are Hispanic women in higher education the nonexistent minority?" EDUCATIONAL RESEARCHER, 9, Oct. 1980, pp. 7–12.

734. Fox, Andrew and others. "In-school Neighborhood Youth Corps. 14/15 year-old black teenage girl project, Memphis, Tennessee." Final report. 1973. ERIC, 175 pp. ED 096 375.

735. Gurin, P. and C. Gaylord. "Educational occupational goals of men and women at black colleges." MONTHLY LABOR REVIEW, 99, Je. 1976, pp. 10–16.

736. Miranda, L. and others. "Concerns of minority women with respect to vocational education." 1977. ERIC, 140 pp. ED 164 633.

737. Nieto-Gomez, Anna. "The needs of the Spanish speaking mujer (women) in Woman-Manpower Training Programs." 1974. ERIC, 10 pp. ED 096 044.

738. Russell, Michele. "Black-eyed blues connections: Teaching Black women." WOMEN'S STUDIES NEWSLETTER, 4, Fall 1976, pp. 6–7.

739. (United Balck Women's Conference). NEW YORK TIMES, 19 Je. 1972, Sec. 2, pp. 18, col 1.

II. WOMEN: EMPLOYMENT

A. EMPLOYMENT STATUS OF WOMEN
1. General

740. Almquist, Elizabeth M. "Women in the work force (review essay)." SIGNS, 2, Summ. 1977, pp. 843–55.
741. American Association of School Administrators. "Women: A significant national resource." 1971. ERIC, 55 pp. ED 082 297.
742. Anderson, Ralph E. and Robert J. Teisine. "Our working women: An underutilized resource." BUSINESS HORIZONS, 16, Feb. 1973, pp. 55–62.
743. Baron, A. S. and R. L. Witte. "The new work dynamic: Men and women in the work force." BUSINESS HORIZONS, 23, Ag. 1980, pp. 56–60.
744. "Changes in the labor force status of women." MONTHLY LABOR REVIEW, 96, Ag. 1973, pp. 76+.
745. Coser, Rose Laub and Gerald Rokoff. "Women in the occupational world: Social disruption and conflict." SOCIAL PROBLEMS, 18, Spr. 1971, pp. 533–54.
746. Crowley, Joan E. and others. "Facts and fiction about the American working woman." 1973. ERIC, 29 pp. ED 074 235.
747. Davis, H. "Employment gains of women by industry, 1968-78." MONTHLY LABOR REVIEW, 103, Je. 1980, pp. 3–9.
748. Deangelo, Lois and Bernice Garcia. "The employable woman conference report." 1977. ERIC, 33 pp. ED 155 086.
749. Dicesare, Constance Bogh. "Changes in the occupational structure of U.S. jobs: Analysis of census data shows that professional, technical, and kindred workers led the job

growth between 1960 and 1970: Women's growth was greatest in clerical and service jobs, already dominated by women." MONTHLY LABOR REVIEW, 98, Mr. 1975, pp. 24–34.

750. Dowdall, Jean A. "Structural and attitudinal factors associated with female labor force participation." SOCIAL SCIENCE QUARTERLY, 55, Je. 1974, pp. 121–30.

751. Duncan, Beverly. "Change in worker/nonworker ratios for women." DEMOGRAPHY, 16, Nov. 1979, pp. 535–48.

752. (Employment picture of women). NEW YORK TIMES, 2 Ja. 1978, pp. 1, col. 2.

753. (Employment status of American women). NEW YORK TIMES, 11 Ap. 1971, pp. 1+, col. 2.

754. Erickson, Julia A. "An analysis of the journey to work for women." SOCIAL PROBLEMS, 24, Ap. 1977, pp. 428–35.

755. Ferber, Marianne A. and Helen M. Lowry. "Woman's place: National differences in the occupational mosaic." JOURNAL OF MARKETING, 41, Jl. 1977, pp. 23–30.

756. (Female employment rates). NEW YORK TIMES, 11 Ja. 1970, Sec. 12, pp. 16, col. 2.

757. Freeman, Leah. "The changing role of women: A selected bibliography." 1977. ERIC, 196 pp. ED 176 139.

758. Garfinkle, S. H. "Occupations of women and black workers." MONTHLY LABOR REVIEW, 98, Nov. 1975, pp. 25–35.

759. Gilbert, D. "Changing female role." NATIONS BUSINESS, 60, Dec. 1972, pp. 39+.

760. Gold, Sonia S. "Alternative national goals and women's employment." SCIENCE, 179, Feb. 1973, pp. 656–60.

761. "Greater activity by women in labor force in recent years points up long-term trend." COMMERCE TODAY, 4, Jl. 1974, pp. 2–3.

762. Grossman, Allyson Sherman. "Women in the labor force (United States): The early years (16-24)." "The middle years (25-54)" by Deborah Pisetzner Klein. "The later years (55 and over)" by Beverly Johnson McEaddy. MONTHLY LABOR REVIEW, 98, Nov. 1975, pp. 3–24.

763. Haber, S. "Trends in work rates of white females, 1890 to 1950." INDUSTRIAL AND LABOR RELATIONS REVIEW, 26, Jl. 1973, pp. 1122–34.

764. Harbeson, Gladys Evans. "Choice and challange for the American woman." 1971. ERIC, 217 pp. ED 097 556.

765. Hartmann, Heidi I. "Women's work in the United States."

CURRENT HISTORY, 70, My. 1976, pp. 215-9+.

766. Haug, Marie R. "Social class measurement and women's occupational roles." SOCIAL FORCES, 52 (1), 1973, pp. 86-98.

767. Heckman, J. J. "Partial survey of recent research on the labor supply of women." AMERICAN ECONOMIC REVIEW, 68, My. 1978, pp. 200-7.

768. Herman, Alexis M. "Progress and problems for working women." LABOR LAW JOURNAL, 30, Ap. 1979, pp. 195-204.

769. Herman, D. D. "More career opportunities for women: Whose responsibility?" PERSONNEL JOURNAL, 53, Je. 1974, pp. 414-7.

770. Hohenshil, Thomas H., ed. "New dimensions in the career development of women." Conference proceedings no. 2. 1974. ERIC, 134 pp. ED 098 437.

771. Holm, J. M. "Employment and women: Cinderella is dead!" NATIONAL ASSOCIATION OF WOMEN DEANS AND COUNSELORS JOURNAL, 34, Fall 1970, pp. 6-13.

772. Jacobs, J. E., comp. "Women and work: A selected, annotated bibliography." EDUCATIONAL HORIZONS, 53, Spr. 1975, pp. 142-4 .

773. Jacobson, Carolyn J. "Women workers: Profile of a growing force." AMERICAN FEDERATIONIST, 81, Jl. 1974, pp. 9-15.

774. Janover, Madeleine and Fran Moirs. "Working women: Expendable (report on Conference on Women and the Workplace, by Society for Occupational and Environmental Health)." OFF OUR BACKS, 6, Jl.-Ag. 1976, pp. 4-5.

775. Jelinek, Mariann. "Career management and women." 1977, ERIC, 21 pp. ED 150 272.

776. Jones, Ethel B. and James E. Long. "Human capital and labor market employment additional evidence for women." JOURNAL OF HUMAN RESOURCES, 14, Sept. 1979, pp. 270-9.

777. Jordan, Ruth. "Full employment: A women's issue." CIVIL RIGHTS DIGEST, 8(2-3), 1976, pp. 26-9.

778. Katzell, Mildren E. and William C. Byham. "Women in the work force. (Confrontation With Change Series)." 1972. ERIC, 76 pp. ED 069 926.

779. Kealiher, Carolyn L. "Women: The wasted resource." PERSONNEL ADMINISTRATOR, 18, Jl.-Ag. 1973, pp. 15-8.

780. Koontz, Elizabeth D. "The progress of the woman worker: An unfinished story." ISSUES IN INDUSTRIAL SOCIETY, 2(1), 1971, pp. 29–31.

781. Koontz, Elizabeth D. "Women as a wasted resource." COMPACT, 4, Ag. 1970, pp. 10–1.

782. Krenkel, Noele and others. "Ad hoc committee on the role and status of women." AREA final report and recommendations. 1975. ERIC, 217 pp. ED 109 126.

783. Lambright, W. Henry. "Womanpower: The next step in manpower policy." PUBLIC PERSONNEL REVIEW, 31 (1), 1970, pp. 25–30.

784. Levitin, Teresa. "Women in the occupational world." 1971. ERIC, 11 pp. ED 056 332.

785. Levitt, Eleanor Sosnow. "Vocational development of professional women: A review." JOURNAL OF VOCATIONAL BEHAVIOR, 1, Oct. 1971, pp. 375–85.

786. Linden, Fabian. "Women in the labor force (United States)." CONFERENCE BOARD RECORD, 7, Ap. 1970, pp. 37–9.

787. Lloyd, C. B. and B. Niemi. "Sex differences in labor supply elasticity: The implications of sectoral shifts in demand (with discussion)." AMERICAN ECONOMIC REVIEW, 68, My. 1978, pp. 78–83, 95–8.

788. McBrearty, James C. "Kitchen revolution: New careers for American women." ARIZONA REVIEW, 21, Ja. 1972, pp. 10–4.

789. McBrearty, James C. "Women in revolt: Assault on employment myths." ARIZONA REVIEW, 19, Nov. 1970, pp. 6–12.

790. McClendon, McKee J. "The occupational status attainment processes of males and females." AMERICAN SOCIOLOGICAL REVIEW, 41, Feb. 1976, pp. 52–64.

791. Maymi, Carmen R. "Women workers and the women's movement." HUMAN ECOLOGY FORUM, 4(2), 1973, pp. 19–20.

792. Oppenheimer, Valerie Kincade. "Demographic influence on female employment and the status of women." AMERICAN JOURNAL OF SOCIOLOGY, 78(4), 1973, pp. 946–61.

793. Pifer, Alan. "Women working: Toward a new society." URBAN AND SOCIAL CHANGE REVIEW, 11(1-2), 1978, pp. 3–11.

794. Pinto, Patrick R. and Jeanne O. Buckmeier, comps. "Problems and issues in the employment of minority, disadvantaged and female groups: An annotated bibliography." 1973. ERIC, 69 pp. ED 083 339.

795. "Portrait of women's new role in employment." US NEWS AND WORLD REPORT, 15 Ja. 1979, pp. 66–7.

796. "Revolution II: Thinking female (on the role and status of women: Seven articles)." COLLEGE AND UNIVERSITY BUSINESS, 48, Feb. 1970, pp. 51–86.

797. Rodenstein, J., comp. "Bibliography on career and other aspects of development in bright women." GIFTED CHILD QUARTERLY, 21, Fall 1977, pp. 421–6.

798. Rounds, James B., Jr., Rene V. Dawis and Lloyd H. Lofquist. "Life history correlates of vocational needs for a female adult sample." JOURNAL OF COUNSELING PSYCHOLOGY, 26, Nov. 1979, pp. 487–96.

799. Rudd, N. M. and P. C. McKenry. "Working women: Issues and implications." JOURNAL OF HOME ECONOMICS, 72, Wint. 1980, pp. 26–9.

800. Schroeder, Paul E. "Women in the world of work: A bibliography of ERIC documents." Bibliography series no. 19. 1973. ERIC, 29 pp. ED 083 479.

801. Schwartz, Felice N. "Converging work roles of men and women." BUSINESS AND SOCIETY REVIEW IN-NOVATION, No. 7, 1973, pp. 71–5.

802. Scott, Ron. "Token women. (Employment situation for women college graduates)." MOTHER JONES, 2, Ag. 1973, pp. 68+.

803. "Seminar/workshops on women in the world of work." Final report. 1974. ERIC, 182 pp. ED 109 561.

804. Simpson, Elizabeth J. "Problems of females in the world of work." THEORY INTO PRACTICE, 14, Feb. 1975, pp. 49–51.

805. Slater, C. and T. Kraseman. "Statistics reveal three distinct phases in growth of women in labor force." BUSINESS AMERICA, 26 Mr. 1979, pp. 20–1.

806. Smith, R. E. "Sources of growth of the female labor force, 1971-75." MONTHLY LABOR REVIEW, 100, Ag. 1977, pp. 27–8.

807. Sorkin, Alan L. "On the occupational status of women, 1870-1970." AMERICAN JOURNAL OF ECONOMICS, 32,

Jl. 1973, pp. 235-44.

808. "Special section: The American women on the move—but
     where?" US NEWS AND WORLD REPORT, 8 Dec. 1975,
     pp. 54-64+.

809. Steffes, Robert B. "An occupational attainment index for
     minorities and women." URBAN LEAGUE REVIEW, 1,
     Ag. 1975, pp. 29-35.

810. Steinem, Gloria. "Where the women workers are. The rise of
     the pink collar ghetto." MS, 5, Mr. 1977, pp. 51-2.

811. Stull, Richard Allen. "New answers to an old question:
     Women's place is in the what?" PERSONNEL JOURNAL,
     52, Ja. 1973, pp. 31-5.

812. Sum, A. M. "Female labor force participations: Why
     projections have been too low." MONTHLY LABOR
     REVIEW, 100, Jl. 1977, pp. 18-24.

813. Sweet, James A. "Women in the labor force." Studies in
     population series. 1973. ERIC, 211 pp. ED 096 399.

814. Szymanski, Albert. "Race, sex and the U.S. working class."
     SOCIAL PROBLEMS, 21, Je. 1974, pp. 706-25.

815. Tavris, Carol. "Women: Work isn't always the answer."
     PSYCHOLOGY TODAY, 10, Sept. 1976, pp. 78-95.

816. "Things are looking up for the white collar women—so they
     say." MANAGEMENT REVIEW, 67, Jl. 1978, pp. 55+.

817. Tully, Andrew. "America is squandering her womanpower."
     NATIONAL BUSINESS WOMAN, 53, Ap. 1972, pp.
     6-7+.

818. U.S. Congress. Joint Economic Committee. Subcommitte on
     Economic Growth. Hearings. *Employment problems of
     women, minorities, and youths: Hearings before the
     Subcommitte on Economic Growth of the Joint Economic
     Committee, Congress of the United States, Ninety-fourth
     Congress, First Session, July 7 and 8, 1975.* Washington,
     DC: GPO, 1974.

819. U.S. Department of Labor. *United States working women: A
     chartbook.* Washington, DC: GPO, 1975.

820. U.S. Equal Employment Opportunity Commission. *Equal
     employment opportunity report, 1973: Job patterns for
     minorities and women in private industry.* Washington,
     DC: GPO, 1975.

821. U.S. Equal Employment Opportunity Commission. *Employ-
     ment profiles of minorities and women in the SMSA*

(Standard metropolitan statistical area's) of 20 large cities. Washington, DC: GPO, 1974.

822. U.S. Women's Bureau. *Background facts on women workers in the U.S.* Washington, DC: GPO, 1970.

823. U.S. Women's Bureau. *1975 Handbook on women workers.* Washington, DC: GPO, 1975.

824. U.S. Women's Bureau. *The role and status of women workers in the United States and Japan: A joint United States—Japan study.* Washington, DC: GPO, 1976.

825. U.S. Women's Bureau. *Why women work.* Washington, DC: GPO, 1970.

826. U.S. Women's Bureau. *Women workers today.* Washington, DC: GPO, 1974.

827. "Up the job ladder—gains for women: Police officer, bank manager, truck driver positions once reserved 'for men only' are now being filled by women; and the trend is picking up speed." US NEWS AND WORLD REPORT, 2 Oct. 1972, pp. 44-6.

828. Vatter, Ethel L. "Structural change in the occupational composition of the female labor force." 1974. ERIC, 55 pp. ED 106 543.

829. Verway, D. I. "Advance to the rear for women." MICHIGAN STATE UNIVERSITY BUSINESS TOPICS, 20, Wint. 1972, pp. 53-62.

830. Vlahos, Mantha. "Survey of the status of women." Institutional research report no. 7. 1975. ERIC, 20 pp. ED 103 082.

831. Waldman, Elizabeth K. "Changes in the labor force activity of women." MONTHLY LABOR REVIEW, 93, Je. 1970, pp. 10-8.

832. Weisskoff, Francine Blau. "Woman's place in the labor market." AMERICAN ECONOMIC REVIEW, 62, My. 1972, pp. 161-76.

833. Wells, Jean A. "Working women (special problems): Women at work in the United States." INDUSTRIAL AND LABOR RELATIONS REPORT, 11, Wint. 1975, pp. 6-11.

834. Wertheimer, Barbara and Anne Nelson. "The American woman at work." PERSONNEL MANAGEMENT, 6(3), 1974, pp. 20-3, 40-1.

835. (Where are women working?) NEW YORK TIMES, 17 Je.

1977, pp. 1, col. 5.

836. (Where women are employed). NEW YORK TIMES, 29 Nov. 1977, pp. 1, col. 1.

837. Williams, Gregory. "The changing U.S. labor force and occupational differentiation by sex." DEMOGRAPHY, 16, Feb. 1977, pp. 73–88.

838. Wisconsin, University of, Madison. Institute for Research on Poverty. *The effect of income and wage rates on the labor supply of prime age women.* 1974. 62 pp. (Available from Institute, 500 Lincoln Drive, Madison, WI 53706.)

839. "Women and the workplace: The implications of occupational segregation." SIGNS, 1(3, Pt. 2), Spr. 1976.

840. "Women in the workplace: A special section." MONTHLY LABOR REVIEW, 97(5), 1974, pp. 3–58.

841. Woodworth, Margaret and Warner Woodworth. "The female takeover: Threat or opportunity." PERSONNEL ADMIN-ISTRATOR, 24(1), 1979, pp. 19–24+.

842. "Working women: Joys and sorrows (Four articles)." US NEWS AND WORLD REPORT, 15 Ja. 1979, pp. 64–74.

843. "Working women: The gains are substantial." SALES AND MARKETING MANAGMENT, 24 Jl. 1978, pp. 66+.

844. Wurtemburg, Gladys V. "The movement created a women's market." MAJORITY REPORT, 13–22 Dec. 1975, pp. 8+.

845. Zbytniewski, J. "Working women: Less time, more money." PROGRESSIVE GROCER, 58, Je. 1978, pp. 56–8+.

2. Reports—Specific Geographic Locations

846. Bone, Jan, ed. "Commission on the Status of Women: Report and recommendations to the governor and the general assembly." Illinois State Commission on the Status of Women. 1975. ERIC, 71 pp. ED 096 595.

847. California. State Commission on the Status of Women. "California women." Report of the California Commission on the Status of Women. 1975. ERIC, 118 pp. ED 156 581.

848. Council on the Economic Status of Women. "Minnesota women: Work and training." 1977. ERIC, 28 pp. ED 151 530.

849. (Employed women in California). NEW YORK TIMES, 19 Feb. 1978, pp. 1, col. 1.

850. Hollman, Kenneth W. and Lewis H. Smith. "Women in Mississippi's labor force." MISSISSIPPI BUSINESS REVIEW, 34, Mr. 1973, pp. 3–8.

851. Huelsman, B. Ryle, "Womanpower in the United States and in Kentucky." 1977, ERIC, 57 pp. ED 176 005.

852. Iowa. Department of Job Service. *Status of women in the Iowa labor market.* 1979. 62 pp. (Available from Department of Job Service, 1000 East Grand Avenue, Des Moines. IA 50319.)

853. Jones, Dorothy M. and others. "The status of women in Alaska, 1977. A preliminary study." 1977. ERIC, 341 pp. ED 138 530.

854. Letlow, Kathlene D. and George S. Tracy. "A research note on occupational changes for Louisana urban females, 1960-1970." JOURNAL OF VOCATIONAL BEHAVIOR, 4, 1974, pp. 333–8.

855. Lilly, Leslie. "Women and work in Appalachia: The waging war." HUMAN SERVICES IN THE RURAL ENVIRONMENT, 1(1), 1979, pp. 40–5.

856. Lockwood, Robert M. "Women working in Texas." TEXAS BUSINESS REVIEW, 49, Dec. 1975, pp. 281–8.

857. Maine. Department of Manpower Affairs. *Women and minority labor force in Maine, statistics, legislation and change.* By Marilyn "Jo" Josephson. 1979. 161 pp. (Available from Department of Manpower Affairs, Augusta, ME 04330.)

858. "Montana women on the move." 1978. ERIC, 87 pp. ED 167 705.

859. Nebraska. Commission on the Status of Women. *Nebraska women's guide to employment.* 1978. 26 pp. (Available from Commission, 301 Centennial Mall South, Lincoln, NE 68509.)

860. New York State. Department of Labor. *Women in the labor force, statistics particularly applicable to affirmative action compliance program, a supplement to minority manpower statistics.* 1972, 28 pp. (Available from Department of Labor, New York, Albany, NY 22130.)

861. Papier, William. *Employment and unemployment among Ohio's women.* 1979. 4 pp. (Available from Ohio Bureau of Employment Services, Division of Research and Statistics, 145 Front Street, Box 1618, Columbus, OH 43216.)

862. *Profile of Nebraska women in employment.* 1977. 103 pp. (Available from Nebraska Commission on the Status of Women, 301 Centennial Mall South, P.O. Box 94985, Lincoln, NE 68509.)

863. "Statistics on minorities and women: Information useful for affirmative action compliance programs in New York State." 1976. ERIC, 133 pp. ED 126 172.

864. U.S. Women's Bureau. *Guide to sources of data on women and women workers for the U.S. and for regions, states and local areas.* Washington, DC: GPO, 1972.

865. U.S. Women's Bureau. *Women workers. Series of reports by states.* Washington, DC: GPO, 1974.

866. "Utah Governor's Commission on the Status of Women: Five year report." 1973. ERIC, 15 pp. ED 152 633.

867. Virginia. Employment Commission. Manpower Research Division. *Report on women in Virginia.* 1978. 62 pp. (Available from Labor Market Analysis Unit, Manpower Research, P.O. Box 1358, Richmond, VA 23211.)

868. Wisconsin. Department of Employment Relations. Division of Human Resource Services. *CETA and Wisconsin women.* 1979. 174 pp. (Available from the Department, 149 East Wilson Street, Madison, WI 53702.)

869. (Women employed in New York State). NEW YORK TIMES, 2 Sept. 1973, pp. 83, col. 2.

3. Career Patterns

a. Mobility

870. Brookshire, Michael L. and Howard H. Lumsden. "Women, jobs and mobility." JOURNAL OF COLLEGE PLACEMENT, 35(3), 1975, pp. 75–9.

871. DeJong, Peter Y. and others. "Patterns of female intergenerational occupational miblity: A comparison with male patterns." AMERICAN SOCIOLOGICAL REVIEW, No. 37, 1971, pp. 774–9 and No. 38, 1971, pp. 806–9.

872. Havens, Elizabeth M. and Judy Corder Tully. "Female intergenerational occupational mobility: Comparison of pattern." Reply by Peter De Jong and others. AMERICAN SOCIOLOGICAL REVIEW, 37, Dec. 1972, pp. 774–9

873. Maynard, Cathleen E. and Robert A. Zawacki. "Mobility and the dual career couple." PERSONAL JOURNAL, 58,

Jl. 1974, pp. 468–72.

874. Moore, K. M. and M. A. D. Sagaria. "Women administrators and mobility: The second struggle." JOURNAL OF NATIONAL ASSOCIATION OF WOMEN DEANS, ADMINISTRATORS AND COUNSELORS, 44, Wint. 1981, pp. 21–8.

875. "More and more women professionals accept career relocation; one company official sees refusal to move as possibly diminishing woman's career potential by as much as 50%." WALL STREET JOURNAL, 13 Sept. 1977, pp. 1, col. 5.

876. Ramsy, Natalie Rogoff. "Patterns of female intergenerational occupational mobility: A comment." AMERICAN SOCIO-LOGICAL REVIEW, 38, Dec. 1973, pp. 806–7; Response, pp. 807–9.

877. Reagan, Barbara B. "Two supply curves for economists? Implications of mobility and career attachment of women." AMERICAN ECONOMIC REVIEW, 65, My. 1975, pp. 100–7.

878. Rosenfeld, Rachel A. "Women's intergenerational occupational mobility." AMERICAN SOCIOLOGICAL REVIEW, 43, Feb. 1978, pp. 36–46.

879. Rosenfeld, Rachel A. and Aage B. Sorensen. "Sex differences in patterns of career mobility." DEMOGRAPHY, 16, Feb. 1979, pp. 89–102.

b. *Other Patterns*

880. Barnes, William F. and Ethel B. Jones. "Manufacturing quit rates revisited: A cyclical view of women's quits." MONTH-LY LABOR REVIEW, 96, Dec. 1973, pp. 53–6.

881. Brown, S. C. "Moonlighting increases sharply in 1977, particularly among women." MONTHLY LABOR RE-VIEW, 10, Ja. 1978, pp. 27–30.

882. Burke, Ronald J. and Douglas S. Wilcox. "Absenteeism and turnover among female telephone operators." PERSONNEL PSYCHOLOGY, 25, Wint. 1972, pp. 639–42.

883. California State Commission on the Status of Women. *Is paraprofessional work a dead-end? Upward mobility and career ladders, Sacramento, 1977.* (Available from Commission, 926 J Street, Room 1003, Sacramento, CA 95814.)

884. Chenoweth, Lillian and Elizabeth Maret-Havens. "Women's labor force participation—a look at some residential

patterns." MONTHLY LABOR REVIEW, 101, Mr. 1978, pp. 38–41.

885. Cooney, R. S. "Changing patterns of female labor force participation." INDUSTRIAL RELATIONS, 16, Oct. 1977, pp. 355–62.

886. Fairbanks, Jane D. and Susan Groag Bell, eds. "Second careers for women. A view from the San Francisco Peninsula." 1971. ERIC, 97 pp. ED 059 429.

887. Federico, S. M. and others. "Predicting women's turnover as a function of extent of met salary expectations and bio-demographic data." PERSONNEL PSYCHOLOGY, 29, Wint. 1976, pp. 559–66.

888. Gottfredson, Gary D. and Denise C. Daiger. "Using a classification of occupations to describe age, sex, and time differences in employment patterns." JOURNAL OF VOCATIONAL BEHAVIOR, 10, Ap. 1977, pp. 121–38.

889. Grossman, Allyson Sherman. "Labor force patterns of single women." MONTHLY LABOR REVIEW, 102, Ag. 1979, pp. 46–8.

890. Grossman, Allyson Sherman. "The labor force patterns of divorced and separated women." MONTHLY LABOR REVIEW, 100, Ja. 1977, pp. 48–53.

891. Harmon, Lenore W. "Anatomy of career commitment in women." JOURNAL OF COUNSELING PSYCHOLOGY, 17, Ja. 1970, pp. 77–80.

892. Holmstrom, Lynda Lytle. "Women's career patterns: Appearances and reality." JOURNAL OF THE NATIONAL ASSOCIATION OF WOMEN DEANS AND COUNSELORS, 36, Wint. 1973, pp. 76–81.

893. Jaffe, A. J. and Jeanne Clare Ridley. "The extent of lifetime employment of women in the United States." INDUSTRIAL GERONTOLOGY, 3, Wint. 1976, pp. 25–36.

894. Jerdee, Thomas H. and Benson Rosen. "Factors influencing the career commitment of women." 1976. ERIC, 15 pp. ED 132 665.

895. Jusenius, Carol J. *Dual career: A longitudinal study of labor market experience of women. Vol. 3.* 1975 (Available from Center for Human Resources Research, Ohio State University, Columbus, OH 43210.)

896. Kahne, H. "Women's occupational choices and lifetime work rhythms: Are we still making progress?" JOURNAL OF

EMPLOYMENT COUNSELING, 16, Je. 1979, pp. 83–93.

897. Kim, Sookon and others. "Dual careers: A longitudinal study of labor market experience of women. Vol. 2." 1972. ERIC, 131 pp. ED 068 713.

898. Kimmel, E. "Women as job changers." AMERICAN PSYCHOLOGIST, 29, Jl. 1974, pp. 536–9.

899. Kummerow, Jean M. and Thomas J. Hummel. "A study of variables relating to women's vocational patterns: A fifteen year follow-up." 1975. ERIC, 18 pp. ED 108 041.

900. Lopata, Helena Znaniecki. "Work histories of American urban women." GERONTOLOGIST, 2(1), 1971, pp. 27–36.

901. Maret-Havens, Elizabeth. "Developing an index to measure female labor force attachment." MONTHLY LABOR REVIEW, 100, My. 1977, pp. 35–8.

902. Mattila, Peter. "Labor turnover and sex discrimination: Working papers." 1974. ERIC, 28 pp. ED 096 407.

903. Meyer, Goldye W. and Steven V. Owen. "Predicting career change of mature, middle-class, married women." 1976. ERIC, 21 pp. ED 122 152.

904. "Myth of female absenteeism." MANAGEMENT REVIEW, 61, Mr. 1972, pp. 58–9.

905. Nero, Sharon A. "An exploratory study of the sociological and psychological impacts of mid-career changes for women." Final report. 1975. ERIC, 52 pp. ED 120 567.

906. Nicholson, N. and P. M. Goodge. "Influence of social, organizational and biographical factors on female absence." JOURNAL OF MANAGEMENT STUDIES, 13, Oct. 1976, pp. 234–54.

907. Rowe, Mary. "Why women take and keep low paying jobs." BUSINESS AND SOCIETY REVIEW, 5, Spr. 1973, pp. 55–60.

908. Schonberger, R. J. "Inflexible working conditions keep women 'unliberated.'" MENTAL HEALTH DIGEST, 4, Mr. 1972, pp. 21–2.

909. Schwartz, E. B. and R. A. Mackenzie. "Time management strategy for dual-career women." BUSINESS QUARTERLY, 42, Aut. 1977, pp. 32–41.

910. Sekscenski, E. S. "Women's share of moonlighting nearly doubles during 1969-79." MONTHLY LABOR REVIEW, 103, My. 1980, pp. 36–42.

911. "Turnover tendencies: Women generally stay on the job

longer than men; men are also more likely to get fired."
WALL STREET JOURNAL, 21 Ag. 1974, pp. 1, col. 5.

912. Vetter, Louise. "Planning ahead for the world of work:
Women's career patterns and their implications." AMERI-
CAN VOCATIONAL JOURNAL, 45, Dec. 1970, pp.
28–30.

913. Viscusi, W. Kip. "Sex differences in worker quitting."
REVIEW OF ECONOMICS AND STATISTICS, 62, Ag.
1980, pp. 388–98.

914. Weaver, Charles N. and Sandra L. Holmes. "On the use of
sick leave by female employees." PERSONNEL ADMINI-
STRATION AND PUBLIC PERSONNEL REVIEW, 1,
Oct. 1972, pp. 46–50.

915. Williams, Martha, Liz Ho, and Lucy Fielder. "Career
patterns: More grist for Women's Liberation." SOCIAL
WORK, 19, Jl. 1974, pp. 463–6.

4. Special Groups

a. Older Women

916. Elkin, Anna. "The emerging role of mature women. Basic
background data in employment and continuing education.
A selected annotated bibliography primarily of free and
inexpensive materials." 1976. ERIC, 27 pp. ED 123 415.

917. Garfinkel, Irwin and Stanley Masters. "The effect of income
and wage rates on the labor supply of older men and
women." 1974. ERIC, 64 pp. ED 105 042.

918. Jacobson, Carolyn J. "Some special problems the older
women worker encounters when seeking employment."
INDUSTRIAL AND LABOR RELATIONS FORUM, 7,
Oct. 1971, pp. 66–73.

919. Jacobson, Dan. "Rejection of the retiree role: A study of
female industrial workers in their 50's." HUMAN RELA-
TIONS, 27, My. 1974, pp. 477–92.

920. Jaslow, Philip. "Employment, retirement and morale among
older women." JOURNAL OF GERONTOLOGY, 31, Mr.
1976, pp. 212–8.

921. McClelland, Diana. "Opening job doors for mature women."
MANPOWER, 5, Ag. 1973, pp. 9–12.

922. Moser, Colette H. "Mature women - the new labor force."
INDUSTRIAL GERONTOLOGY, 1, Spr. 1974, pp. 14–25.

923. Mott, Frank L. "The National Longitudinal Survey mature women's cohort: A socioeconomic overview." 1978. ERIC, 51 pp. ED 155 344.

924. Quinn, Joseph F. *Wage determination and discrimination among older workers. Discussion Paper 468-77.* 1977. 36 pp. (Available from Institute for Research on Poverty, University of Wisconsin, 500 Lincoln Drive, Madison, WI 53706.)

925. Sherman, S. R. "Labor-force status of nonmarried women on the threshold of retirement." SOCIAL SECURITY BULLETIN, 37, Sept. 1974, pp. 3-15.

926. Sommers, Tish, "The compounding impact of age on sex." CIVIL RIGHTS DIGEST, 7, Fall 1974, pp. 2-9.

927. U.S. Congress. House. *National policy proposals affecting midlife women.* Washington, DC: GPO, 1979.

928. U.S. Congress. House. *Status of mid-life women and options for their future.* Washington, DC: GPO, 1980.

929. U.S. Congress. House. Select Committee on Aging. Subcommittee on Retirement Income and Employment. *Age and sex discrimination in employment and review of federal response to employment needs of the elderly.* Washington, DC: GPO, 1976.

930. U.S. Congress. House. Subcommittee on Retirement Income and Employment. *Age and sex discrimination in employment and review of federal response to employment needs of the elderly.* Washington, DC: GPO, 1975.

931. U.S. Women's Bureau. *Mature women workers: A profile.* Washington, DC: GPO, 1976.

932. U.S. Women's Bureau. *Jobfinding techniques for mature women.* Washington, DC: GPO, 1970.

b. Rural Women

933. Emery, Joan. "The farmworker women's equity project." FARMWORKER JOURNAL 1(3), 1979, pp. 33-7.

934. Heaton, C. and P. Martin. "Labor force participation differs significantly for the rural woman." MONTHLY LABOR REVIEW, 102, Ja. 1979, pp. 71-2.

935. Huffman, W. E. "Value of the productive time of farm wives: Iowa, North Carolina, and Oklahoma." JOURNAL OF AGRICULTURAL ECONOMICS, 58, Dec. 1976, pp. 836-41.

936. Maret, Elizabeth and Lillian Chenoweth. "The labor force patterns of mature rural women." RURAL SOCIOLOGY, 44, Wint. 1974, pp. 736–53.

937. Moser, Collette and Deborah Johnson. "Rural women workers in the 20th century: Annotated bibliography." 1973. ERIC, 70 pp. ED 100 570.

938. Sweet, James A. "The employment of rural farm wives." RURAL SOCIOLOGY, 37, Dec. 1972, pp. 553–77.

939. Terry, Geraldine B. and J. L. Charlton. "Changes in labor force characteristics of women in low income rural areas of the South." Southern cooperative series bulletin 185. 1974. ERIC, 52 pp. ED 104 627.

c. Low-Income and Welfare Recipients

940. Ballou, Jacqueline. "Work incentive policies: An evaluation of their effects on welfare women's choice." JOURNAL OF SOCIOLOGY AND SOCIAL WELFARE, 4(6), 1977, pp. 850–63.

941. Chambre, Susan Maizel. "Welfare, work and family structure." SOCIAL WORK, 22, Mr. 1977, pp. 103–9.

942. Chrissinger, M. S. "Factors affecting employment of welfare mothers." SOCIAL WORK, 25, Ja. 1980, pp. 52–6.

943. Cox, Irene. "The employment of mothers as a means of family support (mothers receiving aid under the Aid to Families With Dependent Children programs; based on conference paper)." WELFARE IN REVIEW, 8, Nov.-Dec. 1970, pp. 9–17.

944. Levinson, Perry. "How employable are AFDC women?" WELFARE IN REVIEW, 8, Ap.-Ag. 1970, pp. 12–16.

945. Levy, Frank. "The labor supply of female household heads, or AFDC work incentives don't work too well." JOURNAL OF HUMAN RESOURCES, 14, Wint. 1979, pp. 76–97.

946. Mason, Philip. "Employment, welfare, and mothers' motivation." MANPOWER, 5, Sept. 1973, pp. 28–32.

947. Meyer, J. A. "Impact of welfare benefit levels and tax rates on the labor supply of poor women." REVIEW OF ECONOMICS AND STATISTICS, 57, My. 1975, pp. 236–8.

948. Nichols, Abigail C. "Why welfare mothers work: Implications for employment and training services." SOCIAL SERVICE REVIEW, 53, Sept. 1979, pp. 378–91.

949. Opton, Edward N., Jr. "Factors associated with employment among welfare mothers." 1971. ERIC, 244 pp. ED 058 402.
950. Packer, A. H. "Women's roles and welfare reform (with discussion)." CHALLENGE, 20, Ja. 1978, pp. 45–50.
951. Pembroke, J. D. "Marketing welfare mother's job skills." MANPOWER, 6, Ja. 1974, pp. 28–9.
952. Reid, William J. and Audrey D. Smith. "AFDC mothers view the work incentive program." SOCIAL SERVICE REVIEW, 46, Sept. 1972, pp. 347–62.
953. Rein, Mildred. "Determinants of the work-welfare choice in AFDC." SOCIAL SERVICE REVIEW, 46, Dec. 1972, pp. 539–66.
954. Shea, John R. "Welfare mothers: Barriers to labor force entry." 1972. ERIC, 28 pp. ED 072 279.
955. U.S. Bureau of the Census. *Women and Poverty.* Washington, DC: GPO, 1974.
956. U.S. Women's Bureau. *Employment and economic issues of low-income women: Report of a project.* Washington, DC: GPO, 1978.
957. U.S. Women's Bureau. *Women with low incomes.* Washington, DC: GPO, 1977.
958. Willacy, Hazel M. and Harvey J. Kilaski. "Working women in poverty neighborhoods." MONTHLY LABOR REVIEW, 93(6), 1970, pp. 35–8.

d. Displaced Homemakers

959. Bellevue Community College, Washington. "Vocational orientation course for displaced homemakers." Instructor's manual and final report. 1979. ERIC, 111 pp. ED 185 360.
960. "Displaced homemaker: Symposium." JOURNAL OF HOME ECONOMICS, 71, Summ. 1976, pp. 16–24+.
961. Raimy, E. "Places for displaced homemakers." WORKLIFE MAGAZINE, 2, Jl. 1977, pp. 28–32.
962. Shaw, Lois B. *A profile of women potentially eligible for the displaced homemaker program under the Comprehensive Employment and Training Act of 1978.* 1979. 19 pp (Available from Center for Human Resource Research, College of Administrative Science, Ohio State University, Columbus, OH 43201.)
963. U.S. Congress. House. Select Committee on Aging. Subcommittee on Retirement Income and Employment. Hearing.

Equal opportunity for women: Displaced homemakers and minority women. Washington, DCL GPO, 1976.

964. U.S. Congress. House. Subcommittee on Employment Opportunities. Hearing. *Displaced Homemakers Act.* Washington, DC: GPO, 1977.

965. U.S. Congress. House. Subcommittee on Equal Opportunities. Hearing. *Equal Opportunity for Displaced Homemakers Act.* Washington, DC: GPO, 1976.

966. U.S. Congress. House. Subcommittee on Retirement Income and Employment. Hearing. *Equal opportunity for women. (Displaced homemakers and minority women).* Washington, DC: GPO, 1975.

967. U.S.Congress. Senate. Subcommittee on Employment, Poverty, and Migratory Labor. Hearing. *Displaced Homemakers Act. 1977.* Washington, DC: GPO, 1977.

968. U.S. Women's Bureau. *A guide to coordinating CETA vocational education legislation affecting displaced homemaker program.* Washington, DC: GPO, 1979.

969. U.S. Women's Bureau. *Displaced homemakers: A CETA program model, Fitchburg, Massachusetts.* Washington, DC: GPO, 1978.

970. "Women embark on new careers: The displaced homemakers program, Fort Wayne, Indiana." WORKLIFE MAGAZINE, 3, Oct. 1978, pp. 32+.

971. Wong, J. M. "Displaced homemakers' center." LIFELONG LEARNING, 3, Dec. 1979, pp. 6–7+.

e. Re-entry Women

972. Badenhoop, M. Suzanne and M. Kelly Johansen. "Do re-entry women have special needs?" PSYCHOLOGY OF WOMEN QUARTERLY, 4, Summ. 1980, pp. 591–5.

973. Bergquist, Laura. "Recycling lives. (Women re-entering the work force)." MS, 2, Ag. 1973, pp. 58+.

974. Lacy, Charles L. "Experimental project to prepare mature women for work in community social agencies." VOCATIONAL GUIDANCE QUARTERLY, 18, Je. 1970, pp. 255–8.

975. Roark, Anne C. "Re-entry programs enable women to resume careers in science." CHRONICLE OF HIGHER EDUCATION, 11 Feb. 1980, pp. 3–4.

976. Weinbaum, Batya. "Innovative opportunities for the returning woman." 1977. ERIC, 11 pp. ED 160 750.

f. Minority Women

977. Altenor, Aidan. "The role of occupational status in the career aspiration of black women: A reinterpretation." VOCATIONAL GUIDANCE QUARTERLY, 26, Mr. 1978, pp. 262+.

978. "Black professional women: Forging new careers despite dual standards and doing well, thank you." BLACK ENTERPRISE, 2, Nov. 1974, pp. 35–9.

979. (Black women in blue collar jobs). NEW YORK TIMES, 20 Ja. 1978, pp. 9, col. 4.

980. Dixon-Altenor, Carolyn and Aidan Altenor. "The role of occupational status in the career aspirations of Black women." VOCATIONAL GUIDANCE QUARTERLY, 25, Mr. 1977, pp. 211–6.

981. (Employment of Hispanic women). NEW YORK TIMES, 18 Ap. 1971, pp. 62, col. 4.

982. Epstein, Cynthia Fuchs. "Positive effects of the multiple negative: Sex, race, and professional elites." AMERICAN JOURNAL OF SOCIOLOGY, 78, Ja. 1973, pp. 912–35.

983. Farley, J. and others. "Black women's career aspirations." JOURNAL OF EMPLOYMENT COUNSELING, 14, Sept. 1977, pp. 116–9.

984. Hernandez, Aileen. "Small change for black women." MS, 3, Ag. 1974, pp. 16–8.

985. (Hispanic working women). NEW YORK TIMES, 18 Oct. 1971, pp. 1, col. 6.

986. "Recruiting minority women, No. 2." 1974. ERIC, 4 pp. ED 098 851.

987. Sorkin, Alan L. "Education, occupation, and income of nonwhite women." JOURNAL OF NEGRO EDUCATION, 41, Fall 1972, pp. 343–51.

988. U.S. Women's Bureau. *Fact on women workers of minority races.* Washington, DC: GPO, 1972.

989. U.S. Women's Bureau. *The immigrant woman and her job.* Washington, DC: GPO, 1970.

990. U.S. Women's Bureau. *Minority women workers: A statistical overview.* Washington, DC: GPO, 1977.

991. U.S. Women's Bureau. *Native American women and equal opportunity: How to get ahead in the Federal Government.* Washington, DC: GPO, 1979.

992. Zinn, M.B. "Employment and education of Mexican-

American women: The interplay of modernity and ethnicity in eight families." HARVARD EDUCATIONAL REVIEW, 50, Feb. 1980, pp. 47–62.

g. Offenders

993. North, David S. "Women offenders: Breaking the training mold escape from the past sought through non-traditional jobs." MANPOWER, 7, Feb. 1975, pp. 13–9.

994. U.S. Office of Education. Women's Education Equity Act Program. "Job options: First offender women. A pretrail intervention program." 1979, ERIC, 79 pp. ED 185 355.

995. U.S. Women's Bureau. *Employment needs of women offenders.* Washington, DC: GPO, 1977.

996. "Women cons to learn truck-driving jobs (Nebraska Center for Women)." FLEET OWNER, 72, Nov. 1977, pp. 139+.

h. Young Women and Recent Graduates

997. Baker, Sally Hillsman and Bernard Levenson. "Job opportunities of black and white working-class women." SOCIAL PROBLEMS, 22, Ap. 1975, pp. 510–33.

998. Bartol, K. M. and P. J. Manhardt. "Sex differences in job outcome preferences: Trends among newly hired college graduates." JOURNAL OF APPLIED PSYCHOLOGY, 64, Oct. 1979, pp. 477–82.

999. Bird, Caroline. "Welcome Class of '72, to the female job ghetto." NEW YORK, 29 My. 1972, pp. 31–4.

1000. Luria, Zella. "Recent women college graduates: A study of raising expectations." AMERICAN JOURNAL OF ORTHOPSYCHIATRY, 44, Ap. 1974, pp. 312–26.

1001. Parrish, John B., Hugh Folk and Charles Dodd. "College women and jobs: How well did the Class of '71 do?" JOURNAL OF COLLEGE PLACEMENT, 33, Dec.-Ja. 1973, pp. 69–73.

1002. Roderick, Roger D. and Joseph M. Davis. "Years for decision: A longitudinal study of the educational and labor market experience of young women." Volume 2. 1973. ERIC, 144 pp. ED 076 812.

1003. Shaeffer, Ruth G. "The buyers' market for new college grads: Makes it pay to be a woman, and a specialist." CONFERENCE BOARD RECORD, 12, Feb. 1975, pp. 45–51.

1004. U.S. Department of Labor. Manpower Administration. *Years for decision: A longitudinal study of the educational and labor market experience of young women.* Washington, DC: GPO, 1971.

1005. U.S. Women's Bureau. *Young women and employment: What we know and need to know about the school-work transition: Report of a conference.* Washington, DC: GPO, 1978.

5. Non-Traditional Employment

1006. Association of American Colleges. "Recruiting women for traditionally 'male' careers: Programs and resources for getting women into the men's world." 1977. ERIC, 10 pp. ED 145 256.

1007. Berger, Gertrude. "Females in male intensive professions." SCHOOL COUNSELOR, 27, Mr. 1980, pp. 319–20.

1008. Evans, Van M. "Unisex jobs and nontraditional employment." PERSONNEL, 52, Nov.-Dec. 1975, pp. 31–7.

1009. "Hiring women to do men's work." PROGRESSIVE GROCER, 50, Ja. 1971, pp. 84–8.

1010. Oregon. Governor's Commission for Women. "Women in non-traditional jobs in the mid-Willamette Valley Manpower Consortium." A research project. 1978. ERIC, 32 pp. ED 174 460.

1011. Standley, Kay and Bradley Soule. "Women in male-dominated profession: Contrasts in their personal and vocational histories." JOURNAL OF VOCATIONAL BEHAVIOR, 4, Ap. 1974, pp. 245–85.

1012. U.S. Women's Bureau. *Women in nontraditional jobs, a conference guide: Increasing job options for women.* Washington, DC: GPO, 1978.

1013. U.S. Women's Bureau. *Women in nontraditional jobs, a program model: Denver, better jobs for women.* Washington, DC: GPO, 1978.

6. Future Prospects

1014. Bengs, M. A. "Future belongs to women: An interview with Daniel Bell." WORKING WOMAN, 5, Ap. 1980, pp. 17–9.

1015. Berger, Gertrude, ed. "Changing roles of women; symposium." JOURNAL OF RESEARCH AND DEVELOP-MENT IN EDUCATION, 10, Summ. 1977, pp. 1–76.

1016. "Careers for women in the 70's." 1973. ERIC, 16 pp. ED 079 519.

1017. Gulledge, Earl N. "Career opportunities for women in the 1980's." FLORIDA VOCATIONAL JOURNAL, 4(5), 1979, pp. 10–12.

1018. Hedges, Janice N. "Women workers and manpower demands in the 1970's." MONTHLY LABOR REVIEW, 93, Je. 1970, pp. 19–29.

1019. Koontz, Elizabeth Duncan. "Women and jobs in a changing world." AMERICAN VOCATIONAL JOURNAL, 45, Dec. 1970, pp. 13–15.

1020. Koontz, Elizabeth. "The Women's Bureau looks at the future." MONTHLY LABOR REVIEW, 93, Je. 1970, pp. 3–9.

1021. Maupin, Joyce. "Working women on the move." (Keynote speech at West Coast Conference sponsored by San Francisco Women's Union and Berkeley-Oakland Women's Union, Nov. 1975). UNION W.A.G.E., No. 33, Ja.-Feb. 1976, pp. 1+.

1022. Mott, Frank L. "Racial differences in female labor force participation: Trends and implication for the future." 1978. ERIC, 31 pp. ED 155 345.

1023. Parrish, J. E. "College women and jobs: Another look at the 1970's." JOURNAL OF COLLEGE PLACEMENT, 31, Ap. 1971, pp. 34–8+.

1024. Rohrlich, Laura T. and Ethel L. Vatter. "Women in the world of work: Past, present, and future." WOMEN STUDIES, 1(3), 1973, pp. 263–77.

1025. Rosenblum, Marc. "The great labor force projection debate: Implications for 1980 (Focuses on female labor force participation)." AMERICAN ECONOMIST, 17, Fall 1973, pp. 122–9.

1026. "10 ways to create - not find - jobs in the 80's (Excerpt from epilogue to displaced homemakers: Organizing for a new life by Laurie Shields)." MS, 9, Nov. 1980, pp. 85–8.

1027. U.S. Women's Bureau. Careers for women in the 70's. Washington, DC: GPO, 1973.

1028. "Women and minorities won't achieve job parity with white males by 1985." WALL STREET JOURNAL, 19 Sept. 1979, pp. 1, col. 5.

B. PERSONAL FACTORS

1. Psychological Attributes

a. Personality Factors

1029. Bayes, M. and P. M. Newton. "Women in authority: A sociopsychological analysis." JOURNAL OF APPLIED BEHAVIORIAL SCIENCE, 14, Ja.-Feb.-Mr. 1978, pp. 7–25.

1030. Bielby, Denise Del Vento. "Career sex-atypicality and career involvement of college educated women: Baseline evidence from the 1960's." SOCIOLOGY OF EDUCATION, 51, Ja. 1978, pp. 7–28.

1031. Fenelon, M. E. "Women bring a new perspective to the workforce." MANAGEMENT WORLD, 9, Je. 1980, pp. 1+.

1032. Fitzgerald, Louise F. and John O. Crites. "Toward a career psychology of women: What do we know? What do we need to know?" JOURNAL OF COUNSELING PSYCHOLOGY, 27, Ja. 1980, pp. 44–62.

1033. Greenfeld, S. and others. "Feminine mystique in male-dominated jobs: A comparison of attitudes and background factors of women in male-dominated versus female-dominated jobs." JOURNAL OF VOCATIONAL BEHAVIOR, 17, Dec. 1980, pp. 291–309.

1034. Johnson, F. A. and C. L. Johnson. "Role strain in high-commitment career women." JOURNAL OF THE AMERICAN ACADEMY OF PSYCHOANALYSIS, 4, Ja. 1976, pp. 13–36.

1035. Kaslow, Florence W. and Lita L. Schwartz. "Self-perception of the attractive, successful female professional." INTELLECT, 106, Feb. 1978, pp. 313–5.

1036. Kaufman, D. and M. L. Fetters. "Work motivation and job values among professional men and women: A new accounting." JOURNAL OF VOCATIONAL BEHAVIOR, 17, Dec. 1980, pp. 251–62.

1037. Laws, Judith Long. "Psychological dimensions of women's work force participation." SLOAN MANAGEMENT REVIEW, 15, Sept. 1974, pp. 49–57.

1038. Lemkau, Jeanne Parr. "Personality and background characteristics of women in male-dominated occupations: A

review." PSYCHOLOGY OF WOMEN QUARTERLY,
5, Wint. 1979, pp. 221–40.

1039. Martin, Dorothy R. and David R. Saunders. "An analysis
of personality patterns of women in selected professions."
Final report. 1970. ERIC, 80 pp. ED 038 714.

1040. Miller, Joanne and others. "Women and work: The
psychological effects of occupational conditions." AMERI-
CAN JOURNAL OF SOCIOLOGY, 85, Je. 1974, pp.
66–94.

1041. Putnam, B. A. and J. C. Hansen. "Relationship of self-
concept and feminine role concept to vocational maturity
in young women." JOURNAL OF COUNSELING PSY-
CHOLOGY, 19, Sept. 1972, pp. 436–40.

1042. Tangri, Sandra Schwartz. "Effects of background, personality, college and post-college experiences on women's
post-graduate employment." Final report. 1974. ERIC,
347 pp. ED 101 223.

1043. Yuen, R. K. W. and others. "Vocational needs and
background characteristics of homemaker-oriented women
and careers-oriented women." VOCATIONAL GUI-
DANCE QUARTERLY, 28, Mr. 1980, pp. 250–6.

b. Psychological Barriers

1044. Breedlove, C. J. and V. G. Cicirelli. "Women's fear of
success in relation to personal characteristics and type of
occupation." JOURNAL OF PSYCHOLOGY, 86, Mr.
1974, pp. 181–90.

1045. Cherry, Frances and Kay Deaux. "Fear of success versus
fear of gender-inappropriate behavior." SEX ROLES,
4(1), 1978, pp. 97–101.

1046. Faunce, P. S. "Psychological barriers to occupational
success for women." JOURNAL OF THE NATIONAL
ASSOCIATION OF WOMEN'S DEANS, ADMINI-
STRATORS AND COUNSELORS, 40, Summ. 1977, pp.
140–4.

1047. Gold, Alice Ross. "Reexamining barriers to woman's career
development." AMERICAN JOURNAL OF ORTHO-
PSYCHIATRY, 48, Oct. 1978, pp. 690–702.

1048. Heilman, M. E. and K. E. Kram. "Self-derogating behavior
in women - fixed of flexible: The effects of co-worker's
sex." ORGANIZATIONAL BEHAVIOR AND HUMAN

PERFORMANCE, 22, Dec. 1978, pp. 497–507.

1049. Intons-Peterson, Margaret J. and Holly Johnson. "Sex domination of occupations and the tendencies to approach and avoid success and failure." PSYCHOLOGY OF WOMEN QUARTERLY, 4, Summ. 1980, pp. 526–47.

1050. Jackaway, Rita. "Sex differences in the development of fear of success." CHILD STUDY JOURNAL, 4(2), 1974, pp. 71–80.

1051. Janda, Louis H., Kevin E. O'Grady and Charles F. Capps. "Fear of success in males and females in sex-linked occupations." SEX ROLES, 4(1), 1978, pp. 43–50.

1052. Morgan, S. W. and B. Mausner. "Behavioral and fantasied indicators of avoidance of success in men and women." JOURNAL OF PERSONALITY, 41, Sept. 1973, pp. 457–70.

1053. O'Leary, Virginia E. "Some attitudinal barriers to occupational aspirations in women." PSYCHOLOGICAL BULLETIN, 81, Nov. 1974, pp. 809–26.

1054. Prather, Jane. "Why can't women be more like men: A summary of the socio-psychological factors hindering women's advancements in the professions." AMERICAN BEHAVIORAL SCIENTIST, 15, Nov.-Dec. 1971, pp. 172–82.

1055. Sassen, G. "Success anxiety in women: A constructivist interpretation of its source and its significance." HARVARD EDUCATIONAL REVIEW, 50, Feb. 1980, pp. 13–24.

1056. Schwartz, Ellen Bay. "Psychological barriers to increased employment of women." ISSUES IN INDUSTRIAL SOCIETY, 2(1), 1971, pp. 69–73.

1057. Sutherland, Sharon L. "The unambitious female: Women's low professional aspirations." SIGNS, 3(4), 1978, pp. 774–94.

1058. Williams, D. and M. King. "Sex role attitudes and fear of success as correlates of sex role behavior." JOURNAL OF COLLEGE STUDENT PERSONNEL, 17, Nov. 1976, pp. 480–4.

1059. Wood, M. M. and S. Greenfeld. "Fear of success in high achieving male and female managers in private industry vs. the public sector." JOURNAL OF PSYCHOLOGY, 103, Nov. 1979, pp. 289+.

c. Attitudes Toward Work and Careers

1060. Andrisani, P. J. and M. B. Shapiro. "Women's attitudes toward their jobs: Some longitudinal data on a national sample." PERSONNEL PSYCHOLOGY, 31, Spr. 1978, pp. 15–34.

1061. Bartol, Kathryn M. "Relationship of sex and professional training area to job orientation." JOURNAL OF APPLIED PSYCHOLOGY, 61, Je. 1976, pp. 368–70.

1062. Bratto, Rita and Edward A. Powers. "What the other half thinks: The implications of female perceptions for work demands." 1972. ERIC, 26 pp. ED 072 265.

1063. Brenner, O. C. and Joseph Tomkiewicz. "Job orientation of males and females: Are sex differences declining?" PERSONNEL PSYCHOLOGY, 32, Wint. 1979, pp. 741–50.

1064. Crumley, Wilma and Patricia Sailor. "Careers as viewed by five and ten year graduates of Home Economics and Journalism programs." 1975. ERIC, 12 pp. ED 122 277.

1065. Dodge, Dorothy. "Attitudes of undergraduate women toward careers." Final report. 1974. ERIC, 22 pp. ED 095 571.

1066. Frankel, P. M. "Sex-role attitudes and the development of achievement need in women." JOURNAL OF COLLEGE STUDENT PERSONNEL, 15, Mr. 1974, pp. 114–19.

1067. Hales, Loyde W. and Bradford J. Fenner. "Sex and social class differences in work values." ELEMENTARY SCHOOL GUIDANCE AND COUNSELING, 8, Oct. 1973, pp. 26–32.

1068. Hales, Loyde W. and Keith Yackee. "Self-concepts, sex, and work values." 1974. ERIC, 7 pp. ED 090 459.

1069. Handley, A. A. and William E. Sedlacek. "Characteristics and work attitudes of women working on campus." JOURNAL OF THE NATIONAL ASSOCIATION OF WOMEN DEANS, ADMINISTRATORS AND COUNSELORS, 40, Summ. 1977, pp. 128–34.

1070. Klemmack, David L. and John N. Edwards. "Women's acquisition of stereotyped occupational aspirations." SOCIOLOGY AND SOCIAL RESEARCH, 57, Jl. 1973. pp. 510–25.

1071. Vaughn, Margaret Miller. "Social forms and sex-linked reference groups as determinants of women's alienation in the workplace." UNIVERSITY OF MICHIGAN PAPERS IN WOMEN'S STUDIES, 1, Je. 1974, pp. 149–62.

2. Job Satisfaction and Job Dissatisfaction

1072. Ash, Philip. "Job satisfaction differences among women of different ethnic groups." JOURNAL OF VOCATIONAL BEHAVIOR, 2(2), 1972, pp. 495–507.

1073. Bisconti, Ann Stouffer. "Women: Marriage, career, and job satisfaction" 1978. ERIC, 19 pp. ED 167 909.

1074. Boris, B., Jr. "Job satisfaction and work values for women." JOURNAL OF THE NATIONAL ASSOCIATION FOR WOMEN DEANS, ADMINISTRATORS, AND COUN-SELORS, 37, Summ. 1974, pp. 151–7.

1075. Cantarow, Ellen. "Women workaholics: Beyond the pleasure principle." MOTHER JONES, 4, Je. 1979, pp. 56–62.

1076. "Deep discontent of the working woman." BUSINESS WEEK, 5 Feb. 1979, pp. 28–9.

1077. Dunham, Randall B. and Jeanne B. Herman. "Development of a female faces scale for measuring job satisfaction." JOURNAL OF APPLIED PSYCHOLOGY, 60, Oct. 1975, pp. 629–31.

1078. Glenn, Norval D., Patricia A. Taylor and Charles N. Weaver. "Age and job satisfaction among males and females: A multivariate, multisurvey study." JOURNAL OF APPLIED PSYCHOLOGY, 62, Ap. 1977, pp. 189–93.

1079. (Job dissatisfaction of education women.) NEW YORK TIMES, 22 Dec. 1972, pp. 1, col. 5.

1080. "New survey of the 70's: Women work more, better and enjoy (Roper poll)." WORKING WOMAN, 5, Jl. 1980, pp. 27–9.

1081. Penley, Larry E. and Brian L. Hawkins. "Organizational communication, performance, and job satisfaction as a function of ethnicity and sex." JOURNAL OF VOCA-TIONAL BEHAVIOR, 16, Je. 1980, pp. 368+.

1082. Sauser, W. I., Jr. and C. M. York. "Sex differences in job satisfaction: A reexamination." PERSONNEL PSY-CHOLOGY, 31, Aut. 1978, pp. 537–47.

1083. Shapiro, H. Jack. "Job motivations of males and females, an empirical study." PSYCHOLOGICAL REPORTS, 36, Ap. 1975, pp. 647–54.

1084. Shapiro, H. Jack and Louis W. Stern. "Job satisfaction: Male and female, professional and nonprofessional." PERSONNEL JOURNAL, 54, Jl. 1975, pp. 388–9.

1085. Weaver, Charles N. "Relationships among pay, race, sex, occupational prestige, supervision work autonomy, and job satisfaction in a national sample." PERSONNEL PSYCHOLOGY, 30, Aut. 1977, pp. 437–45.

1086. Weaver, Charles N. "Sex differences in the determinants of job satisfaction." ACADEMIC MANAGEMENT JOURNAL, 21, Je. 1978, pp. 265–74.

1087. Weaver, Charles N. "Sex differences in job satisfaction." BUSINESS HORIZONS, 17, Je. 1974, pp. 43–9.

1088. Weaver, Charles N. and Sandra L. Holmes. "Comparative study of the work satisfaction of females with full-time employment and full-time housekeeping." JOURNAL OF APPLIED PSYCHOLOGY, 60, Feb. 1975, pp. 117–8.

1089. Wright, James D. "Are working women really more satisfied? Evidence from several national surveys." JOURNAL OF MARRIAGE AND THE FAMILY, 40, My. 1978 pp. 301–14.

3. Success

1090. Cunningham, Robert M., Jr. "Women who made it offer insights." COLLEGE AND UNIVERSITY BUSINESS, 4, Feb. 1970, pp. 56–61.

1091. Epstein, Cynthia Fuchs. "Structuring success in women." EDUCATIONAL DIGEST, 39, Feb. 1974, pp. 56–9.

1092. Feather, N. T. "Positive and negative reactions to male and female success and failure in relation to the perceived status and sex typed appropriateness of occupations." JOURNAL OF PERSONALITY AND SOCIAL PSYCHOLOGY, 31, Mr. 1975, pp. 536–48.

1093. Feshbach, Norma A. "Realizing human potential: Focus on women I." EDUCATIONAL HORIZONS, 52(2), 1973-74, pp. 67–71.

1094. Fligstein, Neil and Wendy Wolf. "Sex similarities in occupational status attainment: Are the results due to the restriction of the sample to employed women?" SOCIAL SCIENCE RESEARCH, 7(2), 1978, pp. 197–212.

1095. Garland, Howard. "Sometimes nothing succeeds like success: Reactions to success and failure in sex-linked occupations."

PSYCHOLOGY OF WOMEN, 2, Fall 1977, pp. 50–61.

1096. Hoffman, Lois Wladis. "Early childhood experiences and women's achievement." JOURNAL OF SOCIAL ISSUES, 28(2), 1972, pp. 129–55.

1097. Lewin, E. and V. Olesen. "Lateralness in women's work - new views on success." SEX ROLES, 6, Ag. 1980, pp. 619–30.

1098. Louviere, V. "How women's drive succeeds in a man's world." NATION'S BUSINESS, 64, Ap. 1976, pp. 38+.

1099. Perrucci, Carolyn Cummings. "Gender and achievement: The early careers of college graduates." SOCIOLOGICAL FOCUS, 13, Ap. 1980, pp. 99–112.

1100. Pines, Ayala and Trudy Solomon. "The social psychological double bind of the competent women." 1976. ERIC, 14 pp. ED 159 576.

1101. Shapiro, Laura. "After C-R? Coping with work and success." MOTHER JONES, 9, Jl. 1978, pp. 3–6.

1102. Tidball, M. Elizabeth. "On liberation and competence." EDUCATIONAL RECORD, 57, Spr. 1976, pp. 101–10.

1103. Tomlinson-Keasey, C. "Role variables: Their influence on female motivational constructs." JOURNAL OF COUNSELING PSYCHOLOGY, 21, My. 1974, pp. 232–7.

1104. Waetjen, W. B., J. M. Schuerger and E. B. Schwartz. "Male and female managers: Self-concepts, success and failure." JOURNAL OF PSYCHOLOGY, 103, Sept. 1974, pp. 87–94.

1105. "Who achieves? (Many more Phi Beta Kappa men were in high prestige occupations than PBK women)." HUMAN BEHAVIOR, 5, Ap. 1976, pp. 54+.

C. SOCIAL AND ECONOMIC CLIMATE

1. Employment Discrimination

a. General

1106. Allen, A. Dale, Jr. "What to do about sex discrimination (Job discrimination because of sex)." LABOR LAW JOURNAL, 21, Sept. 1970, pp. 563–76.

1107. Arvey, Richard D. and Stephen J. Musso. "Determining the existence of unfair test discrimination for female clerical workers." PERSONNEL PSYCHOLOGY, 26, Dec. 1973, pp. 559–68.

1108. Bartol, K. M. "Sex structuring of organizations: A search for possible causes." ACADEMIC MANAGEMENT REVIEW, 3, Oct. 1978, pp. 805–15.

1109. Bryant, Willa C. "Discrimination against women in general: Black southern women in particular." CIVIL RIGHTS DIGEST, 4, Summ. 1971, pp. 10–1.

1110. Burton, Gene E. and Dev S. Pathak. "101 ways to discriminate against equal employment opportunity." ADVANCED MANAGEMENT JOURNAL, 41, Ag. 1976, pp. 22–30.

1111. Callis, Philip E. "Minimum height and weight requirements as a form of sex discrimination." LABOR LAW JOURNAL, 25, Dec. 1974, pp. 736–45.

1112. Connelly, Betty Jean and Ann Sullivan. "Discrimination against women in employment practices." ARETE, 1, Spr. 1971, pp. 52–66.

1113. "Discrimination against teenage girls (views of R.C. Sarri)." U S A TODAY, 108, Je. 1980, pp. 10–1.

1114. England, Paula. "Women and occupational prestige: A case of vacuous sex equality." SIGNS, 5, Wint. 1979, pp. 252–65.

1115. Epstein, Cynthia Fuchs. "Encountering the male establishment: Sex-status limits in women's careers in the professions." AMERICAN JOURNAL OF SOCIOLOGY, 75, My. 1970, pp. 965–82.

1116. Eyde, Lorraine D. "Eliminating barriers to career development of women." PERSONNEL AND GUIDANCE JOURNAL, 49, Sept. 1970, pp. 24–7.

1117. Feldberg, Roslyn L. and Evelyn Nakano Glenn. "Male and female: Job versus gender models in the sociology of work." SOCIAL PROBLEMS, 26, Je. 1979, pp. 524–38.

1118. Flanders, Dwight P. and Peggy Engelhardt Anderson. "Sex discrimination in employment: Theory and practice." INDUSTRIAL AND LABOR RELATIONS REVIEW, 26, Ap. 1973, pp. 938–55.

1119. Fretz, C. F. and Joanne Hayman. "Progress for women: Men are still more equal." HARVARD BUSINESS REVIEW, 51, Sept.-Oct. 1973, pp. 133–42.

1120. Fuller, Mary M. "In business the generic pronoun 'he' is non-job related and discriminatory." TRAINING AND DEVELOPMENT JOURNAL, 27, My. 1973, pp. 8–11.

1121. Gackenbach, Jayne I. and Stephen M. Auerback. "On-the-job sex discrimination: Barriers still exist for women." BUSINESS: THE MAGAZINE OF MANAGERIAL THOUGHT AND ACTION, 30, Jan.-Feb. 1980, pp. 24–30.

1122. Grady, John S. "Statistics in employment discrimination." LABOR LAW JOURNAL, 30, Dec. 1979, pp. 748–53.

1123. Hahn, Marilyn C. "Equal rights for women in career development." PERSONNEL, 47, Jl.-Ag. 1970, pp. 55–9.

1124. Hay, Howard C. "The use of statistics to disprove employment discrimination." LABOR LAW JOURNAL, 29, Jl. 1978, pp. 430–40.

1125. Holden, Constance. "NASA: Sacking of top black women stirs concern for equal employment." SCIENCE, 182, Nov. 1973, pp. 804–7.

1126. Jacobson, C. J. "Job problems of women workers." AMERICAN FEDERATIONIST, 84, Feb. 1977, pp. 12–6.

1127. Joyce, N. C. and P. Quickhall. "Women researchers analyze education, job barriers." SCIENCE, 198(4320), 1977, pp. 917–8.

1128. Kentucky. Legislative Research Commission. *Sex discrimination in employment. Research Report No. 171.* 1980. 87 pp. (Available from Legislative Research Commission, State Capitol, Frankfurt, KY 40601.)

1129. Kresge, Pat. "The human dimensions of sex discrimination." AAUW JOURNAL, 64, Feb. 1970, pp. 6–9.

1130. "Lagging behind: Though more women work, job equality fails to materialize." WALL STREET JOURNAL, 6 Jl. 1976, pp. 1, col. 6.

1131. Levitin, Teresa, Robert P. Quinn and Graham L. Staines. "Sex discrimination against the American working woman." AMERICAN BEHAVIORAL SCIENTIST, 15, Nov.-Dec. 1971, pp. 237–54.

1132. Long, James E. "Employment discrimination in the Federal sector." JOURNAL OF HUMAN RESOURCES, 11, Wint. 1976, pp. 86–97.

1133. Luksetich, William A. "Market power and sex discrimination in white-collar employment." REVIEW OF SOCIAL

ECONOMY, 37, Oct. 1979, pp. 211-24.

1134. Lutes, Carol. "Sex discrimination—the reality of women's rights." PROFESSIONAL MANAGEMENT BULLETIN, 12, Feb. 1972, pp. 10-8.

1135. McCune, Shirley. "Thousands reply to opinionaire: Many documented cases of sex discrimination." AAUW JOURNAL, 64, My. 1970, pp. 202-6.

1136. Markus, Maria. "Women and work (I): Feminine emancipation at an impasse." IMPACT OF SCIENCE ON SOCIETY, 22, Jan. 1970, pp. 61-72.

1137. Marshall, G. P. "Sex discrimination and state responsibility." SOCIAL AND ECONOMIC ADMINISTRATION, 9, Ag. 1975, pp. 153-63.

1138. Martin, Walter T. and Dudley L. Poston, Jr. "The occupational composition of white females: Sexism, racism and occupational differentiation." SOCIAL FORCES, 50, Mr. 1972, pp. 349-55.

1139. Medoff, Marshall H. "Market power and employment discrimination." JOURNAL OF HUMAN RESOURCES, 15, Spr. 1980, pp. 293+.

1140. Newland, Kathleen. *Women, men and the division of labor.* 1980. 43 pp. (Available from Worldwatch Institute, 1776 Massachusetts Ave., N. W., Washington, DC 20036.)

1141. Oster, Sharon M. "Industry differences in the level of discrimination against women." QUARTERLY JOURNAL OF ECONOMICS, 89, My. 1975, pp. 215-29.

1142. Osterman, Paul. "Sex discrimination in professional employment: A case study." INDUSTRIAL & LABOR RELATIONS REVIEW, 32, Jl. 1979, pp. 451-64.

1143. Pettigrew, L. Eudora, L. Thomas Keith and Homer C. Hawkins. "Sex discrimination and the American labor market: A perspective." SOCIOLOGICAL FOCUS, 7, Wint. 1973-1974, pp. 71-86.

1144. Reagan, Barbara B. and Betty J. Maynard. "Sex discrimination in universities: An approach through internal labor market analysis." AAUP BULLETIN, 60, Mr. 1974, pp. 13-21.

1145. Robinson, Lora H. "Institutional analysis of sex discrimination: A review and annotated bibliography." 1973. ERIC, 10 pp. ED 076 176.

1146. Rossi, Alice. "Discrimination and demography restrict

women." COLLEGE AND UNIVERSITY BUSINESS, 48, Feb. 1970, pp. 74–8.

1147. Rossi, Alice S. "Job discrimination and what women can do about it." ATLANTIC, 48, Mr. 1970, pp. 99–102.

1148. Schein, V. "Implications and obstacles to full participation of the woman worker." BEST'S REVIEW LIFE/HEALTH INSURANCE EDITION, 72, Ap. 1972, p. 22+.

1149. Schnepper, Jeff A., "Women and occupational segregation." INTELLECT, 105, Je. 1977, pp. 415–7.

1150. "Sex discrimination: The last acceptable prejudice." CONGRESSIONAL QUARTERLY WEEKLY REPORT, 18 Mr. 1972, pp. 597–600.

1151. Stant, Katherine. "Employment problems of women: Causes and cures." ARIZONA REVIEW, 22, My. 1973, pp. 10–3.

1152. U.S. Equal Employment Opportunity Commission. *Employment problems of women: A classic example of discrimination.* Washington, DC: GPO, 1972.

1153. Ward, J. S. "Sex discrimination is essential in industry." JOURNAL OF OCCUPATIONAL MEDICINE, 20, Sept. 1978, pp. 594–6.

1154. (Women and employment discrimination). NEW YORK TIMES, 19 Ap. 1970, pp. 1, col.1.

1155. (Women and job discrimination). NEW YORK TIMES, 25 Sept. 1977, Sec. 4, pp. 7, col. 1.

1156. (Women's Strike for Equality). NEW YORK TIMES, 19 Ag. 1970, pp. 43, col.1.

b. *Discriminatory Attitudes and Sex-role Stereotypes*

1157. Albrecht, Stan L. "Social class and sex-stereotyping of occupations." JOURNAL OF VOCATIONAL BEHAVIOR, 9, Dec. 1976, pp. 321–8.

1158. American Economic Association Committee on the Status of Women in the Economics Profession. "Combatting role prejudice and sex discrimination." AMERICAN ECONOMIC REVIEW, 53, Dec. 1973, pp. 1049–61.

1159. Baldwin, Stephen E. "Subconscious sex bias and labor market reality." LABOR LAW JOURNAL, 30, Jl. 1979, pp. 439+.

1160. Bem, Sandra L. and Daryl J. Bem. "Training the woman to know her place: The social antecedents of women in the world of work." 1973. ERIC, 29 pp. ED 082 098.

1161. Berman, Harriet Katz. "Job bias: The working woman." CIVIL LIBERTIES, 5, Sept. 1973, pp. 2+.

1162. Blau, Francine D. and Wallace E. Hendricks. "Occupational segregation by sex: Trends and prospects." JOURNAL OF HUMAN RESOURCES, 14, Spr. 1979, pp. 197–210.

1163. Burr, E. and others. "Women and the language of inequality." SOCIAL EDUCATION, 36, Dec. 1972, pp. 840–5.

1164. Feather, N. T. and J. G. Simon. "Stereotypes about male and female success and failure at sex-linked occupations." JOURNAL OF PERSONALITY, 44, Mr. 1976, pp. 16–37.

1165. Fox, H. W. and S. R. Renas. "Stereotypes of women in the media and their impact on women's careers. "HUMAN RESOURCES MANAGEMENT, 16, Spr. 1977, pp. 28–31.

1166. Golembiewski, R. T. "Testing some stereotypes about the sexes in organizations: Differential centrality of work?" HUMAN RESOURCE MANAGEMENT, 16, Wint. 1977, pp. 21–4.

1167. Grimm, James W. and Robert N. Stern. "Sex roles and internal labor market structures: The 'female' semi-professions." SOCIAL PROBLEMS, 21, 1974, pp. 690–705.

1168. Hall, G. "Changing sex roles in the labor force." PHI DELTA KAPPAN, 55, Oct. 1973, pp. 135–7.

1169. Haug, Marie R. "Sex role variations in occupational prestige ratings." SOCIOLOGICAL FOCUS, 8, Ja. 1975, pp. 47–56.

1170. Helson, Ravenna. "The changing image of the career woman." JOURNAL OF SOCIAL ISSUES, 28(2), 1972, pp. 33–46.

1171. Hesslebart, Susan. "Attitudes toward women, and their implications for the status of women in public and private employment." GOVERNMENTAL RESEARCH BUL-LETIN, 12, Je. 1975, pp. 1–4.

1173. Kalunian, P. and others. "Changing sex role stereotypes through career development." PSYCHOLOGY IN THE SCHOOLS, 12, Ap. 1975, pp. 230–3.

1174. Kaniuga, N. and others. "Working women portrayed on

evening television programs." VOCATIONAL GUID-
ANCE QUARTERLY, 23, Dec. 1974, pp. 134-7.

1175. Karre, Idahlynn. "Stereotyped sex roles and self-concept:
Strategies for liberating the sexes." COMMUNICATION
EDUCATION, 25, Ja. 1976, pp. 43-52.

1176. Koontz, Elizabeth Duncan. "Fighting stereotypes: Women
want up the career ladder." AMERICAN VOCATIONAL
JOURNAL, 48, My. 1973, pp. 35-6.

1177. Korda, Michael. "Male chauvinism in the office: An hour-
by-hour report." NEW YORK, 22 Ja. 1973, pp. 29-35.

1178. Kotliar, A. "Territorial problems relating to the structure of
employment in terms of sex." PROBLEMS OF ECON-
OMICS, 14, Oct. 1971, pp. 56-74.

1179. Krefting, Linda A. and Philip K. Berger. "Masculinity-
feminity perceptions of job requirements and their relationship to job-sex stereotypes." JOURNAL OF VO-
CATIONAL BEHAVIOR, 15, Oct. 1979, pp. 164-174.

1180. Leppaluoto, Jean R. "Attitude change and sex discrimination: The crunch hypothesis." 1972. ERIC, 11 pp.
ED 071 548.

1181. Linsenmeier, Joan A. W. and Camille B. Wortman.
"Attitudes toward workers and toward their work: More
evidence that sex makes a difference." JOURNAL OF
APPLIED SOCIAL PSYCHOLOGY, 9, Jl.-Ag. 1979, pp.
326-34.

1182. Lirtzman, S. I. and M. A. Wahba. "Determinants of
coalitional behavior of men and women: Sex roles or
situational requirements?" JOURNAL OF APPLIED
PSYCHOLOGY, 56, Oct. 1972, pp. 406-11.

1183. Lyons, L. J. "Four women on sex discrimination: The subtle
but influential villains: Company attitudes." NATIONAL
UNDERWRITER PROPERTY & CASUALTY INSUR-
ANCE EDITION, 4 My. 1977, pp. 2+.

1184. Lyons. L. J. "Sex bias: The villain is subtlety." NATIONAL
UNDERWRITERS LIFE & HEALTH INSURANCE
EDITION, 5 Mr. 1977, pp. 1+.

1185. Macke, Anne Statham, Paula M. Hudis and Don Larrick.
*Sex-role attitudes and employment among women: A
dynamic model of change and continuity.* 1979. 24 pp.
(Available from Ohio State University, College of Administrative Science, Center for Human Resource Research,

Columbus, OH 43201.)

1186. McClellan, Honor Elizabeth Herbst. "Women's roles and careers: Conflict, compromise, or fulfillment." 1973. ERIC, 244 pp. ED 103 750.

1187. Medvene, A. M. and A. Collins. "Occupational prestige and its relationship to traditional and non-traditional views of women's roles." JOURNAL OF COUNSELING PSYCHOLOGY, 21, Mr. 1974, pp. 139–43.

1188. Morrison, Peter A. and Judith P. Wheeler. "Working woman and 'woman's work': A demographic perspective on the breakdown of sex roles." 1976. ERIC, 9 pp. ED 134 808.

1189. Nickerson, Eileen T. "Women as a second-class minority: A case for changing sex-role stereotypes." 1974. ERIC, 16 pp. ED 108 025.

1190. Nolan, Kathleen. "Television programming hurts employment of women and minorities; study reported." MEDIA REPORT TO WOMEN, 8, Ja. 1980, pp. 1+.

1191. O'Donnell, W. J. and K. J. O'Donnell. "Update: Sex-role messages in TV commercials." JOURNAL OF COMMUNICATION, 28, Wint. 1978, pp. 156–8.

1192. O'Leary, V. E. and C. E. Depner. "Alternative gender roles among women: Masculine, feminine, androgenous." INTELLECT, 104, Ja. 1976, pp. 313–5.

1193. Penn, J. R. and M. E. Gabriel. "Role constraints influencing the lives of women." SCHOOL COUNSELOR, 23, Mr. 1976, pp. 252–6.

1194. Rosenbach, W. E., R. C. Dailey and C. P. Morgan. "Perceptions of job characteristics and affective work outcomes for women and men." SEX ROLES, 5, Je. 1979, pp. 267–78.

1195. Schein, V. E. "Sex role stereotyping, ability and performance: Prior research and new directions." PERSONNEL PSYCHOLOGY, 31, Summ. 1978, pp. 259–68.

1196. "Serious about careers? Many male executives still think women aren't." WALL STREET JOURNAL, 10 Jl. 1979, pp. 1, col. 5.

1197. "Sexism: Is the woman teacher discriminated against?" LEARNING: THE MAGAZINE FOR CREATIVE TEACHING, 1, Nov. 1972, pp. 77–84.

1198. Shann, Mary H. "Attitudes of professional men and women toward women's roles in society." 1979. ERIC, 32 pp. ED 169 391.

1199. Shinar, Eva H. "Sexual stereotypes of occupations." JOURNAL OF VOCATIONAL BEHAVIOR, 7, Ag. 1975, pp. 99–111.

1200. Spain, Jane B. "Job stereotyping—a time for change." VITAL SPEECHES, 1 Jl. 1973, pp. 549–51.

1201. Trigg, Linda J. and Daniel Perlman. "Social influences on women's pursuits of a non-traditional career." 1974. ERIC, 22 pp. ED 120 632.

1202. Tyer, Z. E. and C. J. Erdwins. "Relationship of sex role to male-dominated and female-dominated professions." PSYCHOLOGICAL REPORTS, 44, Je. 1979, pp. 1134+.

1203. Vetter, Louise and others. "Sugar and spice is not the answer. A parent handbook on the career implications of sex stereotyping." Research and development series no. 129. 1977. ERIC, 72 pp. ED 147 560.

1204. Wagel, W. H. "Women: The onus of sex stereotyping." PERSONNEL, 54, Nov. 1977, pp. 43–4.

1205. Watkins, Beverly. "This year's freshmen reflect new views of women's role." CHRONICLE OF HIGHER EDUCATION, 12 Ja. 1976, pp. 3–4.

1206. Williams, Gregory. "A research note on trends on occupational differentiation by sex." SOCIAL PROBLEMS, 22, Ap. 1975, pp. 543–7.

1207. Williams, Gregory. "Trends in occupational differentiation by sex." SOCIOLOGY OF WORK AND OCCUPATIONS, 3, Feb. 1976, pp. 38–62.

1208. "Women: Nine reports on role, image, and message; symposium." JOURNAL OF COMMUNICATION, 24, Spr. 1974, pp. 103–55.

2. Family Responsibilities and Conflicts

a. Working Wives—General

1209. Axelson, L. "The working wife: Differences in perception among negro and white males." JOURNAL OF MARRIAGE AND THE FAMILY, 32, 1970, pp. 457–64.

1210. Baqueiro, Armando J. and others. "The labor force decision of married female teachers: A comment." REVIEW OF ECONOMICS & STATISTICS, 58, My. 1976, pp. 241–5.

1211. Bell, Carolyn Shaw. "Age, sex, marriage and jobs."
      PUBLIC INTEREST, 76, Wint. 1973, pp. 76–87.
1212. Bell, Duran. "Why participation rates of black and white
      wives differ." JOURNAL OF HUMAN RESOURCES, 9,
      Fall 1974, pp. 465–79.
1213. Briggs, J. A. "How are you going to get 'em back in the
      kitchen? (You aren't)." FORBES, 15 Nov. 1977, pp.
      177–80+.
1214. Cleland, Virginia and others. "Social and psychological
      influences on employment of married nurses." NURSING
      RESEARCH, 25, Mr.-Ap. 1976, pp. 90–7.
1215. Cooney, Rosemary Santana. "Changing labor force partici-
      pation of Mexican-American wives: A comparison with
      anglos and blacks." SOCIAL SCIENCE QUARTERLY,
      56, Sept. 1975, pp. 252–61.
1216. "Employment and fertility among married women." MET-
      ROPOLITAN LIFE INSURANCE COMPANY. STATI-
      STICAL BULLETIN, 60, Jl. 1979, pp. 14–5.
1217. Fields, Judith M. "A comparison of intercity differences in
      the labor force participation rates of married women in
      1970 with 1940, 1950 and 1960." JOURNAL OF HUMAN
      RESOURCES, 11, Ag. 1976, pp. 568–77.
1218. Gramm, Wendy Lee. "Labor force decision of married
      female teachers: A discriminant analysis approach."
      REVIEW OF ECONOMICS AND STATISTICS, 55,
      Ag. 1973, pp. 341–8.
1219. Gramm, Wendy Lee. "A model of the household supply of
      labor over the life cycle: The labor supply decision of
      married school teachers." 1971. ERIC, 190 pp. ED 081
      976.
1220. Gray, Janet Dreyfus. "Married professional women: How
      they feel about the women's movement." JOURNAL OF
      NATIONAL ASSOCIATION FOR WOMEN DEANS,
      ADMINISTRATORS AND COUNSELORS, 43, Fall
      1979, pp. 26–9.
1221. Hawthorn, Geoffrey and Michael Paddon. "Work, family
      and fertility." HUMAN RELATIONS, 24, Dec. 1971, pp.
      611–28.
1222. Hayghe, H. "Families and the rise of working wives—an
      overview." MONTHLY LABOR REVIEW, 99, My. 1976,
      pp. 12–9.

1223. Hayghe, H. "Labor force activity of married women." MONTHLY LABOR REVIEW, 96, Ap. 1973, pp. 31–6.

1224. Hayghe, H. "Marital and family characteristics of the labor force in March 1973." MONTHLY LABOR REVIEW, 97, Ap. 1974, pp. 21–7.

1225. Heckman, James J. and Robert J. Willis. "A beta-logistic model for the analysis of sequential labor force participation by married women." JOURNAL OF POLITICAL ECONOMY, 85, Feb. 1977, pp. 27–58.

1226. Hughes, Helen MacGill. "Maid of all work or departmental sister-in-law: The faculty wife employed on campus." AMERICAN JOURNAL OF SOCIOLOGY, 78, Ja. 1973, pp. 767–72.

1227. Huth, Carol M. "Married women's work status: The influence of parents and husbands." JOURNAL OF VOCATIONAL BEHAVIOR, 13, Dec. 1978, pp. 272–86.

1228. Johnson, Beverly L. "Changes in marital and family characteristics of workers, 1970-78." MONTHLY LABOR REVIEW, 102, Ap. 1979, pp. 49–52.

1229. Johnson, Beverly L. "Marital and family characteristics of the labor force." MONTHLY LABOR REVIEW, 103, Ap. 1980, pp. 48–52.

1230. Johnson, Beverly L. and H. Hayghe. "Labor force participation of married women, March 1976." MONTHLY LABOR REVIEW, 100, Je. 1977, pp. 32–5.

1231. "Labor force decision of married female teachers." REVIEW OF ECONOMICS AND STATISTICS, 58, My. 1976, pp. 241–5.

1232. Landry, Bart and Margaret Platt Jendrek. "The employment of wives in middle-class black families." JOURNAL OF MARRIAGE AND THE FAMILY, 40, Nov. 1978, pp. 787–97.

1233. Link, C. R. and R. F. Settle. "Labor supply responses of married professional nurses: New evidence." JOURNAL OF HUMAN RESOURCES, 14, Spr. 1979, pp. 256–66.

1234. Mahoney, E. R. and J. G. Richardson. "Perceived social status of husbands and wives: The effects of labor force participation and occupational prestige." SOCIOLOGY AND SOCIAL RESEARCH, 63, Ja. 1979, pp. 364–74.

1235. "Married women in the labor force." METROPOLITAN LIFE INSURANCE COMPANY. STATISTICAL BUL-

LETIN. 55, Ag. 1974, pp. 9–10.

1236. Meador, Raymond L. "On a wife returning to professional work." PUBLIC MANAGEMENT, 55, Feb. 1973, p. 15+.

1237. Mincer, Jacob and Haim Ofek. "The distribution of lifetime labor force participation of married women: Comment." JOURNAL OF POLITICAL ECONOMY, 87, Feb. 1979, pp. 197–212.

1238. Morgenstern, Richard D. and William Hamovitch. "Labor supply of married women in part-time and full-time occupations." INDUSTRIAL AND LABOR RELATIONS REVIEW, 30, Oct. 1976, pp. 59–67.

1239. Nakamura M. and others. "Job opportunities, the offered wage, and the labor supply of married women." AMERICAN ECONOMIC REVIEW, 69, Dec. 1979, pp. 787–805.

1240. Newberry, Phyllis, Myrna M. Weissman and Jerome K. Myers. "Working wives and housewives: Do they differ in mental status and social adjustment?" AMERICAN JOURNAL OF ORTHOPSYCHIATRY, 49, Ap. 1979, pp. 283–91.

1241. Pace, Lois W. "A study of attitudes of married women toward married women's employment." 1970. ERIC, 131 pp. ED 042 989.

1242. Pendleton, Brian F., Margaret M. Poloma and T. Neal Garland. "Scales for investigation of the dual career family." JOURNAL OF MARRIAGE AND THE FAMILY, 42, My. 1980, pp. 269–76.

1243. Pingree, Suzanne and Matilda Butler-Paisley. "Attitudes toward hiring a professional couple: Results of a recent survey." 1974. ERIC, 24 pp. ED 095 738.

1244. Ritter, Kathleen V. and Lowell L. Hargens. "Occupational positions and class identifications of married working women: A test of the asymmetry hypothesis." AMERICAN JOURNAL OF SOCIOLOGY, 80, Ja. 1975, pp. 934–48.

1245. Schonberger, R. J. "Ten million US housewives want to work." LABOR LAW JOURNAL, 21, Je. 1970, pp. 374–9.

1246. Shaw, Lois B. Changes in the work attachment of married women, 1966-1976. 1979. 33 pp. (Available from Center for Human Resource Research, College of Administrative Science, Ohio State University, Columbus, OH 43201.)

1247. Waldman, Elizabeth and others. "Working mothers in the

1970s: A look at the statistics." MONTHLY LABOR REVIEW, 102, Oct. 1979, pp. 39–49.

1248. Weissman, Myrna M. and others. "The faculty wife: Her academic interests and qualifications." AAUP BULLETIN, 58, Sept. 1972, pp. 287–92.

1249. Winter, David G., Abigail J. Stewart and David C. Mc Clelland. "Husband's motives, and wife's career level." JOURNAL OF PERSONALITY AND SOCIAL PSY-CHOLOGY, 35, Mr. 1977, pp. 159–66.

1250. (Working wives). NEW YORK TIMES, 21 Dec. 1978, pp. 20, col. 2.

b. Working Mothers

1251. Beckman, Linda J. "The relative rewards and costs of parenthood and employment for employed women." PSYCHOLOGY OF WOMEN QUARTERLY, 2, Spr. 1978, pp. 215–34.

1252. Berson, Janet S. "Perceived costs of combining career and family roles: The influence of early family history on adult role decisions." 1977. ERIC, 21 pp. ED 156 953.

1253. Darian, Jean C. "Convenience of work and the job constraint of children." DEMOGRAPHY, 12, My. 1975, pp. 245–58.

1254. Darian, Jean C. "Factors influencing the rising labor force participation rates of married women with pre-school children." SOCIAL SCIENCE QUARTERLY, 56, Mr. 1976, pp. 614–30.

1255. Falk, Carol H. "What should a mother do about her career? At home with Philip Lee." WALL STREET JOURNAL, 21 Mr. 1980, pp. 24+.

1256. Gordon, Henry A. and Kenneth C. W. Kammeyer. "The gainful employment of women with small children." JOURNAL OF MARRIAGE AND THE FAMILY, 42, My. 1980, pp. 327–36.

1257. Grossman, Allyson Sherman. "Almost half of all children have mothers in the labor force." MONTHLY LABOR REVIEW, 100, Je. 1977, pp. 41–3.

1258. Hamovitch, William and Richard D. Morgenstern. "Children and the productivity of academic women." JOURNAL OF HIGHER EDUCATION, 48, Nov.-Dec. 1977, pp. 633–45.

1259. Hock, Ellen, Karen Christman and Michael Hock. "Career-related decisions of mothers of infants." FAMILY RELATIONS, 29, Jl. 1980, pp. 325–30.

1260. Hock, Ellen, Karen Christman and Michael Hock. "Factors associated with decisions about return to work in mothers of infants." DEVELOPMENTAL PSYCHOLOGY, 16, Sept. 1980, pp. 535–6.

1261. Lancaster, Jeanette. "Coping mechanisms for the working mother." AMERICAN JOURNAL OF NURSING, 75, Ag. 1975, pp. 1322–3.

1262. Lublin, Joann S. "What should a mother do about her career? Juggling job and junior." WALL STREET JOURNAL, 21 Mr. 1980, pp. 24+.

1263. MacLaury, J. "Senator's reaction to report on working women and children." MONTHLY LABOR REVIEW, 98, Oct. 1975, pp. 36–8.

1264. Nagely, Donna L. "Traditional and pioneer working mothers." JOURNAL OF VOCATIONAL BEHAVIOR, 1, Oct. 1971, pp. 331–41.

1265. Shapiro, David and Frank L. Mott. "Labor supply behavior of prospective and new mothers." DEMOGRAPHY, 16, My. 1979, pp. 199–208.

1266. Sobol, Marion Gross. "A dynamic analysis of labor force participation of married women of childbearing age." JOURNAL OF HUMAN RESOURCES, 8, Fall 1973, pp. 497–505.

1267. Stevens, Gillian and Monica Boyd. "The importance of mother: Labor force participation and intergenerational mobility of women." SOCIAL FORCES, 59, Sept. 1980, pp. 186–99.

1268. Waite, L. J. "Working wives and the family life cycle." AMERICAN JOURNAL OF SOCIOLOGY, 86, Sept. 1980, pp. 272–94.

1269. Waite, Linda J. and Glenna D. Spitze. "Female work orientation and marital events. The transition to marriage and motherhood." 1978. ERIC, 48 pp. ED 169 243.

1270. Waldman, Elizabeth and Kathryn R. Gover. "Children of women in the labor force." MONTHLY LABOR REVIEW, 94, JL. 1971, pp. 19–25.

1271. Waldman, Elizabeth and Kathryn R. Gover. "Family characteristics of women in the labor force." MONTHLY

LABOR REVIEW, 95, Ap. 1972, pp. 4–8.

1272. "When mothers are also managers." BUSINESS WEEK, 18 Ap. 1977, pp. 155–6+.

1273. (Working mothers). NEW YORK TIMES, 1 Feb. 1977, pp. 17, col. 1.

1274. *Working mothers and their children.* Washington, DC: GPO, 1977.

1275. Young, Christabel M. "Work sequences of women during the family life cycle." JOURNAL OF MARRIAGE AND THE FAMILY, 40, My. 1978, pp. 401–12.

c. Role Conflicts

1276. Allen, R. E. and T. J. Keaveny. "Does the work status of married women affect their attitudes toward family life?" PERSONNEL ADMINISTRATION, 24, Je. 1979, pp. 63–6.

1277. Aneshensel, Carol S. and Bernard C. Rosen. "Domestic roles and sex differences in occupational expectations." JOURNAL OF MARRIAGE AND THE FAMILY, 42, Feb. 1980, pp. 121–32.

1278. Clark, Linda Nielsen. "Considerations for married career women." JOURNAL OF NATIONAL ASSOCIATION OF WOMEN DEANS, ADMINISTRATORS, AND COUNSELORS, 40, Feb. 1976, pp. 18–21.

1279. Committee on Status of Women in Academic Profession. "Leaves of absence for child-bearing, child rearing, and family emergencies." AAUP BULLETIN, 3, Ap. 1974, pp. 119–39.

1280. Dalrymple, Julia I. and others. "Preparation for a dual role: Homemaker-wage earner, with adaptations to inner city youth." Final report, vol. 1. 1971. ERIC, 241 pp. ED 058 464.

1281. Farmer, Helen S. and Martin J. Bohn, Jr. "Home-career conflict reduction and the level of career interest in women." JOURNAL OF COUNSELING PSYCHOLOGY, 17, Mr. 1970, pp. 228–32.

1282. Frank, Robert H. "Family location constraints and the geographic distribution of female professionals." JOURNAL OF POLITICAL ECONOMY, 86, Feb. 1978, pp. 117–30.

1283. Gordon, Francine E. and Douglas T. Hall. "Self-image and stereotypes of femininity: Their relationship to women's role conflicts and coping." JOURNAL OF APPLIED PSYCHOLOGY, 59, Ap. 1974, pp. 241-3.

1284. Gramm, Wendy Lee. "Household utility maximization and the working wife." AMERICAN ECONOMIC REVIEW, 65, Mr. 1975, pp. 90-100.

1285. Hall, Douglas T. and Francine E. Gordon. "Career choices of married women: Effects on conflict, role behavior and satisfaction." JOURNAL OF APPLIED PSYCHOLOGY, 58(1), 1973, pp. 42-8.

1286. Hall, F. S. and D. T. Hall. "Dual careers—how do couples and companies cope with the problems?" OR-GANIZATIONAL DYNAMICS, 6, Spr. 1978, pp. 57-77.

1287. Hardesty, Sarah A. and Nancy E. Betz. "The relationship of career salience, attitudes toward women, and demographic and family characteristics to marital adjustment in dual-career couples." JOURNAL OF VOCATIONAL BE-HAVIOR, 17, Oct. 1980, pp. 242+.

1288. Havens, Elizabeth Maret and Jack P. Gibbs. "The relation between female labor force participation and fertility: A theory of variability." SOCIOLOGICAL METHODS & RESEARCH, 3, Feb. 1975, pp. 258-90.

1289. Hedges, Janice Neipert and Jeanne K. Barnett. "Working women and the division of household tasks." MONTHLY LABOR REVIEW, 95, Ap. 1972, pp. 9-13.

1290. Hoffman, Lois Wladis. "The employment of women, education, and fertility." MERRILL-PALMER QUAR-TERLY, 20, Ap. 1974, pp. 99-120.

1291. Knowles, Em Claire. *Dual-career couple relationships: An annotated bibliography.* 1980, 14 pp. (Available from author, Humanities/Social Science Reference De-partment, Shields Library, University of California, Davis, CA 95616.)

1292. Kuiper, S. "Women at work: Young marrieds face the pressures of multiple roles." MANAGEMENT WORLD, 6, Je. 1977, pp. 3-6.

1293. Long, James E. and Ethel B. Jones. "Labor force entry and exit by married women: A longitudinal analysis." REVIEW OF ECONOMICS AND STATISTICS, 62, Feb. 1980, pp. 1-6.

1294. Long, Larry H. "Women's labor force participation and the residential mobility of families." SOCIAL FORCES, 52, Mr. 1974, pp. 342–8.

1295. Lopata, H. Z. and K. F. Norr. "Changing commitments of American women to work and family roles." SOCIAL SECURITY BULLETIN, 43, Je. 1980, pp. 3–14.

1296. Middleton, Lorenzo. "Marriage curbs women's careers in academe, sociologists find." CHRONICLE OF HIGHER EDUCATION, 9 Oct. 1979, p. 1+.

1297. Molm, Linda D. "Sex role attitudes and employment of married women: The direction of causality." SOCIOLOGICAL QUARTERLY, 19, Ag. 1978, pp. 522–33.

1298. Moore, Sylvia F. *The short-term effects of marital disruption on the labor supply behavior of young women.* 1979. 133 pp. (Available from Ohio State University, College of Administrative Science, Columbus, OH 43201.)

1299. Mortimer, Jeylan, Richard Hall and Reuben Hill. "Husbands' occupational attributes as constraints on wives' employment." SOCIOLOGY OF WORK & OCCUPATIONS, 5, Ag. 1978, pp. 285–313.

1300. Neipert, Janice and Jeanne K. Barnett. "Working women and the division of household tasks." MONTHLY LABOR REVIEW, 95, Ap. 1972, pp. 9–14.

1301. Neugarten, Bernice L. "Education and the life cycle." SCHOOL REVIEW, 80, Feb. 1972, pp. 209–16.

1302. Neuman, S. G. "Wife, mother, teacher, scholar, and sex object: Role conflicts of a female academic." INTELLECT, 106, Feb. 1978, pp. 302–6.

1303. Obarr, Jean. "The dual careers of faculty and family: Can they both be done well?" 1978, ERIC, 15 pp. ED 177 989.

1304. Peplau, Letitia Anne and Karen Rook. "Dual career relationships: The college couple perspective." 1978. ERIC, 7 pp. ED 160 939.

1305. Pleck, J. H., G. L. Staines and L. Lang. "Conflicts between work and family life." MONTHLY LABOR REVIEW, 103, Mr. 1980, pp. 29–31.

1306. Pleck, Joseph H. "The work-family role system." SOCIAL PROBLEMS, 24, Ap. 1977, pp. 417–27.

1307. Pospisil, V. C. "Problems of dual-career marriages." INDUSTRY WEEK, 15 Nov. 1976, pp. 86–9.

1308. Preston, Samuel H. and Alan Thomas Richards. "The influence of women's work opportunities on marriage rates." DEMOGRAPHY, 12, My. 1975, pp. 209–22.

1309. Rand, Lorraine M. and Anna Louise Miller. "A developmental cross-sectioning of women's careers and marriage attitudes and life plans." JOURNAL OF VOCATIONAL BEHAVIOR, 2, Jl. 1972, pp. 317–31.

1310. Richardson, John G. "Wife occupational superiority and marital troubles: An examination of the hypothesis." JOURNAL OF MARRIAGE AND THE FAMILY, 41, Feb. 1979, pp. 63–74.

1311. Sampson, Joan M. and others. "Employment status of the wife-mother: Psychological, social, and socioeconomic influencs." HOME ECONOMICS RESEARCH JOURNAL, 3, Je. 1975, pp. 266–79.

1312. Sandell, S. H. "Women and the economics of family migration." REVIEW OF ECONOMICS AND STATISTICS, 59, Nov. 1977, pp. 406–14.

1313. Stake, Jayne E. "Women's self-estimates of competence and the resolution of the career/home conflict." JOURNAL OF VOCATIONAL BEHAVIOR, 14, Feb. 1979, pp. 33–42.

1314. "Unequal commuting. (Women must look to jobs nearer home because of home responsibilities)." HUMAN BEHAVIOR, 6, Nov. 1977, pp. 72+.

1315. Walker, Kathryn E. "Household work time: Its implication for family decisions." JOURNAL OF HOME ECONOMICS, 65, Oct. 1973, pp. 7–11.

1316. "Women at work: Marital relationships often undergo strain when wives get jobs." WALL STREET JOURNAL, 19 Sept. 1978, pp. 1, col. 1.

d. Two-Income Families

1317. Bergmann, Barbara R. and others. "The effect of wives' labor force participation on inequality in the distribution of family income." JOURNAL OF HUMAN RESOURCES, 15, Summ. 1980, pp. 452+.

1318. Danziger, Sheldon. "Do working wives increase family income inequality?" Discussion paper no. 518–78. 1978. ERIC, 15 pp. ED 166 327.

1319. "The economic role of women in family life." FAMILY ECONOMICS REVIEW, Fall 1973, pp. 3–26+.

1320. Ewer, Phyllis A., Eileen Crimmins and Richard Oliver. "An analysis of the relationship between husband's income, family size and wife's employment in the early stages of marriage." JOURNAL OF MARRIAGE AND THE FAMILY, 41, Nov. 1979, pp. 727–38.

1321. "Family investments in human capital: Earnings of women." JOURNAL OF POLITICAL ECONOMY, 82, Mr.-Ap. 1974, pp. S76–S110.

1322. Frazier, Joan. "Banking on women." NEW TIMES, 18 Ap. 1975, pp. 42+.

1323. Hafstrom, J. and M. Dunsing. "Socioeconomic and social-psychological influences on reasons wives work." JOURNAL OF CONSUMER RESEARCH, 5, Dec. 1978, pp. 169–75.

1324. Hayghe, H. "Working wives contribution to family income in 1977." MONTHLY LABOR REVIEW, 102, Oct. 1979, pp. 62–4.

1325. Hiller, Dana V. and William W. Philliber. "Necessity, compatibility and status attainment as factors in the labor force participation of married women." JOURNAL OF MARRIAGE AND THE FAMILY, 42, My. 1980, pp. 347–54.

1326. Horvath, F. W. "Working wives reduce inequality in distribution of family earnings." MONTHLY LABOR REVIEW, 103, Jl. 1980, pp. 51–60.

1327. Kiechel, W., 3d. "Two-income families will reshape the consumer markets." FORTUNE, 10 Mr. 1980, pp. 110–4+.

1328. Leuthold, J. H. "Effect of taxation on the hours worked by married woman." INDUSTRIAL AND LABOR RELATIONS REVIEW, 31, Jl. 1978, pp. 520–6.

1329. Mitchell, O.S. "Labor force activity of married women as a response to changing jobless rates." MONTHLY LABOR REVIEW, 103, Je. 1980, pp. 32–3.

1330. "More working women increasing incomes of U.S. black families." COMMERCE TODAY, 10 Ja. 1972, pp. 22+.

1331. Nussbaum, J. M. "Tax structure and discrimination against working wives." NATIONAL TAX JOURNAL, 25, Je. 1972, pp. 183–91.

1332. Rosen, H. S. "Tax illusion and the labor supply of married women." REVIEW OF ECONOMICS AND STATISTICS, 58, My. 1976, pp. 161–72.

1333. Ryscavage, P. "More wives in the labor force have husbands

with above avarage incomes." MONTHLY LABOR
REVIEW, 102, Je. 1979, pp. 40–9.

1334. Strober, Myra H. "Wives' labor force behavior and family
consumption patterns." AMERICAN ECONOMIC RE-
VIEW, 67, Feb. 1977, pp. 410–7.

1335. "Upward mobility two incomes can buy." BUSINESS
WEEK, 20 Feb. 1978, pp. 80+.

1336. "Women at work: The rich get richer as well-to-do wives
enter the labor force." WALL STREET JOURNAL, 8
Sept. 1978, pp. 1+.

1337. "Working wives becoming major marketing force." AD-
VERTISING AGE, 5 Apr. 1976. pp. 34+.

e. *Women Heads of Households*

1338. Feldman, Harold and Margaret Feldman. "A study of the
effects on the family due to employment of the welfare
mother." 1972. ERIC, 329 pp. ED 060 215.

1339. Honig, Marjorie Hanson. "The impact of the welfare system
on labor supply and family stability: A study of female
heads of families." 1971. ERIC, 157 pp. ED 081 991.

1340. Hooper, J. O. and G. B. March. "Female single parent in
the university." JOURNAL OF COLLEGE STUDENT
PERSONNEL, 21, Mr. 1980, pp. 141–6.

1341. Johnson, Beverly L. "Women who head families: Their
numbers rise, income lags." MONTHLY LABOR RE-
VIEW, 101, Feb. 1978, pp. 32–7.

1342. McEaddy, B. J. "Women who head families: A socioeconomic analysis." MONTHLY LABOR REVIEW, 99,
Je. 1976, pp. 3–9.

1343. Stein, Robert L. "The economic status of families headed by
women." MONTHLY LABOR REVIEW, 93, Dec. 1970,
pp. 3–10.

1344. U.S. Bureau of the Census. Population Division. *Female
family heads: Growth, structure and composition, other
demographic characteristics, economic characteristics,
housing, primary individuals and subfamilies.* Washington,
DC: GPO, 1974.

1345. "Wife is chief breadwinner in 7.4 percent of families."
COMMERCE TODAY, 2 Ap. 1973, pp. 20+.

1346. "Women-headed households growing rapidly." DOLLARS
AND SENSE, 37, My. 1978, pp. 14+.

f. Child Care

1347. *Child care and child development programs, 1977-78, Part 1.* Washington, DC: GPO, 1977.

1348. *Child care: Data and materials.* Washington, DC: GPO, 1977.

1349. *Childcare and preschool: Options for federal support.* Washington, DC: GPO, 1978.

1350. *Children on campus: Survey of pre-kindergarten programs at institutions of higher education in the U.S.* Washington, DC: GPO, 1973.

1351. Day Care and Child Development Council of America. *Resources for day care: A catalog of publications.* 1973. 26 pp. (Available from Day Care and Child Development Council, 1401 K Street, N.W., Washington, DC 20005.)

1352. *Day care services: Industry's involvement.* Washington, DC: GPO, 1971.

1353. (Day care services, problem for working women). NEW YORK TIMES, 30 Nov. 1970, pp. 1+, col. 7.

1354. Ditmore, Jack and W. R. Prosser. "A study of day care's effects on the labor force participation of low-income mothers." Working papers. 1973. ERIC, 113 pp. ED 080 627.

1355. "Employer personnel practices and child care arrangements of working mothers in New York City." 1973. ERIC, 77 pp. ED 094 155.

1356. Husby, Ralph D. "Day care for families on public assistance: Workfare versus welfare." INDUSTRIAL & LABOR RELATIONS REVIEW, 27, Jl. 1974, pp. 503–10.

1357. Sipser, Margaret Ann. "Maternity leave: Judicial and arbitral interpretation, 1970-72." LABOR LAW JOURNAL, 24, Mr. 1973, pp. 173–90.

1358. Smith, Audrey and William J. Reid. "Child care arrangements of AFDC mothers in the Work Incentive Program." CHILD WELFARE, 52, Dec. 1973, pp. 651–61.

1359. U.S. Women's Bureau. *Day care services: Industry's involvement.* Washington, DC: GPO, 1972.

1360. "Who'll baby-sit while mom works?" INDUSTRY WEEK, 7 Ag. 1972, pp. 42+.

1361. "Women at work: Day care is booming." WALL STREET JOURNAL, 15 Sept. 1978, pp. 1+, col. 1.

3. Economic Factors

a. General

1362. *American women workers in a full employment economy.* Washington, DC: GPO, 1977.

1363. Baker, Sally Hillsman and Bernard Levenson. *Earnings prospects of black and white working class women.* 1975. 42 pp. (Available from Sally Hillsman Baker, Sociology Department, Queens College, CUNY, Flushing, NY 11367.)

1364. Bartos, R. "Moving target: The impact of women's employment on consumer behavior." JOURNAL OF MARKETING, 41, Jl. 1977, pp. 31–7.

1365. Bergman, Barbara B. and Irma Adelman. "The 1973 report of the President's Council of Economic Advisors: The economic role of women." AMERICAN ECONOMIC REVIEW, 63, Sept. 1973, pp. 509–14.

1366. Collins, Ruth Harvey. "Why do women work? Because the economy needs them—that's why!" GRADUATE WOMAN, 73, Sept.-Oct. 1979, pp. 12–13.

1367. Corcoran, Mary. "The structure of female wage." AMERICAN ECONOMIC REVIEW, 68, My. 1978, pp. 165–70.

1368. Cronin, D. M. "Women's place in a no-growth society." PUBLIC UTILITIES FORTNIGHTLY, 4 Ja. 1979, pp. 21–3.

1369. *Economic problems of women, Part 1.* Washington, DC: GPO, 1973.

1370. *Economic problems of women, Part 2.* Washington, DC: GPO, 1973.

1371. *Economic problems of women, Part 4.* Washington, DC: GPO, 1974.

1372. "The economic role of women." 1973. ERIC. ED 094 151.

1373. "Effects of the increased labor force participation of women on macroeconomic goals." AMERICAN ECONOMIC REVIEW, 68, My. 1978, pp. 78–98.

1374. Fleisher, Belton M. and George F. Rhodes, Jr. "Fertility, woman's wage rates, and labor supply." AMERICAN ECONOMIC REVIEW, 69, Mr. 1979, pp. 14–24.

1375. Fuchs, Victor R. "Recent trends and long-run prospects for female earning." AMERICAN ECONOMIC REVIEW, 64, My. 1974, pp. 236–42.

1376. Galbraith, John Kenneth. "A new economic role for women? What consequences of emancipation?" CURRENT, No. 155, Oct. 1973, pp. 41–50.

1377. Gennaro, Vincent A. "The earnings picture for women: Slack job markets behind the downward trend." FEDERAL RESERVE BANK OF PHILADELPHIA BUSINESS REVIEW, Jl.-Ag. 1974, pp. 19–22.

1378. Gery, Frank. "The effects of interrupted work life on women's earnings." ARIZONA REVIEW, 24, My. 1975, pp. 1–8.

1379. Gitlow, Abraham L. "Women in the American economy: Today and tomorrow." LABOR LAW JOURNAL, 23, Ap. 1972, pp. 232–7.

1380. Halaby, Charles N. "Job-specific sex differences in organizational reward attainment: Wage discrimination vs. rank segregation." SOCIAL FORCES, 58, Sept. 1979, pp. 108–27.

1381. Hill, Martha S. "The wage effects of marital status and children." JOURNAL OF HUMAN RESOURCES, 14, Ag. 1979, pp. 579+.

1382. Hudis, Paula Marilyn. "The determinants of earnings of men and women in the United States." 1974. ERIC, 194 pp. ED 099 730.

1383. Kentucky. Agricultural Experiment Station. Department of Sociology. *The changing economic status of women in Kentucky, 1950-1975.* 1977. 42 pp. (Available from Agricultural Experiment Station, Lexington, KY 40506.)

1384. Long, James E. "The effect of Americanization on earnings: Some evidence for women." JOURNAL OF POLITICAL ECONOMY, 88, Je. 1980, pp. 620–9.

1385. "More women work, but salaries still lag." INDUSTRY WEEK, 15 Ja. 1973, pp. 17+.

1386. O'Kelly, C. G. "The 'impact' of equal employment legislation on women's earnings." AMERICAN JOURNAL OF ECONOMICS AND SOCIOLOGY, 38, Oct. 1979, pp. 419–30.

1387. Perrucci, Carolyn Cummings. "Income attainment of college graduates: A comparison of employed women and men." SOCIOLOGY AND SOCIAL RESEARCH, 62, Ap. 1978, pp. 361–86.

1388. Rudd, Nancy. "Employment and earnings of women."

FAMILY ECONOMICS REVIEW, Fall 1973, pp. 3–8.

1389. Sandell, Steven H. and David Shapiro. *The theory of human capital and the earnings of women: A re-examination of the evidence.* 1976. 33 pp. (Available from Center for Human Resource Research, College of Administrative Science, Ohio State University, Columbus, OH 43210.)

1390. Sommers, D. "Occupational rankings for men and women by earnings." MONTHLY LABOR REVIEW, 97, Ag. 1974, pp. 34–51.

1391. Struyk, Raymond J. "Explaining variation in hourly wage rates of urban minority group females." JOURNAL OF HUMAN RESOURCES, 8, Summ. 1973, pp. 349–64.

1392. Weiss, E. B. "Female earning power may equal male's as early as 1985." ADVERTISING AGE, 20 Dec. 1971, pp. 26+.

1393. "What economic equality for women requires." AMERICAN ECONOMIC REVIEW, 62, My. 1972, pp. 157–76.

1394. "What's a woman's job worth?" PERSONNEL, 54, Ja. 1977, pp. 6–7.

1395. "Women and the economy." REVIEW OF RADICAL POLITICAL ECONOMICS, 8, Spr. 1976, pp. 1–122.

b. Wage Differentials

1396. Allison, E. K. "Sex-linked earning differentials in the beauty industry." JOURNAL OF HUMAN RESOURCES, 11, Summ. 1976, pp. 383–90.

1397. Anderson, Julie A. and Norma C. Murphy, "An empirical approach to salary discrimination: With case study of sex discrimination in education." EDUCATIONAL RESEARCH QUARTERLY, 2, Spr. 1977, pp. 48–57.

1398. Bergmann, Barbara R. "Occupational segregation, wages and profits when employers discriminate by race or sex." JOURNAL OF POLITICAL ECONOMY, 79, Mr.-Ap. 1971, pp. 294–313.

1399. Bibb, Robert and William H. Form. "The effects of industrial, occupational, and sex stratification on wages in blue-collar markets." SOCIAL FORCES, 55, Je. 1977, pp. 974–96.

1400. Blinder, Alan S. "Wage discrimination: Reduced form and structural estimates." JOURNAL OF HUMAN RE-

SOURCES, 4, Fall 1973, pp. 436–55.

1401. Brown, G. D. "Discrimination and pay disparities between white men and women." MONTHLY LABOR REVIEW, 101, Mr. 1978, pp. 17–22.

1402. Brown, Randall S., Marilyn Moon and Barbara S. Zoloth. "Incorporating occupational attainment in studies of male-female earnings differentials." JOURNAL OF HUMAN RESOURCES, 15, Wint. 1980, pp. 3–28.

1403. Buckley, J. E. "Pay differences between men and women in the same job." MONTHLY LABOR REVIEW, 94, Nov. 1971, pp. 36–40.

1404. Callahan-Levy, Charlene M. and Laurence A. Messe. "Sex differences in the allocation of pay." JOURNAL OF PERSONALITY AND SOCIAL PSYCHOLOGY, 37, Mr. 1979, pp. 433–46.

1405. Cohen, Malcolm S. "Sex differences in compensation." JOURNAL OF HUMAN RESOURCES, 6, Fall 1971, pp. 434–47.

1406. Duncan, Greg J. and Saul Hoffman. "On-the-job training and earnings differences by race and sex." REVIEW OF ECONOMICS AND STATISTICS, 61, Nov. 1979, pp. 594–603.

1407. *The earnings gap between women and men.* Washington, DC: GPO, 1979.

1408. "Earnings of men and women." MONTHLY LABOR REVIEW, 100, Ja. 1977, pp. 2+.

1409. "The economics of discrimination against women: Some new findings." JOURNAL OF HUMAN RESOURCES, 8, Summ. 1973, pp. 383–96.

1410. Ferber, M. A., and B. Kordick. "Sex differentials in the earnings of Ph.D.s." INDUSTRIAL & LABOR RELATIONS REVIEW, 31, Ja. 1978, pp. 227–38.

1411. Frank, Robert H. "Why women earn less: The theory and estimation of differential overqualification." AMERICAN ECONOMIC REVIEW, 68, Je. 1978, pp. 360–73.

1412. Fuchs, Victor R. "Differences in hourly earnings between men and women." MONTHLY LABOR REVIEW, 94, My. 1971, pp. 9–15.

1413. Gordon, Nancy M. and Thomas E. Morton. "Low mobility model of wage discrimination—with special reference to sex differentials." JOURNAL OF ECONOMIC THEORY,

7, Mr. 1974, pp. 241–53.

1414. Gordon, Nancy M., Thomas E. Morton and Ina C. Braden. "Faculty salaries: Is there discrimination by sex, race, and discipline?" AMERICAN ECONOMIC REVIEW, 64, Je. 1974, pp. 419–27.

1415. Gunderson, Morley. "Male-female wage differentials and the impact of equal pay legislation." REVIEW OF ECONOMICS AND STATISTICS, 57, Nov. 1975, pp. 462–9.

1416. Hamilton, Mary Townsend. "Sex and income inequality among the employed." ANNALS OF THE AMERICAN ACADEMY OF POLITICAL AND SOCIAL SCIENCE, 409, Sept. 1973, pp. 42–52.

1417. Henle, P. and P. Ryscavage. "The distribution of earned income among men and women, 1958-77." MONTHLY LABOR REVIEW, 103, Ap. 1980, pp. 3–10.

1418. "In 1970, median income of women workers totaled $5,440, or 59% of the $9,184 median for men." WALL STREET JOURNAL, 27 Ap. 1976, pp. 19+.

1419. Jusenius, C. L. "Influence of work experience, skill requirement, and occupational segregation on women's earnings." JOURNAL OF ECONOMICS AND BUSINESS, 29, Wint. 1977, pp. 107–15.

1420. Kohen, Andrew I. and others. "Women and the economy: A bibliography and a review of the literature on sex differentiation in the labor market." 1975. ERIC, 93 pp. ED 112 099.

1421. McLaughlin, Steven D. "Occupational sex identification and the assessment of male and female earnings inequality." AMERICAN SOCIOLOGICAL REVIEW, 43, Dec. 1978, pp. 909–21.

1422. Magarrell, Jack. "Administrators' salaries rise 8.7 pct; women's pay is lower in most fields." CHRONICLE OF HIGHER EDUCATION, 23 Mr. 1981, pp. 8+.

1423. Malkiel, Burton G. and Judith A. Malkiel. "Male-female pay differentials in professional employment." AMERICAN ECONOMIC REVIEW, 63, Sept. 1973, pp. 693–705.

1424. Mancke, Richard B. "Lower pay for women: A case of economic discrimination?" INDUSTRIAL RELATIONS, 10, Oct. 1971, pp. 316–26.

1425. Moore, W. J. "Impact of children and discrimination on the hourly wage rates of black and white wives." QUART-

ERLY REVIEW OF ECONOMICS AND BUSINESS, 17, Aut. 1977, pp. 43–64.

1426. Mount, Randall I. "Economic and social factors in income inequality: Race and sex discrimination and status as elements in wage differentials." AMERICAN JOURNAL OF ECONOMICS AND SOCIOLOGY, 34, Ap. 1975, pp. 161–74.

1427. Niemi, A. W., Jr. "Sexist earning differences." AMERICAN JOURNAL OF ECONOMICS AND SOCIOLOGY, 36, Ja. 1977, pp. 33–40.

1428. Oaxaca, Ronald L. "Male-female wage differentials in urban labor markets." 1971. ERIC, 157 pp. ED 081 964.

1429. Oaxaca, Ronald L. "Some observations on the economics of women's liberation." CHALLENGE, 19, Jl.-Ag. 1976, pp. 29–33.

1430. O'Neill, June. "The sex differential in earnings and labor market discrimination against women." JOURNAL OF CONTEMPORARY BUSINESS, 2, Summ. 1973, pp. 41–52.

1431. "Rebelling women: The reason; if you wonder why so many women are complaining about discrimination, take a look at almost any payroll." U S NEWS AND WORLD REPORT, 13 Ap. 1970, pp. 35–7.

1432. Roos, Patricia A. "Sexual stratification in the workplace: Male-female differences in economic returns to occupation." 1978. ERIC, 36 pp. ED 160 826.

1433. Roose, J. E. and M. E. Doherty. "Social judgment theoretic approach to sex discrimination in faculty salaries." ORGANIZATIONAL BEHAVIOR & HUMAN PERFORMANCE, 22, Oct. 1978, pp. 193–215.

1434. "Sex differentials in earnings." INDUSTRIAL & LABOR RELATIONS REVIEW, 32, Ap. 1979, pp. 378–86.

1435. Simeral, M. H. "Impact of the public employment program on sex-related wage differentials." INDUSTRIAL & LABOR RELATIONS REVIEW, 31, Jl. 1978, pp. 509–19.

1436. Snyder, D. and P. M. Hudis. "The sex differential in earnings: A further reappraisal: Comment." INDUSTRIAL AND LABOR RELATIONS REVIEW, 32, Ap. 1979, pp. 378–402.

1437. Stevenson, Mary. "Women's wages and job segregation."

POLITICS AND SOCIETY, 4, Fall 1973, pp. 83–96.

1438. Strauss, Robert P. and Francis W. Horvath. "Analyzing economic discrimination against blacks and women with the public use samples." PUBLIC DATA USE, 1, Oct. 1973, pp. 10–8.

1439. Strober, Myra. "Lower pay for women: A case of economic discrimination?" INDUSTRIAL RELATIONS, 11, My. 1972, pp. 279–84.

1440. Suter, Larry E. and Herman P. Miller. "Income differences between men and career women." AMERICAN JOURNAL OF SOCIOLOGY, 78, Ja. 1973, pp. 962–74.

1441. Szymanski, Albert. "The effect of earnings discrimination against women on the economic position of men." SOCIAL FORCES, 56, Dec. 1977, pp. 611+.

1442. Taylor, Patricia A. "Income inequality in the federal civilian government." AMERICAN SOCIOLOGICAL REVIEW, 44, Je. 1979, pp. 468–79.

1443. (Wage disparity for women in employment). NEW YORK TIMES, 8 My. 1978, pp. 1+, col. 3.

1444. Zellner, Harriet. "Discrimination against women, occupational segregation, and the relative wage." AMERICAN ECONOMIC REVIEW, 62, My. 1972, pp. 157–60.

c. Equal Pay for Work of Comparable Value

1445. Bridges, William P. and Richard A. Berk. "Determinants of white collar income: An evaluation of equal pay for equal work." SOCIAL SCIENCE RESEARCH, 3, Sept. 1974, pp. 211–33.

1446. "Equal pay for comparable work grows as a rallying cry for women's groups." WALL STREET JOURNAL, 12 Dec. 1978, pp. 1+.

1447. "Equal pay for women hits retailers." BUSINESS WEEK, 29 Ja. 1972, pp. 76+.

1448. Glucklich, P. and others. "Equal pay: Time to go back to the drawing board." PERSONNEL MANAGEMENT, 9, Ja. 1977, pp. 16–21.

1449. Goldfarb, Robert S. "Explaining male-female differentials for the 'same job'." JOURNAL OF HUMAN RESOURCES, 11, Wint. 1976, pp. 109–17.

1450. U.S. Department of Labor. Equal pay for equal work. Washington, DC: GPO, 1974.

1451. Washington (State). Department of Personnel. *Comparable worth study, September, 1974.* 1975. 30 pp. (Available from Washington Department of Personnel, Olympia, WA 98504.)

d. *Economic Necessity of Work*

1452. Bell, M. E. "Attitudes toward changing economic roles for women." JOURNAL OF INSTRUCTIONAL PSYCHOLOGY, 6, Summ. 1979, pp. 38–40.

1453. Griffiths, Martha. "The economics of being female." TRIAL, 9, Nov.-Dec. 1973, pp. 11–12.

1454. Kahne, Hilda and Andrew I. Kohen. "Economic perspectives on the roles of women in the American economy." JOURNAL OF ECONOMIC LITERATURE, 13, Dec. 1975, pp. 1249–92.

1455. "Most women work because of economic necessity, AFL-CIO study reports." WALL STREET JOURNAL, 24 My. 1977, pp. 1+.

1456. Orrick, A. "Economic experts talk about the impact of inflation and recession for women in the 1980s." WORKING WOMAN, 5, Feb. 1980, pp. 17–9.

1457. Pask, Judith M. "Women and the economy: A selected bibliography." 1977. ERIC, 18 pp. ED 142 905.

1458. U.S. Congress. Economic Joint Committee. *Economic problems of women. Part 1, July 10, 11, and 12, 1973. Part 2, July 24, 25, 26, and 30, 1973. Part 3, Statements for the record.* Washington, DC: GPO, 1973.

1459. U.S. Women's Bureau. *Economic responsibilities of working women.* Washington, DC: GPO, 1979.

1460. "Women hard hit by economic troubles, says NOW leader." INDUSTRY WEEK, 17 Mr. 1975, pp. 19+.

e. *Unemployment and Underemployment*

1461. Barnes, William F. and Ethel B. Jones. "Women's increasing unemployment: A cyclical interpretation." QUARTERLY REVIEW OF ECONOMICS & BUSINESS, 15, Summ. 1975, pp. 61–9.

1462. Bates, Timothy. *Involuntary underemployment among heads of households. Discussion Paper 338-76.* 1976. 25 pp. (Available from Institute for Research on Poverty, University of Wisconsin-Madison, Madison, WI 53706).

1463. *Employment problems of women, minorities, and youths.*
      Washington, DC: GPO, 1975.
1464. Fineshriber, P. H. "Jobless insurance inequities deepen as
      more women enter the labor force." MONTHLY LABOR
      REVIEW, 102, Ap. 1979, pp. 44–5.
1465. Flaim, P. O. "Effect of demographic changes on the nation's
      unemployment rate." MONTHLY LABOR REVIEW,
      102, Mr. 1979, pp. 13–23.
1466. Hopkins, Elaine B. "Unemployed: An academic woman's
      saga." CHANGE, 5, Wint. 1973-1974, pp. 49–53.
1467. "Last hired, first fired." HUMAN BEHAVIOR, 3, Je. 1974,
      pp. 50+.
1468. Morgenstern, Richard D. and Nancy S. Barrett. "The
      retrospective bias in unemployment reporting by sex, race
      and age." JOURNAL OF THE AMERICAN STATIS-
      TICAL ASSOCIATION, 69, Je. 1974, pp. 355–7.
1469. Niemi, B. "Female-male differential in unemployment
      rates." INDUSTRIAL AND LABOR RELATIONS
      REVIEW, 27, Ap. 1974, pp. 331–50.
1470. Olsen, David. "The new cost of being a woman." MOTHER
      JONES, 2, Ja. 1977, pp. 13–4.
1471. "The plight of the female jobless." HUMAN BEHAVIOR, 4,
      Sept. 1975, pp. 51+.
1472. "Retraining teachers who are victims of unemployment."
      NEW YORK TIMES, 6 Ap. 1980, pp. 22+.
1473. "Returning teachers face unemployment." NEW YORK
      TIMES, 15 Feb. 1980, pp. 6+.
1474. Riche-Warren, Mary and others. "A study of the under-
      employment and underutilization of women in Iowa."
      1976. ERIC, 255 pp. ED 154 198.
1475. "Role reversal: Women's jobless rate drops below men's."
      WALL STREET JOURNAL, 5 Nov. 1980, pp. 1+.
1476. Rones, P. L. and C. Leon. "Employment and unemployment
      during 1978: Analysis." MONTHLY LABOR REVIEW,
      102, Feb. 1979, pp. 3–12.
1477. Sandell, Steven H. "Is the unemployment rate of women too
      low? A direct test of the economic theory of job search."
      REVIEW OF ECONOMICS AND STATISTICS, 62,
      Nov. 1980, pp. 634–8.
1478. Sandell, Steven H. "Job search by unemployed women:
      Determinants of the asking wage." INDUSTRIAL &

LABOR RELATIONS REVIEW, 33, Ap. 1980, pp. 368–78.

1479. *Underutilization of women workers.* Washington, DC: GPO, 1971.

1480. "Uneducated and unskilled, women experience unemployment." NEW YORK TIMES, 11 Oct. 1978, pp. 70+.

1481. "Unemployment and women." NEW YORK TIMES, 8 Ag. 1970, pp. 1+.

1482. Wallace, Phyllis A. "Unemployment among black teenage females in urban poverty neighborhoods." 1972. ERIC, 169 pp. ED 081 294.

1483. "Women and unemployment." NEW YORK TIMES, 9 Jl. 1977, pp. 1+.

1484. "Women don't cause unemployment." DOLLARS AND SENSE, 24, Nov. 1976, pp. 6–8.

1485. "Women: Last in, first out in Detroit." BUSINESS WEEK, 16 Feb. 1974, pp. 51+.

D. CONDITIONS IN THE WORKPLACE

1. Recruitment and Hiring

a. Affirmative Action

1486. "Academic institutions and affirmative action programs." INTELLECT, 102, Mr. 1974, pp. 346.

1487. (Affirmative action). NEW YORK TIMES, 24 Sept. 1977, pp. 1, col. 5.

1488. "Affirmative action and employment." ON CAMPUS WITH WOMEN, No. 19, Mr. 1978, pp. 1–3.

1489. (Affirmative action in Connecticut). NEW YORK TIMES, 26 Ap. 1978, sec. 4, pp. 20, col. 1.

1490. (Affirmative action programs affect women). NEW YORK TIMES, 8 Ag. 1976, sec. 6, pp. 14.

1491. Anderson, Betty R. and Martha P. Rogers, eds. *Personnel testing and equal employment opportunity.* Washington, DC: GPO. 1970.

1492. Bell, D. E. and others. "Development of positive affirmative action programs at all levels of higher education employment, development of programs to increase minority and women student enrollment." 1975. ERIC, 84 pp. Ed 125 435.

1493. Bennett, J. E. "Equal opportunities for women—why and how companies should take action." BUSINESS QUART-ERLY, 40, Wint. 1975, pp. 22-9.

1494. Bode, Edward L. "Auditing affirmative action through multiple regression analysis." LABOR LAW JOURNAL, 31, Feb. 1980, pp. 115-20.

1495. Boyle, M. Barbara. "Equal opportunity for women is smart business." HARVARD BUSINESS REVIEW, 73, My.-Je. 1973, pp. 85-95.

1496. Brookmire, D. A. "Designing and implementing your company's affirmative action program." PERSONNEL JOURNAL, 58, Ap. 1979, pp. 232-7.

1497. Craft, James A. "Equal employment opportunity and seniority: Trends and man-power implications." LABOR LAW JOURNAL, 26, Dec. 1975, pp. 750-8.

1498. Cruz, Nestor. "Is equal employment opportunity cost effective?" LABOR LAW JOURNAL, 31, My. 1980, pp. 295-8.

1499. DeFichy, Wendy. "Affirmative action: Equal opportunity for women in library management." COLLEGE AND RESEARCH LIBRARIES, 34, My. 1973, pp. 195-201.

1500. "The drive to open up more careers for women." U S NEWS AND WORLD REPORT, 14 Ja. 1974, pp. 69-70.

1501. Ells, Susan C. "How Polaroid gave women the kind of affirmative action program they wanted." MANAGE-MENT REVIEW, 62, Nov. 1973, pp. 11-3.

1502. Epstein, Ann. "Why we still don't have equal opportunity (EEOC)."MAJORITY REPORT, 22 Ja.- Feb. 1977, pp. 9.

1503. Fields, Cheryl M. "Affirmative action, four years later." CHRONICLE OF HIGHER EDUCATION, 5 Ag. 1974, pp. 1+.

1504. "Firms find few technical workers to fill women quotas." INDUSTRY WEEK, 5 Feb. 1973, pp. 56-8.

1505. Fry, Fred L. "The end of affirmative action." BUSINESS HORIZONS, 23, Feb. 1980, pp. 34-40.

1506. Gaymon, D. "Underutilization in affirmative action pro-grams: What it is and what can we do about it?" PERSONNEL JOURNAL, 58, Jl. 1979, pp. 457-9.

1507. Gery, G. J. "Hiring process: Interviewing women and minorities." SUPERVISORY MANAGEMENT, 20, Oct.

1975, pp. 9–15.

1508. Gery, Gloria J. "Hiring minorities and women: The selection process." PERSONNEL JOURNAL, 53, Dec. 1974, pp. 906–9.

1509. Goldstein, Jinny M. "Affirmative action: Equal employment rights for women in academia." TEACHERS COLLEGE RECORD, 74, 1973, pp. 395–422.

1510. Graham, Peter J. "Affirmative action: Its effects upon intramural-recreational sports department employment policies." 1976. ERIC, 35 pp. ED 129 812.

1511. Hammer, T. H. "Affirmative action programs: Have we forgotten the first-line supervisor?" PERSONNEL JOURNAL, 58, Je. 1979, pp. 384–9.

1512. Herman, Deborah D. "More career opportunities for women: Whose responsibility?" PERSONNEL JOURNAL, 53, Je. 1974, pp. 414–7.

1513. (Higher education and affirmative action). NEW YORK TIMES, 20 Oct. 1978, pp. 58.

1514. Idelson, Evelyn M. *Affirmative action and equal employment: A guidebook for employers.* Washington, DC: GPO, 1974.

1515. Kentucky State Commission on Human Rights, Frankfort. "Employer's manual on affirmative action in employment." 1973. ERIC, 27 pp. ED 109 271.

1516. Kleinschrod, W. R. "Management neglects to plan for cutbacks or hiring under affirmative action." ADMINISTRATIVE MANAGEMENT, 36, Ag. 1975, pp. 23.

1517. Loeb, Jane W., Marianne A. Ferber and Helen M. Lowry. "The effectiveness of affirmative action for women." JOURNAL OF HIGHER EDUCATION, 49, My-Je. 1978, pp. 218–30.

1518. McFeeley, N. D. "Weber versus affirmative action?" PERSONNEL, 57, Ja. 1980, pp. 38–51.

1519. Mitnick, Margery Manesberg. "Equal employment opportunity and affirmative action: A managerial training guide." PERSONNEL JOURNAL, 56, Oct. 1977, pp. 492–7.

1520. National Education Association. "What is affirmative action? Combating discrimination in employment." 1973. ERIC, 20 pp. ED 089 457.

1521. Nebraska State Advisory Committee. U.S. Commission on

Civil Rights. "Private sector affirmative action: Omaha." 1979. ERIC, 52 pp. ED 177 270.

1522. New Haven Public Schools, Connecticut. "The New Haven Department of Education Affirmative Action Plan 1974." 1974. ERIC, 33 pp. ED 099 999.

1523. Nisberg, J. N. "Response to affirmative action planning." PERSONNEL ADMINISTRATOR, 20, Ja. 1975, pp. 27–31.

1524. Nordvall, Robert C. "Affirmative action implementation: Rightness and self-righteousness." JOURNAL OF THE COLLEGE AND UNIVERSITY PERSONNEL ASSOCIATION, 26, Jl.-Ag. 1974, pp. 21–4.

1525. Pati, Gopal C. and Patrick E. Fahey. "Affirmative action program: Its realities and challenges." LABOR LAW JOURNAL, 24, Je. 1973, pp. 351–61.

1526. Pie, B. "Affirmative action—can voluntary approach work." BUSINESS QUARTERLY, 41, Spr. 1976, pp. 15–21.

1527. Rennie, Donald K. "Coming to grips with affirmative action." PERSONNEL ADMINISTRATOR, 18, Sept.-Oct. 1973, pp. 29–31.

1528. Roark, Anne C. "Business graduates find it helps to be female or black—or both." CHRONICLE OF HIGHER EDUCATION, 1 Ag. 1977, pp. 5–6.

1529. Robinson, Donald Allen. "Two movements in pursuit of equal employment opportunity." SIGNS, 4, Spr. 1979, pp. 413–33.

1530. Rosen, Benson and Thomas H. Jerdee. "Coping with affirmative action backlash." BUSINESS HORIZONS, 22, Ag. 1979, pp. 15–20.

1531. Rosenbloom, David H. "Equal employment opportunity: Another strategy." PERSONNEL ADMINISTRATOR, 1, Jl.-Ag. 1972, pp. 38–41.

1532. Salancik, G. R. "Interorganizational dependence and responsiveness to affirmative action: The case of women and defense contractors." ACADEMY OF MANAGEMENT JOURNAL, 22, Je. 1979, pp. 375–403.

1533. Salipante, P. F. and J. D. Aram. "System for individual equity in equal employment opportunity." MONTHLY LABOR REVIEW, 102, Ap. 1979, pp. 46–7.

1534. Schein, Virginia Ellen. "Fair employment of women through personnel research." PERSONNEL JOURNAL, 51, My.

1972, pp. 330–5.

1535. Shulman, Carol Herrnstadt. "Affirmative action: Women's rights on campus." 1972. ERIC, 48 pp. ED 066 143.

1536. Slevin, D. P. "What companies are doing about women's job equality." PERSONNEL, 48, Jl. 1971, pp. 8–18.

1537. Slevin, Dennis. "Full utilization of women in employment: The problem and an action program." HUMAN RESOURCE MANAGEMENT, 12, Spr. 1973, pp. 25–32.

1538. Spiro, Helen and Elizabeth Yermack. "Use of quotas as remedy for discrimination." WOMEN'S RIGHTS LAW REPORTER, 4, Fall 1977, pp. 43–50.

1539. Squires, Gregory D. "Affirmative action or inaction? The pursuit of equal employment opportunity in Cleveland." 1977. ERIC, 83 pp. ED 159 276.

1540. Thornberry, Mary. "Unexpected benefits, expected defeats: Affirmative action for women." 1978. ERIC, 44 pp. ED 162 584.

1541. "Toward a non-sexist personnel opportunity structure: The federal executive bureaucracy." PUBLIC PERSONNEL MANAGEMENT, 8, Jl. 1979, pp. 209–15.

1542. U.S. Equal Opportunity Commission. *Affirmative action and equal employment. A guidebook for employers.* Washington, DC: GPO, 1974.

1543. Weidlein, Edward R. "Affirmative action has little impact on faculty hiring study shows." CHRONICLE OF HIGHER EDUCATION, 27 Ag. 1973, pp. 1+.

1544. Wisconsin, University of, Madison. "An affirmative action program to redress past inequities and to establish a policy of equal treatment and equal opportunity at the University of Wisconsin for all women." 1972. ERIC, 66 pp. ED 067 982.

1545. (Women and affirmative action). NEW YORK TIMES, 18 March 1977, pp. 1, col. 1.

1546. (Women and affirmative action on the job in New York City). NEW YORK TIMES, 26 Ap. 1980, pp. 31, col. 1.

1547. Women's Labor Project and Alliance of Third World Students. "Affirmative action: Minority gains threatened." UNION W.A.G.E., No. 38, Nov.-Dec. 1976, pp. 4–5.

1548. "Women's year sparks nations's effort toward employment equality." COMMERCE TODAY, 8 Dec. 1975, pp. 4–6.

b. Sex Bias

1549. Acker, Joan and Donald R. Van Houten. "Differential recruitment and control: The sex structuring of organizations." ADMINISTRATIVE SCIENCE QUARTERLY, Je. 1974, pp. 152–64.
1550. Britton, J. O. and Kenneth R. Thomas. "Age and sex as employment variables: Views of employment service interviewers." JOURNAL OF EMPLOYMENT COUNSELING, Dec. 1973, pp. 180–6.
1551. Cohen, S. L. "Basis of sex-bias in the job recruitment situation." HUMAN RESOURCE MANAGEMENT, 15, Fall 1976, pp. 8–10.
1552. Cohen, Stephen L. and Kerry A. Bunker. "Subtle effects of sex role stereotypes on recruiters' hiring decisions." JOURNAL OF APPLIED PSYCHOLOGY, 60, Oct. 1975, pp. 566–72.
1553. Dipboye, Robert L., Howard L. Fromkin and Kent Wiback. "Relative importance of applicant sex, attractiveness, and scholastic standing in evaluation of job applicant resumes." JOURNAL OF APPLIED PSYCHOLOGY, 60, Feb. 1975, pp. 39–43.
1554. Galka, Joanne. "Sex bias in help-wanted ads." CHICAGO JOURNALISM REVIEW, 5, Mr. 1972, pp. 9–10.
1555. Rose, G. L. and P. Andiappan. "Sex effects on managerial hiring decisions." ACADEMY OF MANAGEMENT JOURNAL, 21, Mr. 1978, pp. 104–12.
1556. Rosen, Benson and Thomas H. Jerdee. "Effects of applicant sex and difficulty of job on evaluations of candidates for managerial positions." JOURNAL OF APPLIED PSYCHOLOGY, 59, Ag. 1974, pp. 511–2.
1557. Rosen, Benson and Thomas H. Jerdee. "Influence of sex role stereotypes on personnel decisions." JOURNAL OF APPLIED PSYCHOLOGY, 59, Feb. 1974, pp. 9–14.
1558. Warren, Mary Ann. "Secondary sexism and quota hiring." PHILOSOPHY AND PUBLIC AFFAIRS, 6, Spr. 1977, pp. 240–61.
1559. Wiback, Kent and others. "Experimental studies of discrimination in the evaluation of job applicants' resumes: I. Relative importance of sex, attractiveness, and scholastic standing." Paper No. 430. 1973. ERIC, 29 pp. Ed 102 728.

1560. Wolfe, Julie C. "Sex discrimination in hiring graduate academic sociologists: Myths and realities." AMERICAN SOCIOLOGIST, Nov. 1973.
1561. Young, David M., Ernst G. Beier and Steven Beier. "Beyond words: Influence of nonverbal behavior of female job applicants in the employment interview." PERSONNEL AND GUIDANCE JOURNAL, 57, Mr. 1979, pp. 346–50.

2. Benefits

a. Pensions and Retirement

1562. "Actuarial organizations comment on case linking sex bias to pension plan." NATIONAL UNDERWRITER LIFE & HEALTH INSURANCE EDITION, 21 Ja. 1978, pp. 6.
1563. Bergmann, Barbara and Mary Gray. "Equality in retirement benefits." CIVIL RIGHTS DIGEST, 8, Ag. 1975, pp. 24–7.
1564. Bernstein, Merton C. "Forecast of women's retirement income: Cloudy and colder; 25 percent chance of poverty." INDUSTRIAL GERONTOLOGY, 1, Spr. 1974, pp. 1–13.
1565. Bernstein, Merton C. and Lois G. Williams. "Professor Higgins' complaint, or the pension treatment of women who refuse to act like men." EDUCATIONAL RECORD, 55, Fall 1974, pp. 248–56.
1566. Campbell, S. "Delayed mandatory retirement and the working woman." GERONTOLOGIST, 19, Je. 1979, pp. 257–63.
1567. Couglin, Ellen. "Labor Department may delay issuing rule barring pension disparities based on sex." CHRONICLE OF HIGHER EDUCATION, 5 Mr. 1979, pp. 1–6.
1568. Fisher, M.J. "Outlaw pension bias against women (Supreme Court decisions)." NATIONAL UNDERWRITER LIFE & HEALTH INSURANCE EDITION, 29, Ap. 1978, pp. 1+.
1569. Geisel, J. "Sex bias, retirement age, state laws: Court to decide 3 pension cases." BUSINESS INSURANCE, 17 Oct. 1977, pp. 12.
1570. Halperin, Daniel. "Should pension benefits depend upon the sex of the recipient?" AAUP BULLETIN, 62, Ap. 1976, pp. 43–8.
1571. "Is there sex discrimination in pension plans?" NATIONAL

BUSINESS WOMAN, 54, Nov. 1973, pp. 6–8.

1572. Johnson, Carolyn Kitchings and Sharon Price-Bonham. "Women and retirement: A study and implications." FAMILY RELATIONS, 29, Jl. 1980, pp. 380–5.

1573. Judah, Ann. "Pensions, social security inadequate; women get hit the hardest." UNION W.A.G.E., No. 62, Nov.-Dec. 1980, pp. 1+.

1574. Levin, N. A. "Sex discrimination and pension benefits." PENSION WORLD, 12, Jl. 1976, pp. 55–7.

1575. Middleton, Lorenzo. "Judge in Detroit bars sex-based pensions." CHRONICLE OF HIGHER EDUCATION, 15 Oct. 1979, pp. 2.

1576. "Pension plans can't require women to pay more, Supreme Court decides." BUSINESS INSURANCE, 1 My. 1978, pp. 2.

1577. *Pension problems of older women.* Washington, DC: GPO, 1975.

1578. Reno, Virginia. "Women newly entitled to retired-worker benefits: Survey of new beneficiaries." SOCIAL SECURITY BULLETIN, 36, Ap. 1973, pp. 3–26.

1579. Rosen, Benson and Thomas H. Jerdee. "Influence of employee age, sex, and job status on managerial recommendations for retirement." ACADEMY OF MANAGEMENT JOURNAL, 22, Mr. 1979, pp. 169–73.

1580. Schuchat, Theodor. "Sex discrimination and pensions: Labor Department hearings." INDUSTRIAL GERONTOLOGY, 1, Fall 1974, pp. 68+.

1581. U.S. Congress. House. Select Committee on Aging. Subcommittee on Retirement Income and Employment. *Economic problems of aging women: Hearing, July 15, 1975.* Washington, DC: GPO, 1975.

1582. U.S. Congress. House. Select Committee on Aging. Subcommittee on Retirement Income and Employment. *Income security for older women: Path to equality: Report, December 1975.* Washington, DC: GPO, 1976.

1583. "U. S. says pensions unfair to women." NATIONAL UNDERWIRTER LIFE & HEALTH INSURANCE EDITION, 30 Dec. 1978, pp. 1+.

1584. "U. S. says pensions unfair to women." NATIONAL UNDERWRITER LIFE & HEALTH INSURANCE EDITION, 3 Feb. 1979, pp. 13.

1585. *Women and retirement income programs: Current issues of equity and adequacy.* Washington, DC: GPO, 1979.

b. Social Security

1586. Bell, Carolyn Shaw. "Social Security: Society's last discrimination: Whether women are housekeepers or workers, the Social Security System will do them in." BUSINESS & SOCIETY REVIEW, Aut. 1972, pp. 45–7.

1587. Bixby, L. E. "Women and Social Security in the United States." SOCIAL SECURITY BULLETIN, 35, Sept. 1972, pp. 3–11.

1588. *Economic problems of aging women.* Washington, DC: GPO, 1975.

1589. Fisher, M. J. "HEW study: SS biased against women." NATIONAL UNDERWRITER LIFE & HEALTH INSURANCE EDITION, 24 Feb. 1979, pp. 1+.

1590. *Future directions in Social Security. Part 18: Women and Social Security.* Washington, DC: GPO, 1975.

1591. Gelber, S. M. "Social Security and women: A partisan view." INTERNATIONAL LABOUR REVIEW, 112, Dec. 1975, pp. 431–44.

1592. Mallan, L. B. "Women's worklives and future Social Security benefits." SOCIAL SECURITY BULLETIN, 39, Ap. 1976, pp. 3–13.

1593. "Men and women: Changing roles and Social Security." SOCIAL SECURITY BULLETIN, 42, My. 1979, pp. 25–32.

1594. Sass, T. "Demographic and economic characteristics of non-beneficiary widows: An overview." SOCIAL SECURITY BULLETIN, 42, Nov. 1979, pp. 3–14.

1595. Sommers, Tish. "Social Security: A woman's viewpoint." INDUSTRIAL GERONTOLOGY, 2, Ag. 1975, pp. 266–80.

1596. "Task force report on treatment of women under Social Security." SOCIAL SECURITY BULLETIN, 41, My. 1978, pp. 37–9.

1597. U.S. Congress. House. Select Committee on Aging. *Social Security inequities against women, hearings.* Washington, DC: GPO, 1975.

1598. U.S. Congress. Senate. Special Committee on Aging. *Women and Social Security: Adapting to a new era.* Washington, DC: GPO, 1975.

1599. U.S. Task Force on Women and Social Security. *Women and Social Security, adapting to a new era: A working paper prepared for use by the Special Committee on Aging.* Washington, DC: GPO, 1975.

c. *Pregnancy and Maternity Benefits*

1600. Association of American Colleges. Project on the Status and Education of Women. "The Pregnancy Discrimination Act of 1978 and its impact on educational institutions." 1979. ERIC, 7 pp. ED 174 130.

1601. Curran, William J. "Law-medicine notes: Pregnant school-teachers—the right to bear children and the right to work." NEW ENGLAND JOURNAL OF MEDICINE, 2 My. 1974, pp. 1005–6.

1602. Danziger, Joe H. "Mandatory maternity leave of absence policies—an equal protection analysis." TEMPLE UNIVERSITY QUARTERLY, 45, Wint. 1972, pp. 240–58.

1603. Gerner, Jennifer. "Wisconsin maternity leave and fringe benefits: Policies, practices and problems." 1974. ERIC, 184 pp. ED 105 213.

1604. Greenlaw, P. S. and D. L. Foderaro. "Some further implications of the Pregancy Discrimination Act." PERSONNEL JOURNAL, 59, Ja. 1980, pp. 36–43.

1605. King, Paul A. "Maternity benefits question may be finally settled by court ruling." ADMINISTRATIVE MANAGEMENT, 34, Oct. 1973. pp. 10+.

1606. Kistler, Linda and Carol C. McDonough. "Maternity leave: Sharing the costs of motherhood." PERSONNEL, 52, Nov.-Dec. 1975, pp. 57+.

1607. Kistler, Linda and Carol C. McDonough. "Paid maternity leave-benefits may justify the cost." LABOR LAW JOURNAL, 26, Dec. 1975, pp. 782.

1608. *Legislation to prohibit sex discrimination on the basis of pregnancy.* Washington, DC: GPO, 1977.

1609. Lines, P. M. "Update: New rights for pregnant employees." PERSONNEL JOURNAL, 53, Ja. 1979, pp. 33–7.

1610. "Mandatory maternity leave of absence policies—an equal protection analysis." INDUSTRIAL RELATIONS LAW DIGEST, 15, Ja. 1973, pp. 94–108.

1611. "Most firms limit work of expectant mothers." ADMINISTRATIVE MANAGEMENT, 32, Ap. 1971, pp. 50.

1612. Pottker, Janice. *Challenging sex discrimination through the courts: Maternity leave policies.* 1975. 23 pp. (Available from Center for the Study of Sex Differences in Education, 3701 Stewart Dr., Chevy Chase, MD 20015.)

1613. Pottker, Janice and Andrew Fishel. "Sex discrimination as public policy: Maternity leave policies for teachers." EDUCATIONAL FORUM, 39, Nov. 1974, pp. 7–15.

1614. "Pregnancy discharges in the military: The Air Force experience." HARVARD LAW REVIEW, 86, Ja. 1973, pp. 568–94.

1615. Skotzko, E. "Jobless benefits during pregnancy." MONTHLY LABOR REVIEW, 97, Ja. 1974, pp. 73–4.

1616. Skotzko, E. "Pregnancy—a disability?" MONTHLY LABOR REVIEW, 97, My. 1974, pp. 76–7.

1617. "Supreme Court said denying benefits to pregnant workers can be illegal." WALL STREET JOURNAL, 7 Dec. 1977, pp. 5.

1618. Warshaw, L. J. "Non-medical issues presented by the pregnant worker." JOURNAL OF OCCUPATIONAL MEDICINE, 21, Feb. 1979, pp. 89–92.

1619. Weiss, Laura B. "Discrimination banned: Pregnancy disability bill passed by Senate." CONGRESSIONAL QUARTERLY WEEKLY REPORT, 24 Sept. 1977, pp. 2014–5.

d. Other Benefits

1620. Haneberg, R. L. "Employee benefit plans—what constitutes sex discrimination?" RISK MANAGEMENT, 26, Ja. 1979, pp. 11–5.

1621. "Illinois bans sex discrimination by insurers." NATIONAL UNDERWRITER LIFE & HEALTH INSURANCE EDITION, 5 Je. 1976, pp. 6.

1622. King, F. P. "Men, women, and life annuities." JOURNAL OF RISK AND INSURANCE, 43, Dec. 1976, pp. 553–67.

1623. "Labor Department proposes to end sex discrimination in all employee benefits." NATIONAL UNDERWRITER PROPERTY & CASUALTY INSURANCE EDITION, 15 Sept. 1978, pp. 11.

1624. "Missouri cites sex bias in life, health and disability plans." NATIONAL UNDERWRITER LIFE & HEALTH INSURANCE EDITION, 30 Ap. 1977, pp. 22.

1625. "Sex is major factor in cost of disability cover." BUSINESS INSURANCE, 6 Sept. 1976, pp. 8.
1626. "Unisex actuarial tables not answer to ending bias, says life executive." NATIONAL UNDERWRITER LIFE & HEALTH INSURANCE EDITION, 22 Ja. 1977, pp. 2+.

3. Alternative Job Patterns

a. General

1627. Alternative work schedules and part-time career opportunities in the Federal government. Washington, DC: GPO, 1975.
1628. Green, H. L. "Job hours dictate working women's needs." SUPERMARKET BUSINESS, 33, Je. 1978, pp. 23.
1629. Greenwald, Carol S. "Part-time work and flexible hours employment." 1974. ERIC, 12 pp. ED 105 322.
1630. Part-time employment and flexible work hours. Washington, DC: GPO, 1977.
1631. Schwartz, Felice N. "New work patterns for the better use of womanpower." MANAGEMENT REVIEW, My. 1974, pp. 4–12.

b. Part-Time

1632. Bristol, Marie Carosello. "The 20-hour work week." WOMEN: A JOURNAL OF LIBERATION, 2, 1971, pp. 30–1.
1633. Jones, Ethel B. and James E. Long. "Part-week work and human capital investment by married women." JOURNAL OF HUMAN RESOURCES, 14, Ag. 1979, pp. 563–78.
1634. Leon, Carol and Robert W. Bednarzik. "A profile of women on part-time schedules." MONTHLY LABOR REVIEW, 101, Oct. 1978, pp. 3–12.
1635. Long, James E. and Ethel B. Jones. "Part-week work by married women." SOUTHERN ECONOMIC JOURNAL, 46, Ja. 1980, pp. 716–25.
1636. Ostrow, J. "Many women work, but quite a few of them have very short hours." MEDIA DECISIONS, 12, Oct 1977, pp. 82+.
1637. "Part-time professionals: More well-educated women find firms willing to hire them." WALL STREET JOURNAL, 8 Sept. 1972, pp. 28, col. 1.

1638. Weeks, Wendy. "Part-time work: The business view on second-class jobs for housewives and mothers." ATLANTIS, 5, Sept. 1980, pp. 69–88.

1639. Wyper, R. "Back to work—as temporaries." WORKLIFE MAGAZINE, 2, Ap. 1977, pp. 24–6.

c. Flex-Time

1640. "Flexible scheduling." SPOKESWOMAN, 8, Sept. 1977, pp. 14.

1641. King, A. G. "Industrial structure, the flexibility of working hours, and women's labor force participation." REVIEW OF ECONOMICS AND STATISTICS, 60, Ag. 1978, pp. 399–407.

1642. Kuhne, Robert J. and others. "Two views: Changing the workweek. Flexitime. Flexiweek." BUSINESS HORIZONS, 21, Ap. 1978, pp. 39–51.

1643. Martin, Virginia H. "Recruiting women managers through flexible hours." ADVANCED MANAGEMENT JOURNAL, 39, Jl. 1974, pp. 46–53.

1644. Prywes, Ruth W. "A study on the development of a non-standard work day or work week for woman." 1974. ERIC, 395 pp. ED 090 372.

1645. Women Architects, Landscape Architects and Planners. "The case for flexible work schedules." ARCHITECTURAL FORUM, 137, Sept. 1972, pp. 53+.

d. Job Sharing

1646. Frye, Ellen. "Job-sharing, or the myth of what women want." OFF OUR BACKS, 8, Oct. 1978, pp. 4–5.

1647. Lazer, Robert I. "Job sharing as a pattern for permanent part-time work." CONFERENCE BOARD RECORD, 12, Oct. 1975, pp. 57–61.

1648. Olmsted, Barney. "Job sharing—a new way to work." PERSONNEL JOURNAL, 56, Feb. 1977, pp. 78–81.

1649. Perlman, Marsha J. "Two halves equal more than one whole." FRONTIERS, 1, Fall 1975, pp. 58–60.

1650. Taylor, Mary G. and Shirley Foster Hartley. "The two-person career: A classic example." SOCIOLOGY OF WORK AND OCCUPATIONS, 2, Nov. 1975, pp. 354–75.

1651. Winkler, Karen. "Two who share one academic job say the pro's outnumber the con's." CHRONICLE OF HIGHER EDUCATION, 3 Dec. 1979, pp. 3.

4. Unions

a. Participation of Women

1652. Antos, Joseph R., Mark Chandler and Wesley Mellow. "Sex differences in union membership." INDUSTRIAL & LABOR RELATIONS REVIEW, 33, Ja. 1980, pp. 162-9.

1653. Berquist, Virginia A. "Women's participation in labor organizations." MONTHLY LABOR REVIEW, 97, Oct. 1974, pp. 3-9.

1654. Burd, Rachel. "Nurses foil union busters with grassroots strategies." UNION W.A.G.E., No. 60, Jl-Ag. 1980, pp. 1-2.

1655. "Coalition of Labor Union Women declared it will hold their convention in fall 1975 only in a state that has ratified the equal rights amendment." WALL STREET JOURNAL, 25 Mr. 1975, pp. 1, col. 5.

1656. Cornish, Mary. "Women in trade unions." THIS MAGAZINE, 9, Sept.-Oct. 1975, pp. 8-10.

1657. Crothers, Diane. "Unionizing legal workers." WOMEN'S RIGHTS LAW REPORTER, 1, Jl.-Ag. 1971, pp. 22-5.

1658. Crow, Margie. "Coalition of Labor Union Women: Union sisters rise for new woman power." OFF OUR BACKS, 4, Ap. 1974, pp. 1+

1659. Dewey, Lucretia M. "Women in labor unions." MONTHLY LABOR REVIEW, 94, Feb. 1971, pp. 42-8.

1660. Dillon, Joan. "Union women." BOOKLEGGER MAGAZINE, 1, My.-Je. 1974, pp. 20-4.

1661. Dimos, Helen. "The 33 million secretaries, service workers, salesclerks, and factory workers are getting mad and doing something about it!" MS, 8, My. 1980, pp. 44-9.

1662. Goldstein, Mark L. "Blue-collar women and American labor unions." INDUSTRIAL AND LABOR RELATIONS FORUM, 7, Oct. 1971, pp. 1-35.

1663. Haener, Dorothy. "Women into unions: Opening up a closed shop." TRIAL, 9, Nov.-Dec. 1973, pp. 15-7.

1664. LeGrande, L. H. "Women in labor organizations: Their ranks are increasing." MONTHLY LABOR REVIEW, 101, Ag. 1978, pp. 8-14.

1665. Nelson, Anne H. "Working women in organized labor."

SOCIAL SCIENCE RECORD, 23, Fall 1975, pp. 8–15.

1666. Parry, Shirley. "Union organizer." WOMEN: A JOURNAL OF LIBERATION, 3(2), 1972, pp. 51–3.

1667. "The political life of union women." UNION W.A.G.E., 2, Mr.-Ap. 1973, pp. 1+.

1668. Raphael, Edna E. "From sewing machines to politics: The woman union member in the community." 1973. (Available from Pennsylvania State University, 906 Liberal Arts Building, University Park, PA 16802.)

1669. Rein, Marcy. "Same enemy, same fight: Women in the '78 coal strike." OFF OUR BACKS, 8, Oct. 1978, pp. 12.

1670. Reuben, Elaine and Leonore Hoffmann, eds. "Unladylike and unprofessional: Academic women and academic unions." 1975. 54 pp. (Available from Modern Language Association, 62 Fifth Ave., New York, NY 10011.)

1671. "Statewide union women's conference." UNION W.A.G.E., 18, Jl.-Ag. 1973, pp. 1.

1672. Steinem, Gloria. "Getting off the plantation with Lorna, Bessie, Joyce and Bernadette." MS, 9, Ag. 1980, pp. 39–40.

1673. Stern, Marjorie. "An insider's view of the teachers' union and women's rights." URBAN REVIEW, 6, Je.-Jl. 1973, pp. 46–9.

1674. Stern, Marjorie. "Union women organize." AMERICAN TEACHER, 58, Ap. 1974, pp. 13.

1675. Stevens, Wendy. "Women organizing the office." OFF OUR BACKS, 9, Ap. 1979, pp. 10.

1676. Sutton, John R. "Some determinants of women's trade union membership." PACIFIC SOCIOLOGICAL REVIEW, 23, Oct. 1980, pp. 377–92.

1677. Tarr-Whelan, Linda. "Women workers and organized labor." SOCIAL POLICY, 9, My.-Je. 1978, pp. 13–7.

1678. Tempkin, Tanya. "CLUW: strategy within." OFF OUR BACKS, 5, Ja.-Feb. 1976, pp. 2–3.

1679. "Union women want leadership roles; avoid activist push." INDUSTRY WEEK, 15 Dec. 1975, pp. 9–10.

1680. (Unionization of women). NEW YORK TIMES, 25 Je. 1978, pp. 1, col. 1.

1681. Wertheimer, Barbara H. *Search for a partnership role: Women in labor unions today.* n.d. (Available from New York State School of Industrial and Labor Relations,

Cornell University, Ithaca, NY 14853.)

1682. Wertheimer, Barbara H. "38 million women denied union benefits." NEW DIRECTIONS FOR WOMEN, 9, My.-Je. 1980, pp. 8+.

1683. "Women in unions—how much progress?" DOLLARS AND SENSE, 41, Nov. 1978, pp. 9.

1684. "Women workers: Gaining power, seeking more." U S NEWS AND WORLD REPORT, 13 Nov. 1972, pp. 104–7.

1685. "Wow fights 'Coffee, tea or else' policy." MAJORITY REPORT, 16–29 Ap. 1977, pp. 8.

b. Bargaining and Strikes

1686. American Association of University Professors. Committee on Academic Freedom and Tenure. "On processing complaints of discrimination on the basis of sex." AAUP BULLETIN, 63, Ap. 1977, pp. 231–6.

1687. Block, R. N. "Legal and traditional criteria in the arbitration of sex discrimination grievances." ARBITRATION JOURNAL, 32, Dec. 1977, pp. 241–55.

1688. D'Anne, Denise. "Homemakers' contract threatened." UNION W.A.G.E., No. 52, Mr.-Ap. 1979, pp. 5–6.

1689. Elkins, R. Edison and Marvin Rogoff. "Collective bargaining and affirmative action." PUBLIC MANAGEMENT, 55, Jl. 1973, pp. 17–9.

1690. Fischbach, Donald F. "Union liability for sex discrimination." INDUSTRIAL RELATIONS DIGEST, 15, Jl. 1972, pp. 114–23.

1691. Fratkin, Susan. "Collective bargaining and affirmative action." JOURNAL OF THE COLLEGE AND UNIVERSITY PERSONNEL ASSOCIATION, 26, Jl.-Ag. 1975, pp. 53–62.

1692. Goldman, Jane. "Unions, women and economic justice: Litigating union sex discrimination." WOMEN'S RIGHTS LAW REPORTER, 4, Fall 1977, pp. 3–26.

1693. Jenkins, Maxine. "Women in the San Francisco City Strike." UNION W.A.G.E., 23, My.-Je. 1974, pp. 6–7.

1694. Kanda, Kathy. "Women on strike at Head Ski." FRONTIERS, 1, Fall 1975, pp. 1+.

1695. Orenbach, Kenneth B. "A new twist to an old dispute: The arbitration of grievances involving race, sex, or religious discrimination in the public sector." INDUSTRIAL AND LABOR RELATIONS FORUM, 8, My. 1972, pp. 35–53.

1696. Sandler, B. "Women on the campus and collective bargaining: It doesn't have to hurt to be a woman in labor." JOURNAL OF THE COLLEGE AND UNIVERSITY PERSONNEL ASSOCIATION, 25, Spr. 1974, pp. 82–89.

1697. Schmeller, Kurt R. "Collective bargaining and women in higher education." COLLEGE AND UNIVERSITY JOURNAL, 12, My. 1973, pp. 34–6.

1698. Sherman, Malcolm J. "Affirmative action and the AAUP." AAUP BULLETIN, 61, Dec. 1975, pp. 293–303.

1699. Sibble, Edward Matson. "Remedies for labor union sex discrimination." GEORGETOWN LAW JOURNAL, 63, Mr. 1975, pp. 939–54.

1700. Smith, Arthur B. "The impact on collective bargaining of equal employment opportunity remedies." INDUSTRIAL AND LABOR RELATIONS REVIEW, 28, Ap. 1975, pp. 376–94.

1701. Smith, Georgina M. "Faculty women at the bargaining table." AAUP BULLETIN, 59, Dec. 1973, pp. 402–6.

1702. Weiss, Lenore. "TWU downs TWA: Women flight attendants backbone of strike." UNION W.A.G.E., 21, Ja.-Feb. 1974, pp. 1.

1703. (Women's strike for equality). NEW YORK TIMES, 27 Ag. 1970, pp. 1, col. 2.

5. Sexual Harrassmant

1704. Association of American Colleges. Project on the Status and Education of Women. "Sexual harassment: A hidden issue." 1978. ERIC, 8 pp. ED 157 481.

1705. "Blue collar women: Harassed, forced out. WREE clearing house to collect data and push for protection." WREE-VIEW, 3, Sept.-Oct. 1978, pp. 1.

1706. "Fighting lechery on campus." TIME, 4 Feb. 1980, pp. 84.

1707. Ginsberg, Gilbert J. and Jean Galloway Koreski. "Sexual advances by an employee's supervisor: A sex discrimination violation of Title VII?" EMPLOYEE RELATIONS LAW JOURNAL, 3, Summ. 1977, pp. 83–93.

1708. Josephson, N. "Sexual harassment on the job: Why more and more women are fighting back." GLAMOUR, 78, My. 1980, pp. 288–9+.

1709. Lindsey, Karen. "Sexual harassment on the job and how to stop it." MS, 6, Nov. 1977, pp. 47–8.

1710. Marske, C. E. and others. "Combatting sexual harassment: A new awareness." U S A TODAY, 108, Mr. 1980, pp. 45–8.

1711. Povorney, Karen. "Women organizing to fight abuse: Sexual harassment used to keep women in their 'place'." UNION W.A.G.E., No. 61, Sept.-Oct. 1980, pp. 2–3.

1712. Renick, J. C. "Sexual harassment at work: Why it happens, what to do about it." PERSONNEL JOURNAL, 59, Ag. 1980, pp. 658–62.

1713. Sawyer, Sandra and Arthur A. Whatley. "Sexual harassment: A form of sex discrimination." PERSONNEL ADMINISTRATOR, 25, Ja. 1980, pp. 36–8+.

1714. "Sexual harassment by supervisors and fellow employees worries employers." WALL STREET JOURNAL, 27 Nov. 1979, pp. 1, col. 5.

1715. *Sexual harassment in the federal government.* Washington, DC: GPO, 1979.

1716. "Sexual harassment lands companies in court." BUSINESS WEEK, 1 Oct. 1979, pp. 120+.

1717. (Sexual harassment of women on the job). NEW YORK TIMES, 27 Sept. 1978, pp. 44.

1718. Seymour, William C. "Sexual harassment: Finding a cause of action under Title VII." LABOR LAW JOURNAL, 30, Mr. 1979, pp. 139–56.

1719. Somers, P. A. and J. Clementson-Mohr. "Sexual extortion in the workplace." PERSONNEL ADMINISTRATION, 24, Ap. 1979, pp. 23–8.

1720. White, S. "Office pass (continued): A case of sexual harassment in the Environmental Protection Agency!" ACROSS THE BOARD, 15, Mr. 1978, pp. 48–51.

6. Health and Safety

1721. Baker, Beth. "Beware! Your job may be hazardous to your health." WREE-VIEW, 3, Nov.-Dec. 1978, pp. 3.

1722. "Cyanamid attacked over sterilization of female workers." CHEMICAL MARKETING REPORTER, 8 Ja. 1979, pp. 3+.

1723. Diamond, Mimi. "Reproductive hazards on the job: OSHA

conference stresses unity." WREE-VIEW, 4, Ap.-Je. 1979, pp. 5.

1724. "Dilemma of regulating reproductive risks." BUSINESS WEEK, 29 Ag. 1977, pp. 76–7+.

1725. "Employers are charged with sidestepping safety." BUSINESS INSURANCE, 26 Jl. 1976, pp. 11.

1726. Gomberg, E. S. "Women, work, and alcohol: Disturbing trend." SUPERVISORY MANAGEMENT, 22, Dec. 1977, pp. 16–20.

1727. "Growing furor over women's safety on the job." U S NEWS & WORLD REPORT, 2 Ag. 1976, pp. 56.

1728. Hauenstein, Louise S., Stanislav V. Kasl and Ernest Harburg. "Work status, work satisfaction, and blood pressure among married black and white women." PSYCHOLOGY OF WOMEN, 1, Summ. 1977, pp. 334–49.

1729. Haynes, S. G. and M. Feinleib. "Working women and heart disease." SCIENCE NEWS, 9 Feb. 1980, pp. 86.

1730. Kassel, Paula. "Five submit to sterilization to avoid losing their jobs." NEW DIRECTIONS FOR WOMEN, 8, Ja. 1979, pp. 1+.

1731. Lehmann, Phyllis. "Protecting women out of their jobs." SCIENCE FOR THE PEOPLE, 9, Nov.-Dec. 1977, pp. 30–3.

1732. Lublin, Joann S. "Cost of equality?" WALL STREET JOURNAL, 14 Ja. 1980, pp. 1+.

1733. Newman, John F. and others. "Women in the labor force and suicide." SOCIAL PROBLEMS, 21, Fall 1973, pp. 220–30.

1734. Osborne, Robin and Deborah Farson. "No job is safe these days—corporate policy: Forced sterilization." UNION W.A.G.E., No. 52, Mr.-Ap. 1979, pp. 8–9.

1735. Root, N. and J. R. Daley. "Are women safer workers: A new look at the data." MONTHLY LABOR REVIEW, 103, Sept. 1980, pp. 3–10.

1736. Seminario, M. "Women workers: Hazards on the job." AMERICAN FEDERATIONIST, 85, Ag. 1978, pp. 18–23.

1737. Stellman, Jeanne M. "The hidden health toll: A cost of work to the American woman." CIVIL RIGHTS DIGEST, 10, Fall 1977, pp. 32–41.

1738. Welch, Susan and Alan Booth. "Employment and health among married women with children." SEX ROLES, 3, Ag. 1977, pp. 385–97.
1739. "Women claim Cyanamid forced strilization." CHEMICAL & ENGINEERING NEWS, 8 Ja. 1979, pp. 6.

7. Management Practices

a. General

1740. Bass, Bernard M., Judith Krusell, and Ralph A. Alexander. "Male managers' attitudes toward working women." AMERICAN BEHAVIORAL SCIENTIST, 15, Nov.-Dec. 1971, pp. 221–36.
1741. Biles, G. E. and H. A. Pryatel. "Myths, management and women." PERSONNEL JOURNAL, 57, Oct. 1978, pp. 572+.
1742. Boer, P. M. "Women in the workforce—reflecting a new era for management." MANAGEMENT WORLD, 9, Je. 1980, pp. 8–10.
1743. Rosen, Benson and Thomas H. Jerdee. "On-the-job sex bias: Increasing managerial awareness." PERSONNEL ADMINISTRATION, 22, Ja. 1977, pp. 15–18.
1744. "Women at work: Management practices change to reflect role of women employees." WALL STREET JOURNAL, 13 Sept. 1978, pp. 1, col. 1.
1745. Young, J. W. "Subordinate's exposure or organizational vulnerability to the superior: Sex and organizational effects." ACADEMY OF MANAGEMENT JOURNAL, 21, Mr. 1978, pp. 113–22.

b. Sex Differences

1746. Aery, S. "Organizational effectiveness and the woman administrator." NASPA JOURNAL, 15, Fall 1977, pp. 43–7.
1747. "Are women managers different from men?" MANAGEMENT REVIEW, 69, Dec. 1980, pp. 52.
1748. Baird, John E., Jr., and Patricia Hayes Bradley. "Styles of management and communication: A comparative study of men and women." COMMUNICATION MONOGRAPHS, 46, Je. 1979, pp. 101–11.

1749. Day, David R. and Ralph M. Stogdill. "Leader behavior of male and female supervisors: A comparative study." PERSONNEL PSYCHOLOGY, 25, Summ. 1972, pp. 353–60.

1750. Haccoun, D. M. and others. "Sex differences in the appropriateness of supervisory styles: A nonmanagement view." JOURNAL OF APPLIED PSYCHOLOGY, 63, Feb. 1978, pp. 124–7.

1751. Humphreys, L. W. and W. A. Shrode. "Decision-making profiles of female and male managers." MSU BUSINESS TOPICS, 26, Aut. 1978, pp. 45–51.

1752. Lannon, J. M. "Male v. female values in management." MANAGEMENT INTERNATIONAL REVIEW, 17(1), 1977, pp. 9–12.

1753. Maidalton, R. R. and S. Feldman-Summers. "Effect of employee gender and behavioral style on the evaluations of male and female banking executives." JOURNAL OF APPLIED PSYCHOLOGY, 64, Ap. 1979, pp. 221–6.

1754. "Rating the executive." HUMAN BEHAVIOR, 6, Feb. 1977, pp. 46.

1755. Renwick, P. A. "Effects of sex differences on the perception and management of superior-subordinate conflict: An exploratory study." ORGANIZATIONAL BEHAVIOR & HUMAN PERFORMANCE, 19, Ag. 1977, pp. 403–15.

1756. Schein, Virginia Ellen. "The relationship between sex role stereotypes and requisite management characteristics." JOURNAL OF APPLIED PSYCHOLOGY, 57, Ap. 1973, pp. 95–100.

1757. Schein, Virginia Ellen. "Relationships between sex role stereotypes and requisite management characteristics among female managers." JOURNAL OF APPLIED PSY-CHOLOGY, 60, Je. 1975, pp. 340–4.

1758. Vaden, R. E. and N. B. Lynn. "Administrative person: Will women bring a differing morality to management?" UNIVERSITY OF MICHIGAN BUSINESS REVIEW, 31, Mr. 1979, pp. 22–5

1759. Wolf, Wendy C. and Neil D. Fligstein. "Sex and authority in the workplace: The causes of sexual inequality." AMERICAN SOCIOLOGICAL REVIEW, 44, Ap. 1979, pp. 235–52.

c. Performance Evaluation

1760. Hamner, W. Clay and others. "Race and sex as determinants of ratings by potential employers in a simulated work-sampling task." JOURNAL OF APPLIED PSYCHOLOGY, 59, Dec. 1974, pp. 705–11.

1761. Mischel, H. N. "Sex bias in the evaluation of professional achievements." JOURNAL OF EDUCATIONAL PSYCHOLOGY, 66, Ap. 1974, pp. 157–66.

1762. Munson, C. E. "Evaluation of male and female supervisors." SOCIAL WORK, 24, Mr. 1979, pp. 104–11.

1763. Rose, G. L. "Sex effects on effort attributions in managerial performance evaluation." ORGANIZATIONAL BEHAVIOR & HUMAN PERFORMANCE, 21, Je. 1978, pp. 367–78.

1764. Rosen, Benson and Thomas H. Jerdee. "Effects of applicant's sex and difficulty of job on evaluations of candidates for managerial positions." JOURNAL OF APPLIED PSYCHOLOGY, 59, Ag. 1974, pp. 511–2.

1765. Rosen, Benson and Thomas H. Jerdee. "Effects of employee's sex and threatening versus pleading appeals on managerial evaluations of grievances." JOURNAL OF APPLIED PSYCHOLOGY, 60 Ag. 1975, pp. 442–5.

1766. Rosen, Benson and Thomas H. Jerdee. "Influence of sex-role stereotypes on evaluations of male and female supervisory behavior." JOURNAL OF APPLIED PSYCHOLOGY, Feb. 1973, pp. 44–8.

1767. Thomsen, D. J. "Eliminating pay discrimination caused by job evaluation." PERSONNEL, 55, Sept. 1978, pp. 11–22.

1768. Turner, Barbara F. and Castellano B. Turner. "Race and sex differences in evaluating women." 1974. ERIC, 12 pp. ED 101 233.

d. Promotion

1769. Albrecht, M. "Women resistance to promotion and self-directed growth." HUMAN RESOURCE MANAGEMENT, 17, Spr. 1978, pp. 12–7.

1770. Lyon, C. D. and T. N. Saario. "Women in public education: Sexual discrimination in promotions." PHI DELTA KAPPAN, 55, Oct. 1973, pp. 120–3.

1771. Rosen, Benson and Thomas H. Jerdee. "Influence of sex

role stereotypes and personnel decisions." JOURNAL OF APPLIED PSYCHOLOGY, 59, Feb. 1974, pp. 9–14.

1772. Rosenberg, DeAnne. "Clearing the way for the growth of women subordinates." SUPERVISORY MANAGEMENT, Ja. 1976, pp. 9–13.

1773. "Women at Pitney Bowes demand and win promotion policies." MANAGEMENT ADVISOR, 10, Mr. 1973, pp. 8–9.

8. Cooperation Among Women

a. Professional Organizations

1774. Cowan, Ruth B. and Sarah Slavin Schramm. "The American Political Science Association grievance procedure in the context of sex discrimination." POLITICAL SCIENCE, 9, Ag. 1976, pp. 420–1.

1775. Friedlaender, A. F. "Committee on the status of women in the economics profession." AMERICAN ECONOMIC REVIEW, 69, My. 1979, pp. 414–21.

1776. Greenleaf, Elizabeth A. "The status of the National Association of Women Deans and Counselors in March 1972." NATIONAL ASSOCIATION OF WOMEN DEANS AND COUNSELORS, 36, Fall 1972, pp. 36–40.

1777. Maupin, Joyce. *Working women and their organizations— 150 years of struggle.* 1974. 33 pp. (Available from UNION W.A.G.E., P.O. Box 462, Berkeley, CA 94701.)

1778. Oltman, Ruth M. "Women in the professional caucuses." AMERICAN BEHAVIORAL SCIENTIST, 15, Nov.-Dec. 1971, pp. 281–302.

1779. "Our living history: Reminiscences of black participation in NAWDAC." JOURNAL OF NATIONAL ASSOCIA-TION OF WOMEN DEANS, ADMINISTRATORS, AND COUNSELORS, 43, Wint. 1980, pp. 3–13.

1780. Schwartz, Neena B. "Why women form their own profes-sional organizations." JOURNAL OF THE AMERICAN MEDICAL WOMEN'S ASSOCIATION, 28, Ja. 1973, pp. 12–5.

1781. Soldwedel, B. J. "Profile and status of N.A.W.D.A.C. members." JOURNAL OF NATIONAL ASSOCIATION OF WOMEN DEANS, ADMINISTRATORS, AND COUNSELORS, 40, Summ. 1977, pp. 123–7.

1782. Vithayathil, Teresa. "Women in the I.A.S." JOURNAL OF THE NATIONAL ACADEMY OF ADMINISTRATION, 16, Oct.-Dec. 1971, pp. 91–8.

1783. "Women's units in 60 organizations." CHRONICLE OF HIGHER EDUCATION, 16 My. 1977, pp. 11.

b. Networks and Mentors

1784. Farley, J. and J. D. Kelly. "Woman's job roster: Is it helping?" JOURNAL OF NATIONAL ASSOCIATION OF WOMEN DEANS, ADMINISTRATORS, AND COUNSELORS, 39, Summ. 1976, pp. 190–5.

1785. Halcomb, R. "Mentors and the successful woman." ACROSS THE BOARD, 17, Feb. 1980, pp. 13–8.

1786. "Mentors for women: Like it or not, it's a two-way street." MANAGEMENT REVIEW, 69, Je. 1980, pp. 6.

1787. Price, M. "Professional women help each other climb." INDUSTRY WEEK, 9 Jl. 1979, pp. 29–30+.

1788. Shapiro, E. C. and others. "Moving up: Role models, mentors, and the patron system." SLOAN MANAGEMENT REVIEW, 19, Spr. 1978, pp. 51–8.

1789. Welch, M. S. "How to start a women's network: How one network started." WORKING WOMAN, 5, Mr. 1980, pp. 82–3.

1790. Welch, M. S. "Networking: It could be your key to job survival, success." VOGUE, 170, Mr. 1980, pp. 155–6.

9. Legal Issues, Legislation and Regulations

a. Title VII

1791. Bernstein, Merton C. and Lois G. Williams. "Title VII and the problem of sex classifications in pension programs." COLUMBIA LAW REVIEW, 74, Nov. 1974, pp. 1203–30.

1792. Binder, Denis. "Sex discrimination in the airline industry: Title VII flying high." CALIFORNIA LAW REVIEW, 59, Sept. 1971, pp. 1091–112.

1793. Eastwood, Mary Jane. "Employment discrimination and Title VII of the Civil Rights Act of 1964." HARVARD LAW REVIEW, 84, Mr. 1971, pp. 1109–80.

1794. Edwards, H. T. "Sex discrimination under Title VII: Some unresolved issues." LABOR LAW JOURNAL, 24, Jl. 1973, pp. 411–23.

1795. Gilbreath, J. I. "Sex discrimination and Title VII of the Civil Rights Act." PERSONNEL JOURNAL, 56, Ja. 1977, pp. 23–6.

1796. Hill, M., Jr. "Sex discrimination under Title VII and the constitution: A legal analysis." LABOR LAW JOURNAL, 29, Sept. 1978, pp. 570–81.

1797. Perry, Lowell W. "The mandate and impact of Title VII." LABOR LAW JOURNAL, 26, Dec. 1975, pp. 743–9.

1798. Safren, Miriam A. "Title VII and employee selection technique." PERSONNEL, 50, Ja.-Feb. 1973, pp. 26–35.

1799. Sape, George P. and Thomas J. Hart. "Title VII reconsidered: The Equal Employment Opportunity Act of 1972." GEORGE WASHINGTON LAW REVIEW, 40, 1972, pp. 824–89.

1800. Spiegelman, Paul J. "Bona fide seniority systems and relief from 'Last hired, first fired' layoffs under Title VII." EMPLOYEE RELATIONS LAW JOURNAL, 2, Ag. 1976, pp. 141–54.

1801. Walsh, E. B. "Sex discrimination and the impact of Title VII." LABOR LAW JOURNAL, 25, Mr. 1974, pp. 150–4.

1802. White, David M. and Richard L. Francis. "Title VII and the masters of reality: Eliminating credentialism in the American labor market." GEORGETOWN LAW JOURNAL, 64, Jl. 1976, pp. 1213–44.

1803. Wilcox, Jonathan J. "The sex discrimination provisions of Title VII: A maturing controversy." PACIFIC LAW JOURNAL, 3, Ja. 1972, pp. 37–62.

b. Equal Rights Amendment

1804. (ERA). NEW YORK TIMES, 22 Oct. 1978, pp. 82.

1805. *The "Equal Rights" Amendment.* Washington, DC: GPO, 1970.

1806. *Equal Rights Amendment extension.* Washington, DC: GPO, 1977.

1807. "Equal rights for women: ABC's of the big fight." U S NEWS & WORLD REPORT, 26 Mr. 1973, pp. 34–6.

1808. Foss, S. K. "Equal rights amendment controversy: Two worlds in conflict." QUARTERLY JOURNAL OF SPEECH, 65, Oct. 1979, pp. 275–88.

1809. "Fury of women scorned leads to boycott of convention cit-

ies in anti-ERA states." WALL STREET JOURNAL, 3
Nov. 1977. pp. 1, col. 5.

1810. Huber, Joan, Cynthia Rexroat and Glenna Spitze. "A cru-
cible of opinion of women's status: ERA in Illinois."
SOCIAL FORCES, 57, Dec. 1978, pp. 549–65.

1811. "Losing momentum: Movement to ratify equal-rights proposal slowed by opposition." WALL STREET JOURNAL,
26 Jl. 1974, pp. 1, col. 1.

1812. Loutzenhiser, J. "ERA boycott and the Sherman act."
AMERICAN BUSINESS LAW JOURNAL, 17, Wint.
1980, pp. 507–19.

1813. Martin, D. L. "Women against ERA: The loyalist opposition." LEARNING, 6, My./Je. 1978, pp. 33.

1814. Murray, Pauli. "The Negro woman's stake in the Equal
Rights Amendment." HARVARD CIVIL RIGHTS—
CIVIL LIBERTIES LAW REVIEW, 6, Mr. 1971, pp.
253–9.

1815. Rabin, Jack and Donald B. Dodd. "The 'ERA' comes to
New Columbia." 1973. ERIC, 14 pp. ED 099 301.

1816. "Sex discrimination and equal protection: Do we need a
constitution amendment?" HARVARD LAW REVIEW,
84, Ap. 1971, pp. 1499–1524.

1817. Sherman, Malcomb J. "Institutions and equal rights."
WALL STREET JOURNAL, 7 My. 1975, pp. 20.

1818. U.S. Congress. House. Committee on the Judiciary. *Equal
rights for men and women 1971: Hearings, March 24-
April 5, 1971, on H.J. Resolution 35, 208, and related
bills.* Washington, DC: GPO, 1971.

1819. U.S. Congress. Senate. Committee on the Judiciary. *The
"equal rights" amendment: Hearings, May 5-7, 1970, on
S.J. Resolution 61.* Washington, DC: GPO, 1970.

1820. U.S. Congress. Senate. Committee on the Judiciary. *Equal
rights 1970: Hearings, September 9-1, 1970, on S. J. Resolution 61 and S.J. Resolution 231.* Washington, DC:
GPO, 1970.

c. *Equal Employment Opportunity Act*

1821. Beller, Andrea H. "The effect of economic conditions on the
success of equal employment opportunity laws: An application to the sex differential in earnings." REVIEW OF
ECONOMICS AND STATISTICS, 62, Ag. 1980, pp.

379–87.
1822. Brown, William, III. "The Equal Employment Opportunity Act of 1972—the light at the top of the stairs." PERSONNEL ADMINISTRATION, 35, Je. 1972, pp. 4ff.
1823. Carey, William A. "Litigation involving sex discrimination under the Equal Employment Opportunity Act." WOMEN LAWYERS JOURNAL, 60, Wint. 1974, pp. 21–9.
1824. *Equal opportunity and full employment, part 1.* Washington, DC: GPO, 1975.
1825. *Equal opportunity and full employment, part 2.* Washington, DC: GPO, 1975.
1826. *Oversight on Federal enforcement of equal employment opportunity laws.* Washington, DC: GPO, 1978.
1827. Read, John C. "Equal employment opportunity under federal contracts." LABOR LAW JOURNAL, 28, Ja. 1977, pp. 3–12.

d. Equal Pay Act

1828. "Closing pay gap for women: New rules." U S NEWS AND WORLD REPORT, 14 Ag. 1972, pp. 69.
1829. Feldman, Edwin B. "Sex, money and the Equal Pay Act." NATION'S SCHOOLS, 91, Ap. 1973, pp. 56–8+.
1830. Moran, Robert D. "Reducing discrimination: Role of the Equal Pay Act." MONTHLY LABOR REVIEW, 93, Je. 1970, pp. 30–4.
1831. Sangerman, H. "Look at the Equal Pay Act in practice." LABOR LAW JOURNAL, 22, My. 1971, pp. 259–65.
1832. Tessaro, Edward. "Equal pay act allows for some salary differentials." MODERN NURSING HOME, 28, Je. 1972, pp. 4+.

e. Other Legislation and Regulations

1833. *Achieving the goals of the Employment Act of 1946, Thirtieth anniversary review. Vol. 1: Employment. Paper No. 6: Impact of macroeconomic conditions on employment opportunities for women.* Washington, DC: GPO, 1977.
1834. Adams, A. E. "Labor department plans new rules on hiring and promoting women." BANKING, 64, Nov. 1971, pp. 13.
1835. Adams, A. E. "Labor department stiffens rules on whom you hire, how you hire." BANKING, 64, Dec. 1971, pp. 12.

1836. Baron, A. S. and E. T. Reeves. "How effective has affirmative action legislation been?" PERSONNEL ADMINISTRATOR, 22, Ja. 1977, pp. 47-9.

1837. "Califano endorses preferential treatment: Calls it constitutional and moral obligation that need not result in reverse discrimination." CHRONICLE OF HIGHER EDUCATION, 28 Mr. 1977, pp. 11.

1838. Carlson, Elliot. "States revising labor laws for women, even without equal rights amendment." WALL STREET JOURNAL, 3 Sept. 1970, pp. 7.

1839. *Coming decade: American women and human resources policies and programs, 1979, Part 1.* Washington, DC: GPO, 1979.

1840. Draper, Virginia. "A historical sketch of the major labor law developments that have occurred as a result of the Civil Rights Act of 1964 and the activities of the Equal Employment Opportunity Commission." HOWARD LAW JOURNAL, 18(1), 1973, pp. 29-87.

1841. Eastwood, Mary. "Fighting job discrimination: Three federal approaches." FEMINIST STUDIES, 1, Summ. 1972, pp. 75-103.

1842. Education Commission of the States. *A handbook of state laws and policies affecting equal rights of women in education.* 1975. 125 pp.

1843. "Education, credit, sports—barriers to women keep falling." U S NEWS & WORLD REPORT, 21 Jl. 1975, pp. 21-2.

1844. Feldman, Edwin. "Female employees have law on their side." COLLEGE AND UNIVERSITY BUSINESS, 54, My. 1973, pp. 54-5.

1845. *A guide to Federal laws prohibiting sex discrimination.* Washington, DC: GPO, 1974.

1846. "Guidelines proposed to protect women's jobs." CHEMICAL WEEK, 13 Feb. 1980, pp. 18-9.

1847. Hallam, Charlotte B. "Legal tools to fight sex discrimination." LABOR LAW JOURNAL, 24, Dec. 1973, pp. 803-9.

1848. *Handling of discrimination complaints in the Senate, Part 2.* Washington, DC: GPO, 1978.

1849. Hook, Janet. "Labor Department would revise affirmative action rules." CHRONICLE OF HIGHER EDUCATION, 14 Ja. 1980, pp. 17.

1850. Hughes, Marija Matich. "The sexual barrier; legal and economic aspects of employment." 1970. ERIC, 43 pp. ED 065 701.

1851. Hughes, Marija Matich. "The sexual barrier; legal and economic aspects of employment. Supplement 1." 1971. ERIC, 40 pp. ED 065 702.

1852. Hughes, Marija Matich. "The sexual barrier; legal and economic aspects of employment. Supplement 2." 1972. ERIC, 79 pp. ED 965 703.

1853. "Labor Department sets goal of 25% women in apprenticeship." AIR CONDITIONING, HEATING & REFRIGERATION NEWS, 16 Ap. 1979, pp. 1+.

1854. "Lady's law vanishes." NATION'S BUSINESS, 59, Dec. 1971, pp. 62.

1855. *Laws on sex discrimination in employment.* Washington, DC: GPO, 1973.

1856. (Legislative reform for women's rights). NEW YORK TIMES, 20 Oct. 1971. pp. 27, col. 2.

1857. Moller, Vicki. "The majority that doesn't rule." PACIFIC BUSINESS, 62, Ja.-Feb. 1972, pp. 10-5.

1858. Moore, Mack A. "Proposed federal legislation for temporary labor services." LABOR LAW JOURNAL, 26, Dec. 1975, pp. 767-81.

1859. Munts, Raymond and David C. Rice. "Women workers: protection or equality." INDUSTRIAL AND LABOR RELATIONS REVIEW, 24, Oct. 1970, pp. 3-13.

1860. "New women's job standards may hike costs, alter practices." INDUSTRY WEEK, 24 Ap. 1972, pp. 21-2.

1861. "Outcry over minority contracting." BUSINESS WEEK, 2 Je. 1980, pp. 36.

1862. *Oversight hearings on Federal enforcement of EEO laws.* Washington, DC: GPO, 1979.

1863. Pryor, Betty and others. "Sex discrimination and contract compliance. Beyond the legal requirements." 1972. ERIC, 12 pp. ED 065 050.

1864. Ratner, R. S. "Paradox of protection: Maximum hours legislation in the United States." INTERNATIONAL LABOUR REVIEW, 119, Mr. 1980, pp. 185-98.

1865. Roark, Anne. "U.S. Civil Rights Office called failure in enforcing law prohibiting sex bias." CHRONICLE OF HIGHER EDUCATION, 8 Dec. 1980, pp. 11+.

1866. Rubenfeld, Stephen A. and Dennis D. Strouble. "Arbitration and EEO issues." LABOR LAW JOURNAL, 30, Ag. 1979, pp. 489–94.

1867. Sassower, Doris L. "The legal rights of professional women." CONTEMPORARY EDUCATION, 43, Feb. 1972, pp. 205–8.

1868. Sassower, Doris L. "Women, power, and the law." AMERICAN BAR ASSOCIATION JOURNAL, 62, My. 1976, pp. 613–6.

1869. "Sex discrimination and contract compliance beyond the legal requirement." EDUCATIONAL RECORD, 53, Summ. 1972, pp. 265–6.

1870. Sherry, John E. H. "Law and the women employee: The innkeeper's economic and legal responsibilities." HOTEL & RESTAURANT ADMINISTRATION QUARTERLY, 14, Nov. 1973, pp. 85–113.

1871. Shulman, Carol Herrnstadt. "Federal laws: Nondiscrimination and faculty employment." 1975. ERIC, 63 pp. ED 109 979.

1872. Smith, L. "EEOC's bold foray into job evaluation." FORTUNE, 11 Sept. 1978, pp. 58–60+.

1873. Soule, Bradley and Kay Standley. "Perceptions of sex discrimination in law." AMERICAN BAR ASSOCIATION JOURNAL, 59, Oct. 1973, pp. 1144–7.

1874. Stead, Bette Ann. "Real equal opportunity for women executives." BUSINESS HORIZONS, 17, Ag. 1974, pp. 87–92.

1875. Stillman, N. G. "Women in the workplace: A legal perspective." JOURNAL OF OCCUPATIONAL MEDICINE, 20, Sept. 1978, pp. 605–9.

1876. Terlin, Rose. "A working woman's guide to her job rights." 1974. ERIC, 41 pp. Ed 109 328.

1877. Thorp, Cary D., Jr. "Fair employment practices: The compliance jungle." PERSONNEL JOURNAL, 52, Je. 1973, pp. 642–9.

1878. Tinsley, Adrian. "Academic women, sex discrimination, and the law." 1975. 30 pp. (Available from Modern Language Association, 62 Fifth Ave., New York, NY 10011.)

1879. U.S. Commission on Civil Rights. *A guide to federal laws and regulations prohibiting sex discrimination.* Washington, DC: GPO, 1976.

1880. U.S. Equal Employment Opportunity Commission. *Guidelines on discrimination because of sex.* Washington, DC: GPO, 1972.

1881. U.S. Equal Employment Opportunity Commission. *Toward fair employment and the EEOC.* Washington, DC: GPO, 1973.

1882. U.S. Congress. House. Committee on Education and Labor. *Discrimination against women: Hearings, Pt. 1, June 17-30, 1970, on Section 805 of H.R. 16098.* Washington, DC: GPO, 1970.

1883. U.S. Congress. House Committee on Education and Labor. *Oversight hearings on discrimination against women: Hearings, April 26-May 10, 1972.* Washington, DC: GPO, 1973.

1884. U.S. Women's Bureau. *A working woman's guide to her job rights.* Washington, DC: GPO, 1975.

1885. "Veterans' preference and the equal protection clause." WOMEN'S RIGHTS LAW REPORTER, 3, Spr.-Summ. 1977, pp. 175-83.

1886. "What are the protective laws?" UNION W.A.G.E., No. 14, Nove.-Dec. 1972, pp. 1+.

1887. Willborn, Steven L. "Public sector pattern or practice enforcement under Reorganization Plan No. 1 of 1978." LABOR LAW JOURNAL, 31, Ja. 1980, pp. 27-36.

1888. Winkler, Karen J. "Office for Civil Rights blasted in GAO report: Senator Bayh calls findings, 'truly appalling'." CHRONICLE OF HIGHER EDUCATION, 11 Ap. 1977, pp. 11.

1889. Women in the Work Force. *What every woman worker should know about discrimination.* 1980. 15 pp. (Available from Women in the Work Force, P.O. Box 2234, 842 South Main Street, High Point, NC 27271.)

1890. Women in the Work Force. *What every woman worker should know about minimum wage and overtime laws.* 1980. 11 pp. (Available from Women in the Work Force, P.O. Box 2234, 842 South Main Street, High Point, NC 27261.)

1891. Women in the Work Force. *What every woman worker should know about The National Labor Relations Act.* 1980. 15 pp. (Available from Women in the Work Force, P.O. Box 2234, 842 South Main Street, High Point, NC 27261.)

1892. "Women's liberation counts a victory: New federal guidelines set a tough tone on sex discrimination." BUSINESS WEEK, 13 Je. 1970, pp. 98–100.

1893. "Women's rights handbook. California Department of Justice Information Pamphlet No. 9." 1976. ERIC, 70 pp. ED 160 697.

1894. Yaffe, Barbara and Byron Yaffe. "State protective legislation: An anachronism under Title VII?" ISSUES IN INDUSTRIAL SOCIETY, 2(1), 1971, pp. 54–61.

f. Specific Cases

1895. Clark, D. L. "Discrimination suits: A unique settlement." EDUCATIONAL RECORD, 58, Summ. 1977, pp. 233–49.

1896. "The courts back women on job equality: Women have won 178 of 208 lower court cases and 14 of 30 appeals." BUSINESS WEEK, 25 Nov. 1972, pp. 44+.

1897. Crothers, Diane. "The AT & T settlement." WOMEN'S RIGHTS LAW REPORTER, 1, Summ. 1973, pp. 5–13.

1898. "EEOC finds *Newsday* discrimination in job classification and promotion." MEDIA REPORT TO WOMEN, 1 Ja. 1977, pp. 10.

1899. "Group of female construction workers filed suit charging Labor Department condoned pattern of sex discrimination." WALL STREET JOURNAL, 17 My. 1976, pp. 13. col. 2.

1900. Jacobs, R. B. "Manhart case: Sex-based differentials and the application of Title VII to pensions." LABOR LAW JOURNAL, 31, Ap. 1980, pp. 232–46.

1901. Mellow, J. P., Jr. "Addison-Wesley agrees to $360,000 sex-bias accord." PUBLISHERS WEEKLY, 11 Ap. 1980, pp. 10.

1902. Nickel, H. "Dante in the Federal inferno." FORTUNE, 2 Je. 1980, pp. 78–80+.

1903. Portwood, James D. and Karen S. Koziara. "In search of equal employment opportunity: New interpretations of Title VII." LABOR LAW JOURNAL, 30, Je. 1979, pp. 353–60.

1904. Rourke, Nancy. "The New York telephone settlement: A study in contrast." WOMEN'S RIGHTS LAW REPORTER, 1, Summ. 1973, pp. 15–7.

1905. Rush, Floyd L. "The impact on employment procedures of the Supreme Court decision in the Duke Power Case." PERSONNEL JOURNAL, 50, Oct. 1971, pp. 777–83.

1906. "Sex-bias case citing Merrill Lynch, Pierce, Fenner & Smith gets class action status." WALL STREET JOURNAL, 9 Je. 1975, pp. 11, col. 2.

1907. Shaffer, Butler D. "Some economic considerations in sex discrimination cases." LABOR LAW JOURNAL, 26, My. 1975, pp. 290–300.

1908. "$60,000 won by women employees who sued KOA stations in Colorado." MEDIA REPORT TO WOMEN, 1 Ja. 1979, pp. 1–2.

1909. Stephens, John L. "Bank assails government's motives, methods, and allegations in EEO action." ABA BANKING JOURNAL, 72, Ja. 1980, pp. 18+.

1910. "Suit demands US probe sex bias in Southwest." CHRONICLE OF HIGHER EDUCATION, 19 Ja. 1976, pp. 10.

1911. "Supreme Court held that law giving veterans a preference for government jobs doesn't amount to constitutional discrimination against women." WALL STREET JOURNAL, 6 Je. 1979, pp. 6, col. 2.

1912. Swanson, Susan. "Reverse discrimination, & other lies: *Weber vs Kaiser:. . .*women's brief." OFF OUR BACKS, 9, Ap. 1979, pp. 8–9.

1913. "US finds for AT & T in equal employment case." CPA JOURNAL, 49, Ap. 1979, pp. 72–3.

1914. "Uniroyal, Inc. was barred from doing business with the federal government as the result of a job-discrimination case." WALL STREET JOURNAL, 2 Jl. 1979, pp. 6, col. 1.

1915. "Veterans' public employment preference as sex discrimination: *Anthony v. Massachusetts* and *Branch v. DuBois.*" HARVARD LAW REVIEW, 90, Feb. 1977, pp. 805–14.

1916. Wehrwein, A. C. "Woman chemist gets $100,000 in settlement of sex-bias suit." CHRONICLE OF HIGHER EDUCATION, 28 Ap. 1980, pp. 1+.

1917. Whol, Lisa C. "Liberating Ma Bell." MS, 2, 1973, pp. 52+.

1918. "Women charge discrimination at Chase." BANKING, 68, Mr. 1976, pp. 24.

1919. "Women scientists sue HEW." CHEMICAL AND ENGINEERING NEWS, 3 Ap. 1972, pp. 8.

1920. "Women suing New York Times win class action status in federal court." MEDIA REPORT TO WOMEN, 1 My. 1977, pp. 1+.

E. OCCUPATIONS

1. Clerical Work

1921. Arvey, Richard D. and Stephen J. Musso. "Determining the existence of unfair test discriminations for female clerical workers." PERSONNEL PSYCHOLOGY 26, Dec. 1973, pp. 559–68.

1922. Benet, Mary Kathleen. "Everybody's gal Friday: How a lot of nice women get into offices in the first place." MS, 1, My. 1973, pp. 78–9.

1923. Benet, Mary Kathleen. "A view from the secretarial ghetto." ADIMINISTRATIVE MANAGEMENT, 34, Nov. 1973, pp. 24–6.

1924. Bowen, Donald B. "Work values of women in secretarial-clerical occupations." AMERICAN JOURNAL OF COMMUNITY PSYCHOLOGY, 1, Ja.-Mr. 1973, pp. 83–90.

1925. Culver, Gordan and Elsie Devans. "A career in the secretarial occupations." BUSINESS EDUCATION FORUM, 26(8), 1972, pp. 3–6.

1926. Dreyfack, Raymond. "Is today's secretary on the way out?" NATION'S BUSINESS, 61, Spr. 1973, pp. 87–8.

1927. Fiore, Michael V. "The secretarial role in transition." SUPERVISORY MANAGEMENT, 16, Nov. 1971, pp. 22–7.

1928. Gordon, Robert. "We asked your secretary." CASE AND COMMENT, 77, My.-Je. 1972, pp. 35–7.

1929. Gottlieb, Karen. "Drowning in the typing pool." BLACK MARIA, 2, Spr. 1979, pp. 13–24.

1930. Palmer, Phyllis M. and Sharon L. Grant. *The status of clerical workers.* (Available from Business and Professional Women's Foundation, 2012 Massachusetts Avenue, N.W. Washington, DC 20036.)

1931. "Personal business (What bugs your secretary most about her job)." BUSINESS WEEK, 25 Nov. 1972, pp. 73.

1932. Prather, Jane E. "When the girls move in: A social analysis of the feminization of the bank teller's job." JOURNAL

OF MARRIAGE AND THE FAMILY, 33, Nov. 1971. pp. 777–82.

1933. Roderick, Roger D. and John R. Shea. "Typing, shorthand, and occupational assignments of women: Some black-white differentials." 1972. ERIC, 25 pp. ED 076 802.

1934. "Secretary is becoming an endangered species." FORBES, 11 Dec. 1978, pp. 61–2.

1935. Strong, Marsha K. "Mother types at home." MOTHER EARTH NEWS, 54, Nov. 1978, pp. 80.

1936. "Suddenly, a new shortage of secretaries." BUSINESS WEEK, 8 Ag. 1977, pp. 84–5.

1937. Tepper, Harold. "The private secretary: A company liability." MANAGEMENT REVIEW, 62, Feb. 1973, pp. 23–32.

1938. Thompson, Louise. "Making waves in the secretarial pool." MAJORITY REPORT, 19 Mr.-l Ap. 1977, pp. 5.

1939. Twifel, Minna and Ellen Birdseye. "The secretary." WOMEN: A JOURNAL OF LIBERATION, 2, 1971, pp. 33–8.

1940. Vaughan, E. J. "Women can hold down own wages if they seek mostly clerical work." NATIONAL UNDERWRITER LIFE AND HEALTH INSURANCE EDITION, 28 Je. 1974, pp. 19+.

2. Crafts and Trades

1941. "Blue-Collar Women: More female workers get skilled trade jobs." WALL STREET JOURNAL, 13 Nov. 1978, pp. 1+.

1942. "Just 1.9% of the 175,303 construction trades apprentices registered at the end of 1978 were women." WALL STREET JOURNAL, 12 Feb. 1980, pp.1+.

1943. Lederer, M. "Plumber's here and he's a woman." AMERICAN EDUCATION, 40, Feb. 1975, pp. 36–8.

1944. Lehmann, P. "Women journey into the skilled trades." WORKLIFE MAGAZINE, 2, Ag. 1977, pp. 26–31.

1945. Minter, Charlotte and Roseann Cacciola. "The welder is a woman." COMMUNITY AND JUNIOR COLLEGE JOURNAL, 47, Nov. 1976, pp. 6–7.

1946. "Move over lads, more Josephines are coming." AIR CONDITIONING, HEATING AND REFRIGERATION NEWS, 28 My. 1973, pp. 129.

1947. Rich, J. "Supervising the woman craftworker." SUPERVI-

SION, 40, My. 1978, pp. 4–5.

1948. Smith, Karen. "Lower pay, harder work - long struggles for women book binders." UNION W.A.G.E., 23, My.-Je. 1974, pp. 11.

1949. "Tools for a woman's trade. (Working with tools designed for average man's hands difficult for women)." HUMAN BEHAVIOR, 6, Oct. 1977, pp. 72+.

1950. "Two gals prefer hanging ductwork over routine secretarial chores." AIR CONDITIONING, HEATING AND REFRIGERATION NEWS, 13 Ag. 1973, pp. 16.

1951. U.S. Equal Employment Opportunity Commission. *Minorities and women in referral units in building trades.* Washington, DC: GPO, 1974. 54 pp.

1952. U.S. Women's Bureau. *Steps to opening the skilled trades to women.* Washington, DC: GPO, 1974.

3. Paid Domestic Work

1953. "Black women for wages for housework. Local women seek wages for housework." MAJORITY REPORT, 2-15 Ap. 1977, pp. 9.

1954. Christensen, Ethlyn. "Household employment: Restructing the occupation." ISSUES IN INDUSTRIAL SOCIETY, 2(1), 1971, pp. 47–53.

1955. Grossman, Allyson Sherman. "Women in domestic work: Yesterday and today." MONTHLY LABOR REVIEW, 103, Ag. 1980, pp. 17–21.

1956. Hulett, Josephine and Janet Dewart. "Household help wanted—female." MS 1, Fall 1972, pp. 45-9+.

1957. Katz, Donald R. "Carolyn Reed and the backstairs revolt (household workers)." NEW YORK, 11 Je. 1979, pp. 45-50.

1958. Matilla, J. P. "The effect of extending minimum wages to cover household maids." JOURNAL OF HUMAN RESOURCES, 8, Summ. 1973, pp. 365–82.

1959. Peterson, Calvin R. "The cleaning lady." JOURNAL OF HUMANISTIC PSYCHOLOGY, 18, Sp. 1978, pp. 63-4.

1960. Roberts, Ellen. "Women and work: The household workers fight." ESSENCE, 4, Ap. 1974, p. 12.

1961. Ryan, Sheila. "Chambermaids: A profile of some women's work." SOCIAL POLICY, 7, Mr.-Ap. 1977, pp. 36–40.

1962. Walker, Kathryn E. "Economic discrimination and household work." HUMAN ECOLOGY FORUM, 4(2), 1974, pp. 21–3.

1963. Washington, Marie, Christine Wacek and Joyce Maupin. "Household workers demand $5 mimimum wage." UNION W.A.G.E., No. 54, Jl.-Ag. 1979, pp. 8.

1964. *Women private household workers: A statistical and legislative profile.* Washington, DC: GPO, 1978.

4. Education

a. Elementary and Secondary School Faculty

1965. Brophy, Jere E. and Thomas L. Good. "Feminization of American elementary schools." PHI DELTA KAPPAN, 54, Ap. 1973, pp. 564–6; Reply D.F. Smith, 54, Je. 1973, pp. 703–4; Rejoiner, 55, Sept. 1973, pp. 73–5.

1966. Fishel, Andrew and Janice Pottker. "Women teachers and teacher power." URBAN REVIEW, 6, Nov.-Dec. 1973, pp. 40–4.

1967. Greaball, Leon C. and John A. Olson. "Role dissatisfaction and career contingencies among female elementary teachers." JOURNAL OF THE PERSONNEL ASSOCIATION FOR TEACHER EDUCATION, 11, Je. 1973, pp. 131–8.

1968. Lebowitz, R. "Women elementary school teachers and the feminist movement." ELEMENTARY SCHOOL JOURNAL, 80, My. 1980, pp. 239–45.

1969. Lee, Patrick C. "Male and female teachers in elementary schools: An ecological analysis." TEACHERS COLLEGE RECORD, 75, Sept. 1973, pp. 79–98.

1970. Love, R. B. "Oakland public schools: Showcase for affirmative action." PHI DELTA KAPPAN, 61, Nov. 1979, pp. 191–3.

1971. Main, Cecil. "Characteristics of a group of women science teachers." SCHOOL SCIENCE AND MATHEMATICS, 73, Ap. 1973, pp. 286–90.

1972. Nolte, M. C. "Women in education: A long, long way to go." AMERICAN SCHOOL BOARD JOURNAL, 160, Oct. 1973, pp. 38–40.

1973. Nolte, M. Chester, ed. "Gender and sexual mores in educational employment. A legal memorandum." 1974. ERIC, 7 pp. ED 108 369.

1974. Sopher, Valerie. "Focus on education: Battle fatigue (Stress of schoolworkers and day care workers)." UNION W.A.G.E., No. 55, Sept.-Oct. 1979, pp. 5.

1975. (Women in the teacher profession). NEW YORK TIMES, 16 Oct. 1973, pp. 47+, col. 3.

b. Post-Secondary School Faculty

1976. Babey-Brooke, Anna M. and R. B. Amber."Discrimination against women in higher education. A 15 year survey. Promotional practices at Brooklyn College CUNY: 1955-1970, all ranks—tenured and untenured." 1970. ERIC, 27 pp. ED 044 089.

1977. Bayer, Alan E. and Helen S. Astin. "Sex differentials in the academic reward system." SCIENCE, 188, My. 1975, pp. 796–802.

1978. Bergmann, Barbara R. and Myles Maxfield, Jr. "How to analyze the fairness of faculty women's salaries on your own campus." AAUP BULLETIN, 61, Oct. 1975, pp. 262–8.

1979. Bradley, J. and J. Silverleaf. "Women teachers in further education." EDUCATIONAL RESEARCH, 22, Nov. 1979, pp. 15–21.

1980. Committee on the Status of Women. "Data on women in departments of political science." PS, 7, Wint. 1974, pp. 38–41.

1981. Eble, E.E. "Strengthening the position of women faculty members." NATIONAL ASSOCIATION OF WOMEN DEANS AND COUNSELORS JOURNAL, 35, Summ. 1972, pp. 165–6.

1982. Ekstrom, Ruth B. "Issues in the recruitment, professional development, promotion, and remuneration of women faculty." Research memorandum. 1978. ERIC, 23 pp. ED 161 318.

1983. "Fact File: Status of female faculty members, 1979-80. Men and women compared in number, salary level and percentage with tenure." CHRONICLE OF HIGHER EDUCATION, 29 Sept. 1980, pp. 8.

1984. Farber, Stephen. "The earnings and promotion of women faculty." AMERICAN ECONOMIC REVIEW, 67, Mr. 1977, pp. 199–217.

1985. Farley, Jennie. "Men, women, and work satisfaction on

campus." CORNELL JOURNAL OF SOCIAL RELA-
TIONS, 9, Spr. 1974, pp. 17–33.

1986. "Female professors still get paid less than their male coun-
terparts." WALL STREET JOURNAL, 5 Dec. 1978, pp.
1+.

1987. Ferber, M. A. and others. "Economic status of women
faculty: A reappraisal." JOURNAL OF HUMAN
RESOURCES, 13, Summ. 1978, pp. 385–401.

1988. Ferber, Marianne and Jane W. Loeb. "Performance,
rewards, and perceptions of sex discrimination among
male and female faculty." AMERICAN JOURNAL OF
SOCIOLOGY, 78, Ja. 1973, pp. 995–1002.

1989. Fields, C. M. "Courts are rejecting most charges of sex bias
made by women professors." CHRONICLE OF HIGHER
EDUCATION, 26 Sept. 1977, pp. 1+.

1990. Gallup, Jane Marie. "Financial barriers to participation in
postsecondary education perceived by New York State
employed women." 1980. ERIC, 153 pp. ED 176 653.

1991. Gray, M. "Climbing the academic ladder - doctoral women
scientist in academe." ACADEME, 66(1), 1980, pp.
39–40.

1992. Harlan, Anne and others. "Sex, productivity and reward in
academe." 1974. ERIC, 13 pp. ED 097 619.

1993. Harris, A. S. "Women in college art departments and muse-
ums." ART JOURNAL, 32, Summ. 1973, pp. 417–19.

1994. Harris, Ann Sutherland. "The second sex in academe."
AAUP BULLETIN, 56, Sept. 1970, pp. 283–95.

1995. Heilburn, Carol. "Men over 40, women under 40: These two
seemingly unlikely groups hold the power to give women a
larger role on college faculties." CHRONICLE OF
HIGHER EDUCATION, 15 Nov. 1976, pp. 32.

1996. Hicks, Laurabeth H. "The mature, married black female in
academe." 1974. ERIC, 6 pp. ED 106 711.

1997. Hoffman, Emily P. "Faculty salaries: Is there discrimination
by sex, race, and discipline?" AMERICAN ECONOMIC
REVIEW, 66, Mr. 1976, pp. 196–8.

1998. Holden, Christine. "Women in Michigan: Academic sexism
under seige." SCIENCE, 178, Nov. 1972, pp. 841–3.

1999. Holden, Christine. "Women in Michigan: Parlaying rights
into power." SCIENCE, 178, Dec. 1972, pp. 962–5.

2000. Hornig, Lilli S. "Untenured and tenuous: The status of

women faculty." ANNALS OF THE AMERICAN
ACADEMY OF POLITICAL AND SOCIAL SCIENCE,
448, Mr. 1980, pp. 115–25.

2001. "In 'The Academic Game' it's hard for women to get ahead."
CHRONICLE OF HIGHER EDUCATION, 26 Nov.
1979, pp. 19.

2002. Jaffe, Lorna. "Women's place in academe." MIDWEST
QUARTERLY, 15, Oct. 1973, pp. 16–30.

2003. Johnson, George E. and Frank P. Stafford. "The earnings
and promotion of women faculty." AMERICAN ECO-
NOMIC REVIEW, 64, Dec. 1974, pp. 888–903.

2004. Johnson, Robert C., Jr. "Affirmative action and the academic profession." ANNALS OF THE AMERICAN
ACADEMY OF POLITICAL AND SOCIAL SCIENCE,
448, Mr. 1980, pp. 102–14.

2005. Kimmel, Ellen B. "The status of faculty women: A method
for documentation and correction of salary and rank
inequities due to sex." 1972. ERIC, 21 pp. ED 074 996.

2006. Koch, J. V. and J. F. Chizinar. "Sex discrimination and
affirmative action in faculty salaries." ECONOMIC
INQUIRY, 14, Mr. 1976, pp. 16–24.

2007. Ladd, Everett Carll, Jr. and Seymour Martin Lipset.
"Faculty women: Little gain in status, 1975. Ladd-Lipset
survey of U.S. professoriate." CHRONICLE OF HIGHER
EDUCATION, 29 Sept. 1975, pp. 2.

2008. Lauter, Nancy A. and Daniel Dietrich. "Woman's place in
academe - an ERIC report." ENGLISH EDUCATION, 3,
Spr. 1972, pp. 169–73.

2009. Leslie, David W. and Ronald B. Head. "Part-time faculty
rights." EDUCATIONAL RECORD, 60, Wint. 1979, pp.
46–67.

2010. Long, J. Scott, Paul D. Allison and Robert McGinnis.
"Entrance into the academic career." AMERICAN
SOCIOLOGICAL REVIEW, 44, Oct. 1979, pp. 816–31.

2011. McAllester, Susan, ed. "A case for equity: Women in English departments." 1971. ERIC, 100 pp. ED 057 020.

2012. Magarrell, Jack. "Colleges give bigger raises to women but
men's average pay is still higher." CHRONICLE OF
HIGHER EDUCATION, 8 Dec. 1980, pp. 1+.

2013. Magarrell, Jack. "More women on faculties: Pay still lags."
CHRONICLE OF HIGHER EDUCATION, 29 Sept.

1980, pp. 8.

2014. Marting, Leeda and K. Sue Foley. "Women in broadcasting education." JOURNAL OF BROADCASTING, 19, Wint. 1975, pp. 31–42.

2015. Marwell, Gerald, Rachel Rosenfeld and Seymour Spilerman. *Residence location, geographic mobility, and the attainment of women in academia. Discussion paper 359–76.* 1976. 31 pp. (Available from Institute Research on Poverty, University of Wisconsin, Madison, WI 53706.)

2016. Menninger, Sally Ann and Clare Rose. "Women scientist and engineers in American academia." INTERNATIONAL JOURNAL OF WOMEN'S STUDIES, 3, My.-Je. 1980, pp. 292–9.

2017. Miner, Anne S. "Academic employment of women at Stanford." 1972. ERIC, 43 pp. ED 063 893.

2018. Miyares, Javier and Glenwood C. Brooks, Jr. "Some data on the status of women in the state public postsecondary education institutions." 1977. ERIC, 17 pp. ED 158 685.

2019. Moore, Kathryn M. and Peter A. Wollitzer. "Recent trends in research on academic women: A bibliographic review and analysis." 1979. ERIC, 28 pp. ED 176 618.

2020. National Education Association. "The status of women faculty and administrators in higher education institutions, 1971-1972." 1973. ERIC, 8 pp. ED 080 034.

2021. "National report: Opportunities for women in higher education." INTELLECT, 102, Ja. 1974, pp. 208–19.

2022. "Newest campus crusade: Equal rights for women." U S NEWS AND WORLD REPORT, 13 Dec. 1971, pp. 79–81.

2023. Oltman, Ruth M. "Campus 1970, 'Where do women stand?' " Research report of a survey on women in academe. 1970. ERIC, 47 pp. ED 046 336.

2024. Patterson, Michelle. "Alice in wonderland: A study of women faculty in graduate departments of sociology." AMERICAN SOCIOLOGIST, 6, Ag. 1971, pp. 226–34.

2025. "Percentage of women professors is four times national average in women's college survey." 1976. ERIC, 9 pp. ED 126 791.

2026. Pingree, S. and others. "Writers see gains, losses in women faculty status." JOURNALISM EDUCATION, 32, Jl.

1977, pp. 32–5.

2027. Rawls, R. L. and J. L. Fox. "Women in academic chemistry find rise to full status difficult." CHEMICAL AND ENGINEERING NEWS, 56, Sept. 1978, pp. 26–32.

2028. Rose, Clare and others. "Responsiveness vs. resources: The implementation and impact of affirmative action programs for women scientists in postsecondary education." Air forum paper 1978. 1979. ERIC, 30 pp. ED 161 389.

2029. Rose, Clare and others. "The study of the academic employment and graduate enrollment patterns and trends of women in science and engineering." Summary report. 1979. ERIC, 44 pp. ED 169 866.

2030. "Sex bias fades in the hiring of new Ph. D's California study claims." WALL STREET JOURNAL, 3 Je. 1975, pp. 1+, col. 5.

2031. Shaffer, M. K. "Faculty awareness: Key to women's advancement." DELTA KAPPA GAMMA BULLETIN, 43, Summ. 1977, pp. 36–43.

2032. Silverstein, Michael. "The development of identity: Power and sex roles in academia." JOURNAL OF APPLIED BEHAVIORAL SCIENCE, 8, Sept.-Oct. 1972, pp. 536–63.

2033. "Stalemate or progress: A follow-up survey on the status of women in New Jersey higher education." 1973. ERIC, 33 pp. ED 077 465.

2034. Steinbach, Sheldon E. "Equal employment opportunity on campus: Issues in 1974." JOURNAL OF THE COLLEGE AND UNIVERSITY PERSONNEL ASSOCIATION, 25, Jl.-Ag. 1974, pp. 1–9.

2035. Tanur, J. M. and R. L. Coser. "Pockets of poverty in the salaries of academic women." AAUP BULLETIN, 64, Mr. 1978, pp. 26–30.

2036. Theodore, Athena. "Academic women in protest." 1974. ERIC, 79 pp. ED 091 989.

2037. Weidman, Carla Sue and John C. Weidman. "The woman professor of education: Social and occupational characteristics." 1975. ERIC, 24 pp. ED 104 893.

2038. Weitzman, Lenore and others. "Women on the Yale faculty." 1971. ERIC, 33 pp. ED 056 636.

2039. Westervelt, Esther M. "Essay review: Opportunities for women in higher education - their current participation, prospects for the future, and recommendations for action." HARVARD EDUCATIONAL REVIEW, 44, My. 1974, pp. 295–313.

2040. Winkler, Karen J. "Woman historians have greater access to some jobs but remain concentrated in underpaid ranks." CHRONICLE OF HIGHER EDUCATION, 12 Ja. 1981, pp. 8.

2041. "Woman trainers avidly sought by colleges to treat female athletes." WALL STREET JOURNAL, 20 Je. 1976, pp. 1+, col. 5.

2042. "Women lost ground on college faculties in 1975, survey by American Association of University Professors showed." WALL STREET JOURNAL, 13 Jl. 1976, pp. 1+, col. 5.

2043. "Women professors: Where are they?" M B A, 11, Sept. 1972, pp. 38+.

2044. "WPS: A Committee on the Status of Women in Political Science." Report on the status of women in political science. WESTERN POLITICAL QUARTERLY, 28, Je. 1975, pp. 387–90.

2045. Young, Carlotta Joyner, Doris Layton MacKenzie and Carolyn Wood Sherif. "In search of token women in academia." PSYCHOLOGY OF WOMEN, 4, Summ. 1980, pp. 508–25.

c. *Administration*

2046. Adkison, J. A. and J. D. Bailey. "Increasing women's participation in education, administration." EDUCATION DIGEST, 46, Feb. 1981, pp. 10–3.

2047. Arter, Margaret Helen. "The role of women in administration in state universities and land grant colleges." 1972. ERIC, 3 pp. ED 086 085.

2048. Clement, Jacqueline P. "Where are the women superintendents?" SOUTHERN JOURNAL OF EDUCATIONAL RESEARCH, 7, Wint. 1973, pp. 1–6.

2049. Cochran, J. "How do women administrators view job satisfaction and discrimination?" JOURNAL OF NATIONAL ASSOCIATION OF WOMEN DEANS, ADMINISTRATORS, AND COUNSELORS, 41, Wint. 1978, pp. 67–8.

2050. Coffin, Gregory C. and Ruth B. Ekstrom. "Aspirations, experience, and roadblocks to the hiring of women in educational administration." 1977. ERIC, 10 pp. ED 151 966.

2051. Collins, Lorraine. "About those few females who scale the heights of school management." INTEGRATED EDUCATION, 15, Ja.-Feb. 1977, pp. 19–21.

2052. Dale, C. T. "Women are still missing persons in administrative and supervisory jobs." EDUCATIONAL LEADERSHIP, 31, Nov. 1973, pp. 123–7.

2053. Dale, Charlene T. and others. "Wanted - more women. Where are the women superintendents." 1973. ERIC, 29 pp. ED 084 620.

2054. Dias, Sally L. "The aspiration levels of women for administrative careers in education: Predictive factors and implications for effecting change." 1976. ERIC, 70 pp. ED 119 376.

2055. Doughty, R. N. "Black women in school administration." INTEGRATED EDUCATION, 15, Jl.-Ag. 1977, pp. 34–7.

2056. Fishel, Andrew and Janice Pottker. "Performance of women principals: A review of behavioral and attitudinal studies." JOURNAL OF NATIONAL ASSOCIATION FOR WOMEN DEANS, ADMINISTRATORS, AND COUNSELORS, 3, Spr. 1975, pp. 110–7.

2057. Fishel, Andrew and Janice Pottker. "Women in educational governance: A statistical portrait." EDUCATIONAL RESEARCHER, 3, Jl.-Ag. 1974, pp. 4–7.

2058. Fishel, Andrew and Janice Pottker. "Women lose out: Is there sex discrimination in school administration." CLEARING HOUSE, 47, Mr. 1973, pp. 387–9.

2059. Frasher, J. M. and R. S. Frasher. "Educational administration: A feminine profession." EDUCATIONAL ADMINISTRATION QUARTERLY, 15, Spr. 1979, pp. 1–3.

2060. Freedman, I. "Women in educational administration (New York)." EDUCATION DIGEST, 45, Mr. 1980, pp. 34–5.

2061. Howard, Suzanne. "Why aren't women administering our schools? The status of women public school teachers and the factors hindering their promotion into administration." Wanted: More women series. 1975, ERIC, 54 pp. ED 126 592.

2062. Hulett, Sarah A. "Women administrators in Missouri." SCHOOL AND COMMUNITY, 63, Ja. 1977, pp. 16.

2063. Jackson, Dorothy J. "Effectiveness of training institute for women administrators: A preliminary investigation." 1979.

ERIC, 20 pp. ED 171 183.

2064. Kalvelage, Joan. "The decline in female elementary principals since 1928: Riddles and clues." 1978. ERIC, 22 pp. ED 163 594.

2065. Kaye, Bernard W. "Moving women into educational administration." 1975. ERIC, 23 pp. ED 105 549.

2066. Kimmel, E. D. Harlow and M. Topping. "Training women for administrative roles." EDUCATIONAL LEADERSHIP, 37, Dec. 1979, pp. 229-31.

2067. Koontz, Elizabeth Duncan. "The best kept secret of the past 5,000 years; women are ready for leadership in education." Fastback series no. 2. 1972. ERIC, 47 pp. ED 062 725.

2068. Kuh, George D. "Entry-level employment prospects for women in college-student personnel work." PERSONNEL AND GUIDANCE JOURNAL, 57, Feb. 1979, pp. 296-8.

2069. Kurner, M. E. "Vanishing ladies: Women princpals today." DELTA KAPPA GAMMA BULLETIN, 43, Summ. 1977, pp. 56-9.

2070. Levandowski, B. S. "Women in educational administration: Where do they stand?" NASSP BULLETIN, 61, Sept. 1977, pp. 101-6.

2071. Lyman, K. D. and J. J. Speizer. "Advancing in school administration: A pilot project for women." HARVARD EDUCATIONAL REVIEW, 50, Feb. 1980, pp. 25-35.

2072. Mickish, Ginny. "Can women function as successfully as men in the role of elementary principal." Research reports in educational administration. 1971. ERIC, 20 pp. ED 062 679.

2073. Mosley, Myrtis Hall. "Black women administrators in higher education: An endangered species." JOURNAL OF BLACK STUDIES, 10, Mr. 1980, pp. 295-310.

2074. Niedermayer, Gretchen and Vicki W. Kramer. "Women in administrative positions in public education." A position paper. 1974. ERIC, 72 pp. ED 096 742.

2075. O'Brien, Gael M. "Trials of women's-college presidents." CHRONICLE OF HIGHER EDUCATION, 1 Ag. 1977, pp. 8-9.

2076. Ortiz, F. I. "Scaling the hierarchical system in school administration: A case analysis of a female administrator."

URBAN REVIEW, 11, Fall 1979, pp. 111–26.

2077. Pallante, J. J. and C. L. Hilton. "Authority positions for women: Principalships in public education." CONTEMPORARY EDUCATION, 48, Summ. 1977, pp. 206–10.

2078. Porter-Gehrie, Cynthia. "The female high school principal: Key factors in successful career advancement." 1979. ERIC, 27 pp. ED 170 914.

2079. Sandeen, Arthur. "Minority and women staff members: NASPA (National Association of Student Personnel Administrators)." NASPA JOURNAL, 11, Jl. 1973, pp. 2–14.

2080. Schmuck, Patricia Ann. "Sex differentiation in public school administration." Wanted More Women Series. 1975. ERIC, 130 Ppp. ED 126 593.

2081. "Sex equality in educational administration." Executive handbook. 1975. ERIC, 29 pp. ED 111 098.

2082. Silvestri, M. J. and P. L. Kane. "How affirmative is action for administrative positions in higher education." JOURNAL OF HIGHER EDUCATION, 46, Jl.-Ag. 1975, pp. 445–50.

2083. Stockard, J. "Public prejudice against women school administrators: The possibility of change." EDUCATIONAL ADMINISTRATION QUARTERLY, 15, Fall 1979, pp. 83–96.

2084. Strober, Myra H. and David Tyack. "Why do women teach and men manage?" A report on research on schools. SIGNS, 5, Spr. 1980, pp. 494–503.

2085. TenElshof, Annette and E. Tomlinson. "Alleviating stress for women administrators." JOURNAL OF THE NATIONAL ASSOCIATION FOR WOMEN DEANS, ADMINISTRATORS, AND COUNSELORS, 44, Wint. 1981, pp. 37–41.

2086. "Women: A significant and national resource." 1971. ERIC, 50 pp. ED 082 297.

2087. "Women administrators found unequal in pay, status." CHRONICLE OF HIGHER EDUCATION, 27 Je. 1977, pp. 8.

2088. Women in educational administration. WEECN Resource Roundup. 6 pp., 1979. (Available from Women's Educational Equity Act Program, U.S. Department of Education, Washington, DC 20202.)

2089. *Women in higher education administration.* September 1978. 6 pp. (Available from Project on the Status and Education of Women, Association of American Colleges, Washington, DC. 20009.)

d. Librarians and Archivists

2090. American Library Association. "Status of women in libraries: A task force meets in Detroit." LIBRARY JOURNAL, 95, Ag. 1970, pp. 2635.

2091. Braunagel, J. S. "Job mobility of men and women librarians and how it affects advancement." AMERICAN LIBRARIES, 10, Dec. 1970, pp. 643–7.

2092. Carpenter, Raymond L. and Kenneth D. Shearer. "Sex and salary survey; selected statistics of large public libraries in the United States and Canada." LIBRARY JOURNAL, 15 Nov. 1972, pp. 3682–5.

2093. Carpenter, Raymond L. and Kenneth D. Shearer. "Sex and salary update." LIBRARY JOURNAL, 15 Ja. 1974, pp. 101–7.

2094. Crawford, Miriam. "Women in archives: A program for action." AMERICAN ARCHIVIST, 36, Ap. 1973, pp. 223–32.

2095. Deutrich, Mabel. "Ms. versus Mr. Archivist." AMERICAN ARCHIVIST, 36, Ap. 1973, pp. 171–81.

2096. Deutrich, Mabel E. "Women in archives: A summary report of the Committee on the Status of Women in the Archival Profession." AMERICAN ARCHIVIST, 38, Ja. 1975, pp. 43–6.

2097. Freivogel, Elsie Freeman. "Women in archives: The status of women in the academic professions." AMERICAN ARCHIVIST, 36, Mr. 1973, pp. 183–201.

2098. Goldstein, Rachael K. and others. "The status of women in the administration of health science libraries (United States)." MEDICAL LIBRARY ASSOCIATION BULLETIN, 63, Oct. 1975, pp. 386–95.

2099. Lee, David L. and Janet E. Hall. "Female library science students and the occupational stereotype: Fact or fiction?" COLLEGE AND RESEARCH LIBRARIES, 34, Sept. 1973, pp. 265–7.

2100. Lipow, Anne and others. "A report on the status of women employed in the library of the University of California,

Berkeley, with recommendations for affirmative action."
1971. ERIC, 61 pp. ED 066 163.

2101. Luethe, Marie. "The status of women and ethnic minorities
employed in the libraries of the California State University and college system." 1974. ERIC, 51 pp. ED 127 984.

2102. Schiller, Anita R. "The disadvantaged majority: Women
employed in libraries." AMERICAN LIBRARIES, 1, Ap.
1970, pp. 345-9.

2103. Sellen, Betty-Carol and Joan K. Marshall, eds. "Women in
a woman's profession: Strategies." 1974, ERIC, 98 pp. ED
114 056.

2104. Wahba, Susanne Patterson. "Job satisfaction of librarians:
A comparison between men and women." COLLEGE
AND RESEARCH LIBRARIES, 36, Ja. 1975, pp. 45-51.

2105. Yates, E. G. "Sexism in the library profession." LIBRARY
JOURNAL, 15 Dec. 1979, pp. 2615-19.

5. Health Care

a. Nurses

2106. Boston Nurses' Group. "The false promise: Professionalism
in nursing." SCIENCE FOR THE PEOPLE, 10, My.-Je.
1978, pp. 20-34; 20, Jl.-Ag. 1978, pp. 23-33.

2107. Cleland, V. "Sex discrimination: Nursing's most pervasive
problem." AMERICAN JOURNAL OF NURSING, 71,
Ag. 1971, pp. 1542-7.

2108. Elmore, J. A. "Black nurses—their service and their struggle." AMERICAN JOURNAL OF NURSING, 76, Mr.
1976, pp. 435-7.

2109. Fields, Cheryl. "Faculty jobs are plentiful for nurses with
graduate degrees." CHRONICLE OF HIGHER EDU-
CATION, 3 Mr. 1980, pp. 6.

2110. Fottler, Myron D. "Attitudes of female nurses toward the
male nurse: A study of occupational segregation."
JOURNAL OF HEALTH AND SOCIAL BEHAVIOR,
17, Je. 1976, pp. 98-110.

2111. Heide, Wilma Scott. "Nursing and women's liberation: A
parallel." AMERICAN JOURNAL OF NURSING, 73,
My. 1973, pp. 824-7.

2112. Kelley, L. K. and J. M. Baker. "Women in nursing and academic tenure." JOURNAL OF NURSING EDUCA-

TION, 19, Feb. 1980, pp. 41–8.

2113. Link, C.R. and R. F. Settle. "Financial incentive and labor supply of married professional nurses: An economic analysis." NURSING RESEARCH, 29, Jl.-Ag. 1980, pp. 238–43.

2114. Muhlenkamp, A. F. and Jean L. Parsons. Characteristics of nurses: An overview of recent research published in a nursing research periodical." JOURNAL OF VOCATIONAL BEHAVIOR, 2, Jl. 1972, pp. 261–73.

2115. (Women in the nursing profession). NEW YORK TIMES, 13 My. 1977, pp. 90, Col. 1.

b. Doctors

2116. Benedek, E. P. and E. Poznanski. "Career choices for the woman psychiatric resident." AMERICAN JOURNAL OF PSYCHIATRY, 137, Mr. 1980, pp. 301–5.

2117. Bewley, B. R. and T. H. Bewley. "Hospital doctors' career structure and misuse of medical woman powers." LANCET, 2, Ag. 1975, pp. 270–2.

2118. Calmes, S. H. "Coping skills for women in medicine." EDUCATIONAL HORIZONS, 58, Spr. 1980, pp. 150–5.

2119. Cartwright, L. K. "Career satisfaction and role harmony in a sample of young women physicians." JOURNAL OF VOCATIONAL BEHAVIOR, 12, Ap. 1978, pp. 184–96.

2120. Cartwright, Lillian Kaufman. "Continuity and noncontinuity in the careers of a sample of young women physicians." JOURNAL OF THE AMERICAN MEDICAL WOMEN'S ASSOCIATION, 32, Sept. 1977, pp. 316–21.

2121. Cuca, J. M. "Specialization and career preferences of women and men recently graduated from United States medical schools." JOURNAL OF THE AMERICAN MEDICAL WOMEN'S ASSOCIATION, 34(11), 979, pp. 426+.

2122. Ducker, D. G. "The effect of two sources of role strain on women physicians." SEX ROLES, 6, Ag. 1980, pp. 549–60.

2123. Ehrenreich. B. "Gender and objectivity in medicine." INTERNATIONAL JOURNAL OF HEALTH SERVICES, 4, Fall 1974, pp. 617–23.

2124. Finseth, Katherine Aldin. "Overcoming barriers to women in medicine: A model program." JOURNAL OF THE

AMERICAN MEDICAL WOMEN'S ASSOCIATION, 33, Ja. 1978, pp. 33-7.

2125. Heins, Marilyn and others. "A profile of the woman physician." JOURNAL OF THE AMERICAN MEDICAL WOMEN'S ASSOCIATION, 32, Nov. 1977, pp. 421-7.

2126. Herman, M. W. and J. Veloski. "Career expectations of women and men in medical school." NEW ENGLAND JOURNAL OF MEDICINE, 302(18), 1980, pp. 1035-6.

2127. Hesselbart, Susan. *Women doctors win and male nurses lose: A study of sex role and occupational stereotypes.* 1976. 17 pp. (Available from author, Department of Sociology, Florida State University, Tallahassee, FL 32306.)

2128. Jacobson, Beverly and Wendy Jacobson. "Only eight percent: A look at women in medicine (United States)." CIVIL RIGHTS DIGEST, 7, Summ. 1975, pp. 20-7.

2129. Jolly, H. Paul and Thomas A. Larson. "women physicians on United States medical school faculties." JOURNAL OF MEDICAL EDUCATION, 50, Ag. 1975, pp. 825-8.

2130. Kehrer, B. H. "Factors affecting the incomes of men and women physicians: An exploratory analysis." JOURNAL OF HUMAN RESOURCES , 11, Fall 1976, pp. 526-45.

2131. Mandelbaum, Dorothy Rosenthal. "Education, medical training and the practice variable related to the career persistence of women physicians." JOURNAL OF THE AMERICAN MEDICAL WOMEN'S ASSOCIATION, 34, Oct. 1979, pp. 384-6+.

2132. Mandelbaum, Dorothy Rosenthal. "The nonpersistence of women MD's: A new diagnosis." INTERNATIONAL JOURNAL OF WOMEN'S STUDIES, 2, Sept-Oct. 1979, pp. 443-51.

2133. Mandelbaum, Dorothy Rosenthal. "Personality variables related to the career persistence of women physicians." JOURNAL OF THE AMERICAN MEDICAL WOMEN'S ASSOCIATION, 34, Je. 1979, pp. 255-6+.

2134. *Medicine—a woman's career.* 1973. 11 pp. (Available from American Medical Women's Association, Inc., 1740 Broadway, New York, NY 10019.)

2135. Neumann, K. "Physician's viewpoint: It really doesn't matter if the RPh happens to be a female (honest)!" AMERICAN DRUGGIST, 180, Jl. 1979, pp. 13.

2136. Ortiz, Flora Ida. "Women and medicine: The process of

professional incorporation." JOURNAL OF THE AMERI-
CAN MEDICAL WOMEN'S ASSOCIATION, 30, Ja.
1975, pp. 18–30.

2137. Owens, Arthur. "Women doctors: Still earning less, but try-
ing harder." MEDICAL ECONOMICS, 22 Mr. 1976, pp.
154–7.

2138. Pennell, Maryland Y. and Josephine E. Rinshaw. "Distribution of women physicians, 1970." JOURNAL OF THE
AMERICAN MEDICAL WOMEN'S ASSOCIATION,
27, Ap. 1972, pp. 197–203.

2139. Redman, Helen C. "Women in American radiology."
JOURNAL OF THE AMERICAN MEDICAL WO-
MEN'S ASSOCIATION, 27, Spr. 1972, pp. 475–81 .

2140. Ruben, R. J. "Women in medicine: Past, present and
future." JOURNAL OF THE AMERICAN MEDICAL
WOMEN'S ASSOCIATION, 27, My. 1972, pp. 251–9.

2141. Scadron, Arlene. "Women MDs bone up on leadership
skills." NEW DIRECTIONS FOR WOMEN, 9, My.-Je.
1980, pp. 4–5.

2142. Spurlock, Jeanne. "New recognition for women in APA."
AMERICAN JOURNAL OF PSYCHIATRY, 132, Je.
1975, pp. 647–8.

c. *Other Practitioners*

2143. Appelbaum, Alan L. "Women in health care administration.
Much remains to be done." HOSPITALS, 49, Ag. 1975,
pp. 52–9.

2144. Farnsworth, Ellen. "Sex and size of home affect administrators' salaries." MODERN NURSING HOME, 29, Jl.
1972, pp. 4+.

2145. Glaser, M. "Women pharmacists: Ready for a more active
role?" DRUG TOPICS, 15 Ag. 1977, pp. 41–3+.

2146. Kirk, K. W., R. W. Johnson and R. A. Ohvall. "Interests of
women pharmacists." VOCATIONAL GUIDANCE
QUARTERLY, 22, Mr. 1974, pp. 200–8.

2147. Koslow, Sally Platkin. "Women in health careers: It's a nat-
ural!" FAMILY HEALTH, 7, Jl. 1975, pp. 41–42+.

2148. Lebowitz, Ann. "A study of the participation of women in
the health care industry labor force." Executive summary.
1977. ERIC, 22 pp. ED 156 917.

2149. Linn, Erwin L. "Women dentists: Career and family."

SOCIAL PROBLEMS, 18, Wint. 1971, pp. 393–404.
2150. "Minorities and women in the health fields: Applicants, students and workers." 1974. ERIC, 52 pp. ED 120 525.
2151. "Nationally speaking on being a member of a 'feminine'profession." AMERICAN JOURNAL OF OCCUPATIONAL THERAPY, 29, Nov.-Dec. 1975, pp. 597–600.
2152. Navarro, Vincente. "Women in health care." NEW ENGLAND JOURNAL OF MEDICINE, 20 Feb. 1975, pp. 398–402.
2153. U.S. Department of Health, Education & Welfare. Bureau of Health Manpower. *Minorities & women in the health fields.* Washington, DC: GPO, 1976.
2154. U.S. Department of Health, Education and Welfare. *Women in health careers.* Washington, DC: GPO, 1976.
2155. U.S. Health Resources Administration. *Women in health careers: Status of women in health careers in the United States and other selected countries.* Washington, DC: GPO, 1976.
2156. U.S. Women's Bureau. *Why not be a medical technologist? Careers for women.* Washington, DC: GPO, 1971.
2157. Van Dusen, Karen. "Women environmental health professionals." JOURNAL OF ENVIRONMENTAL HEALTH, 38, Nov.-Dec. 1975, pp. 155–8.
2158. "Women say stereotypes block them from pharmacy's best careers." AMERICAN DRUGGIST, 175, Je. 1977, .pp. 60–1.
2159. Yokopenic, Patricia A. and others. "Professional communication networks: A case study of women in the American public health association." SOCIAL PROBLEMS, 22, Ap. 1975, pp. 493–509.
2160. Zincone, L. H., Jr. and F. A. Close. "Sex discrimination in a paramedical profession (physical therapist)." INDUSTRIAL & LABOR RELATIONS REVIEW, 32, Oct. 1978, pp. 74–85.

6. Industrial and Blue-Collar Workers

2161. Agassi, Judith Buber. "Women who work in factories." DISSENT, 18, Wint. 1972, pp. 233–9.
2162. Belli, C. "Women on move in auto industry." AUTOMOTIVE NEWS, 24 Ja. 1977, pp. 15+.
2163. Bernard, Jacqueline. "A meeting of the (women) miners."

(First National Conference of Women Coal Miners, Charleston, West Virginia). MS, 8, Nov. 1979, pp. 33.

2164. Birchall, D. and R. Wild. "Job characteristics and attitudes of female manual workers—research note." HUMAN RELATIONS, 30, Ap. 1977, pp. 335–42.

2165. Bridges, William P. "Industry marginality and female employment: A new appraisal." AMERICAN SOCIOLOGICAL REVIEW, 45, Feb. 1980, pp. 58–75.

2166. Brown, Stephen. "Women shipbuilders: Just doing a job." MANPOWER, 7, Mr. 1975, pp. 10–3.

2167. Buck, Rinker. "The new sweatshops: A penny for your collar (garment workers)." NEW YORK, 29 Ja. 1979, pp. 40–6.

2168. Clark, G. "Mechanics find woman doing the instructing." AUTOMOTIVE NEWS, 20 Mr. 1978, pp. 26.

2169. Crow, Margie and Anne Williams. "Working in construction (Washington, D.C. organization)." OFF OUR BACKS, 6, Jl.-Ag. 1976, pp. 6–7.

2170. Deyo, Frederic C. "The single female factory worker and her peer group." HUMAN ORGANIZATION, 39, Sept. 1980, pp. 80–3.

2171. "Feminists demand equal opportunity in industry." MANAGEMENT REVIEW, 59, Nov. 1970, pp. 20–3.

2172. Hardin, H. "Women in rugged plant jobs: A progress report (Special intake program)." TELEPHONY, 28 Mr. 1977, pp. 62–3+.

2173. "Hardships that blue-collar women face." BUSINESS WEEK, 14 Ag. 1978, pp. 86+.

2174. Hart, Holly. "Facotry Girl." WOMEN: A JOURNAL OF LIBERATION, 2(1), 1971, pp. 24–6.

2175. Hawes, Mandy. "Small potatoes for women: Working in the canneries." UNION W.A.G.E., No. 37, 1976, pp. 1+.

2176. Healy, Jon M. "Women in PT (power transmission equipment) apply the feminine touch." INDUSTRIAL DISTRIBUTION, 62, Oct. 1972, pp. 31–4.

2177. Heimberg, Marilyn. "Exchange your eraser for overalls?" ESSENCE, 6, Mr. 1976, pp. 57+.

2178. Heisler, Dina. "Blue collar women with nerves of steel." WREE-VIEW, 4, Ja.-Mr. 1979, pp. 1+.

2179. Heisler, Dina. "WREE interviews women in construction: Tradeswomen break new ground." WREE-VIEW, 5, Mr.-

Ap. 1980, pp. 1+.

2180. Henderson, N. J. "Profile of a decade: Stress on women in the industry." AIR CONSITIONING, HEATING AND REFRIGERATION NEWS, 4 Feb. 1980, pp. 3+.

2181. "Labor's women: Year-end review; 1970." AMERICAN LABOR, 4, Dec. 1970-Ja. 1971, pp. 37–42.

2182. Lyle, Jerolyn R. and Jane L. Ross. "Women in industry: Employment patterns of women in corporate America." 1973. ERIC, 157 pp. ED 103 604.

2183. Mettler. A. "Textile woman: An expanding role." TEXTILE INDUSTRIES, 141, Oct. 1977, pp. 24–5.

2184. "Militant women mining the coalfields." BUSINESS WEEK, 25 Je. 1979, pp. 30–1.

2185. Pohl, Constance. "Women take a short walk on a long pier (efforts to be hired as cargo checkers and stevedores)." MAJORITY REPORT, 11 Nov-31 Dec. 1978, pp. 1.

2186. Price, Tom. "The women in the mines." NEW TIMES, 18 Oct. 1974, pp. 52+.

2187. "Rubber firms ponder restricting women's jobs." BUSINESS INSURANCE, 12 Dec. 1977, pp. 67.

2188. Rubin, M. "Suburbanization of industry and its effect upon labor force participation rates of suburban women." AMERICAN REAL ESTATE AND URBAN ECONOMIC ASSOCIATION JOURNAL, 5, Spr. 1977, pp. 111–27.

2189. Sandler, B. R. "You've come a long way, maybe: Or why it still hurts to be a woman in labor." CURRENT ISSUES IN HIGHER EDUCATION ANNUAL SERIES, No 4, 1979, pp. 11–14.

2190. "Sex bias in longshoring." MONTHLY LABOR REVIEW, 97, Je. 1974, pp. 62.

2191. Tabor, Martha. "First National Women Coal Miners' Conference." (June 8-10, 1979. Institute, West Virginia). OFF OUR BACKS, 9, Ag.-Sept. 1979. pp. 20–1.

2192. Terkel, S. "Being the woman in one of America's most scorned families: Blue collar workers." TODAY'S HEALTH, 50, Feb. 1972, pp. 48–53+.

2193. Tobias, Sheila and Lisa Anderson. "Whatever happened to Rosie the Riveter?" MS, 1, Je. 1973, pp. 92+.

2194. U.S. Equal Employment Opportunity Commission. *Hearings before Equal Employment Opportunity Commission on utilization of minority and women workers in certain major industries held in Houston, Texas, June 2-4, 1970.* Washington, DC: GPO, 1971.

2195. U.S. Equal Employment Opportunity Commission. *Promise vs. performance: A study of equal employment opportunity in the nation's electric and gas utilities.* Washington, DC: GPO, 1972.

2196. Walshok, Mary L. "Nontraditional blue collar work among urban women." 1975. ERIC, 18 pp. ED 124 854.

2197. Wells, Jean A. "Automation and women workers." 1970. ERIC, 16 pp. ED 050 227.

2198. West, Karen. "How to get a blue collar." MS, 5, My. 1977, pp. 62–5.

2199. White, P. "Women instructors learn pole climbing and quickly become better teachers." TELEPHONY, 17 Ja. 1977, pp. 112–3.

2200. "Women fill more blue-collar jobs in processing plants." OIL AND GAS JOURNAL, 3 Je. 1974, pp. 75.

2201. "Women miners may soon make up 20% of Kentucky's coalfield work force." WALL STREET JOURNAL, 4 Ja. 1977, pp. 1, col. 5.

2202. "Women out do men in material handling jobs." FACTORY MANAGEMENT, 4, Oct. 1971, pp. 46.

7. Legal Profession

2203. Baker, Joan E. "Women as lawyers. Employment discrimination against women lawyers." AMERICAN BAR ASSOCIATION JOURNAL, 59, Sept. 1973, pp. 1029–32.

2204. Durkin, M. and A. L. Rhodes. "Shift in female participation in the legal profession by state: 1960-1970." WOMEN LAW JOURNAL, 65, Fall 1979, pp. 11–20+.

2205. Hoke, Mardon. "Women in law." WOMEN: A JOURNAL OF LIBERATION, 2(4), 1972, pp. 17.

2206. LaRussa, Georgina W. "Portia's decision: Women's motives for studying law and their career satisfaction as attorneys." PSYCHOLOGY OF WOMEN, 1, Summ. 1977, pp. 350–64.

2207. Leverzey, Beth and Joan Anderson. "Trials of a woman lawyer." WOMEN'S RIGHTS LAW REPORTER, 1, Wint. 1974, pp. 38–40.

2208. Ness. Susan and Fredrica Wechsler. "Women judges—why

so few?" GRADUATE WOMAN, 73, Nov.-Dec. 1979,
pp. 10–12.
2209. Pfeiffer, Sophie Douglass. "Women lawyers in Rhode
Island." AMERICAN BAR ASSOCIATION JOURNAL,
61, Je. 1975, pp. 740+.
2210. Sassower, Doris L. "Women in the law: The second
hundred years." AMERICAN BAR ASSOCIATION
JOURNAL, 57, Ap. 1971, pp. 329–32.
2211. (Women lawyers). NEW YORK TIMES, 16 My. 1977, pp.
1, col. 1.

8. Business

a. Management

2212. Athanassiades, John C. "Myths of women in management:
What every businessman ought to know about women but
may be afraid to ask." ATLANTA ECONOMIC REVIEW,
25, My.-Je. 1975, pp. 4-9.
2213. Badawy, M. K. "How women managers view their role in
the organization." PERSONNEL ADMINISTRATOR,
23, Feb. 1978, pp. 60 .
2214. Baldrige, Letitia. "When women move up to executive jobs
(excerpts from interview)." U S NEWS AND WORLD
REPORT, 24 Mr. 1980, pp. 67+.
2215. Barnes, Marian and Sheribel Rothenberg. "The search for
women managers: Fiction or reality." EMPLOYEE RE-
LATIONS LAW JOURNAL, 1, Ag. 1975, pp. 280-92.
2216. Baron, A. S. "New data on women managers." TRAINING
AND DEVELOPMENT JOURNAL, 32, Nov. 1978, pp.
12-13.
2217. Bender, Marvin. "Women at Avon: No room at the top."
BUSINESS AND SOCIETY REVIEW, 5, Wint. 1972-73,
pp. 19-24.
2218. "Big jump in the ranks of female directors." BUSINESS
WEEK, 10 Ja. 1977, pp. 49-50.
2219. "Bringing women into computing management." E D P
ANALYZER, 14, Ag. 1976, pp. 1-14.
2220. Brown, Linda Keller. "Women and business management."
SIGNS, 5, Wint. 1979, pp. 266-88.
2221. Deaux, Kay. "Women in management: Causal explanations
of performance." 1974. ERIC, 15 pp. ED 098 476.

2222. "Double standard for women managers' pay." BUSINESS WEEK, 28 Nov. 1977, pp. 61+.

2223. Duckworth, T. A. "Women in management—fable or fact?" PERSONNEL ADMINISTRATOR, 18, Jl.-Ag. 1973, pp. 19-22.

2224. Ekberg-Jordan, Sandra. "The woman manager: Opportunities and obstacles." AAUW JOURNAL, 69, Ap. 1976, pp. 6-12.

2225. Forgionne, G. A. and C. C. Nwacukwu. "Acceptance of authority in female-managed organizational positions." UNIVERSITY OF MICHIGAN BUSINESS REVIEW, 29, My. 1977, pp. 23-8.

2226. Gordon, F. E. and M. H. Strober. "Initial observations on a pioneer cohort: 1974 Women MBAs." SLOAN MANAGEMENT REVIEW, 19, Wint. 1978, pp. 15-23.

2227. Grambs, Jean Dresden. "Women and administration: Confrontation or accommodation." THEORY INTO PRACTICE, 15(4), 1976, pp. 293-300.

2228. Grant, Linda. "Here come the MBA's." WORKING WOMAN, 2, Sept. 1972, pp. 18-24.

2229. Hackamack, Lawrence C. and Alan B. Solid. "The woman executive: There is still ample room for progress." BUSINESS HORIZONS, 15, Ap. 1972. pp. 89-93.

2230. Hay, C. D. "Women in management: The obstacles and opportunities they face." PERSONNEL ADMINISTRATOR, 25, Ap. 1980, pp. 31-9.

2231. Jensen, Beverly. "Black and female too: Career women find that the road to the top may be paved with racism, sexism, and sometimes both (experiences of several black women executives)." BLACK ENTERPRISE, 6, Jl. 1976, pp. 26-9.

2232. Jewell, D. O. and C. R. Pollard. "Women on the executive ladder: Performance is the first criterion." ATLANTA ECONOMIC REVIEW, 26, Nov. 1976, pp. 9+.

2233. Johnson, R. P. "Having women in management makes good business sense." FOOD SERVICE MARKETING, 38, Nov. 1976, pp. 12+.

2234. Lloyd, B. V. "Textile women proving managerial prowess." TEXTILE INDUSTRIES, 143, Feb. 1979, pp. 26+.

2235. Mahon, G. "MBA is still a ticker to what those speed-writing schools call 'mo pay'." MADEMOISELLE, 86,

My. 1980, pp. 66+.

2236. Matthews, Mildred. "The life and times of a woman administrator." AMERICAN VOCATIONAL JOURNAL, 50, Sept. 1975, pp. 36-41.

2237. Miner, J. B. "Motivational potential for upgrading among minority and female managers." JOURNAL OF APPLIED PSYCHOLOGY, 62, Dec. 1977, pp. 691+.

2238. Mirides, E. and A. Cote. "Women in management: Strategies for removing the barriers." PERSONNEL ADMINISTRATOR, 25, Ap. 1980, pp. 25-8.

2239. "More women move into the boardroom." BUSINESS WEEK, 1 Mr. 1976, pp. 26+.

2240. "100 top corporate women." BUSINESS WEEK, 21 Je. 1976, pp. 56-60+.

2241. Orr, L. H. "Out of the typing pool and onto the board: A list of women directors." BUSINESS AND SOCIETY REVIEW, No. 21, Summ. 1977, pp. 27-33.

2242. Orth, Charles D. and Frederic Jacobs. "Women in management: Pattern for change." HARVARD BUSINESS REVIEW, 49, Jl.-Ag. 1971, pp. 139-47.

2243. Overton, E. "What makes an executive woman." WORKING WOMAN, 5, Ja. 1980, pp. 35-8+.

2244. Powell, G. N. "Career development and the woman manager - a social power perspective." PERSONNEL JOURNAL, 57, My.-Je. 1980, pp. 22-32.

2245. Reif, W. E., J. W. Newstrom and R. M. Monczka. "Exploding some myths about women managers." CALIFORNIA MANAGEMENT REVIEW, 17, Summ. 1975, pp. 72-9.

2246. Riccardi, Toni and others. "Careers and management: Strategies for women professionals." Pre-conference seminar (Cincinnati, Ohio, March 24-25, 1979). 1979. ERIC, 81 pp. ED 177 311.

2247. Robertson, W. "Top women in big business." FORTUNE, 98, Jl. 1978, pp. 58–62+.

2248. Robertson, W. "Women MBA's. Harvard '73 - how they're doing." FORTUNE, 98, Ag. 1978, pp. 50-4.

2249. Robertson, Wyndham. "The ten highest-ranking women in big business." FORTUNE, 87, Ap. 1973, pp. 81-9.

2250. Robinson, Donald. "Female bigshots in Fortune's top 500." NEW WOMAN, 1, Ap.-My. 1972, pp. 88–91+.

2251. Schwartz, Eleanor Brantley and James J. Rago, Jr. "Beyond tokenism: Women as true corporate peers." BUSINESS HORIZONS, 16, Dec. 1973, pp. 69–76.

2252. Stanek, L. W. "Women in management: Can it be a renaissance for everybody?" MANAGEMENT REVIEW, 69, Nov. 1980, pp. 44–8.

2253. Terborg, J. R. "Women in management: A research review." JOURNAL OF APPLIED PSYCHOLOGY, 62, Dec. 1977, pp. 647–64.

2254. Terborg, J. R. and others. "Organizational and personal correlates of attitudes toward women as managers." ACADEMIC MANAGEMENT JOURNAL, 20, Mr. 1977, pp. 89–100.

2255. Terborg, James R. "Integration of women into management positions: A research review." 1976. ERIC, 31 pp. ED 132 708.

2256. Uehling, Barbara S. "Women and the psychology of management." 1973. ERIC, 7 pp. ED 089 562.

2257. Veiga, J. F. and J. N. Yanouzas. "What women in management want - ideal vs. real." ACADEMY OF MANAGEMENT JOURNAL, 19, Mr. 1976, pp. 137+.

2258. Wagel, W. H. "Women: Profile of the female officer." PERSONNEL JOURNAL, 54, Nov. 1977, pp. 45+.

2259. "Who are the women in the board rooms?" (A roster, arranged by company). BUSINESS AND SOCIETY REVIEW, No. 15, Wint. 1975-76, pp. 5–10.

2260. "Why so few women have made it to the top." BUSINESS WEEK, 5 Je. 1978, pp. 99–100+.

2261. "Women executives: A selected annotated bibliography." 1970. ERIC, 29 pp. ED 057 286.

2262. "Women executives sit on 25% of corporate boards of directors, according to a survey of 501 companies by Korn-Ferry, New York." WALL STREET JOURNAL, 21 Mr. 1978, pp. 1, col. 5.

2263. "Women in banking: Will she be your new management trainee?" SAVINGS AND LOAN NEWS, 91, Jl. 1970, pp. 40–5.

2264. "Women mean business. (Managerial women are motivated by same career rewards as are men)." HUMAN BE-HAVIOR, 6, Mr. 1977, pp. 49+.

2265. Woods, Marion M. "What does it take for a woman to

make it in management?" PERSONNEL JOURNAL, 54,
Ja. 1975, pp. 38–41+.

b. Banking

2266. Archibald, Kathleen A. "Sizing up the future of women in
banking." BANKING, 66, Jl. 1973, pp. 28–30.
2267. "Bank women make strides in pay and position." A B A
BANKING JOURNAL, 71, My. 1979, pp. 240+.
2268. "Donna Pillar: First woman CMB (Certified mortgage
banker)." MORTGAGE BANKER, 40, Feb. 1980, pp.
27+.
2269. "Feminist credit unions appear to be moving even faster than
women's banks." WALL STREET JOURNAL, 13 My.
1976, pp. 1, col. 5.
2270. Giges, Nancy. "Bankwomen: The atmosphere is changing."
M B A (MASTERS IN BUSINESS ADMINISTRA-
TION), 6, Mr. 1972, pp. 5+.
2271. Kulczycky, M. "Women at the top: Why so few?"
SAVINGS AND LOAN NEWS, 93, Je. 1977, pp. 68–73.
2272. Larwood, Laurie, David Zalkind and Jeanne Legault.
"Bank job: A field study of sexually discriminatory
performances on a neutral role task." JOURNAL OF
APPLIED SOCIAL PSYCHOLOGY, 5, Ja.-Mr. 1975,
pp. 68–74.
2273. Mathis, Marilyn and David H. Jones. "Finding more
women and minorities for management level jobs."
BANKING, 66, Mr. 1974, pp. 94–100.
2274. "Now a rush by women to start their own banks." U S
NEWS AND WORLD REPORT, 27 Oct. 1975, pp. 61–2.
2275. "Path up for women bankers. (Simmons College)." BUSI-
NESS WEEK, 13 Je. 1977, pp. 105+.
2276. Roebling, Mary G. "The outlook for women in banking."
MICHIGAN BUSINESS REVIEW, 24, Nov. 1972, pp.
14–9.
2277. "Shortchanged: Minorities and women in banking (United
States)." ECONOMIC PRIORITIES REPORT, 3, Sept.-
Oct. 1972, pp. 3–29.
2278. Tesar, J. "Anti-discriminatory women's banks: One even has
a man president (First Women's of California's R.
Henry)." BANKING, 69, Oct. 1977, pp. 66–7.
2279. "Women and minorities make big gains in status in

banking." A B A BANKING JOURNAL, 22, Oct. 1980, pp. 20+.

2280. "Women in mortgage banking: An update." MORTGAGE BANKER, 40, Feb. 1980, pp. 24-5.

c. *Insurance*

2281. Boynton, N. D. and others. "New female agent." BESTS REVIEW LIFE/HEALTH INSURANCE EDITION, 78, Dec. 1977, pp. 22+.

2282. Carson, E. H. "Women directors and officers of insurance companies." BESTS REVIEW LIFE/HEALTH INSURANCE EDITION, 78, Dec. 1977, pp. 16+.

2283. "LIMRA: Women agents doing well." NATIONAL UNDERWRITER. LIFE EDITION, 10 Sept. 1977, pp. 22+.

2284. McLean, G. "Ohio panel aiming to bring more women into life sales posts (Ohio Association of Life Underwriters)." NATIONAL UNDERWRITER. LIFE EDITION, 26 Nov. 1977, pp. 1+.

2285. Pilla, B. A. "Women in business (Prudential Insurance)." TRAINING AND DEVELOPMENT JOURNAL, 31, Nov. 1977, pp. 22-5.

d. *Accounting*

2286. Barcelona, Constance T., Clara C. Lelievre and Thomas W. Lelievre. "The professions's underutilized resource: The woman CPA." JOURNAL OF ACCOUNTANCY, 140, Nov. 1975, pp. 58-64.

2287. Cooper, S. K. and others. "Women and careers in accounting." CPA JOURNAL, 47, My. 1977, pp. 71-3.

2288. Dunlop, Anna. "Women accountants." ACCOUNTANTS DIGEST, 39, Je. 1974, pp. 230-1.

2289. Hoffman, Miona E. "Women who should be in accounting." NATIONAL PUBLIC ACCOUNTANT, 18, My. 1973, pp. 8-11.

2290. Rankin, D. "Women accountants are scarcely adding up." BUSINESS AND SOCIETY REVIEW, No. 25, 1978, pp. 59-61.

2291. Rayburn, L. Gayle. "Recruitment of women accountants." JOURNAL OF ACCOUNTING, 132, Nov. 1971, pp. 51-7.

2292. Rayburn, L. Gayle. "The woman accountant: An asset to the accounting profession." NATIONAL PUBLIC ACCOUNTANT, 19, Oct. 1974, pp. 12–6.

2293. Rayburn, L. Gayle. "Careers for women in accounting." JOURNAL OF EMPLOYMENT COUNSELING, 13, Sept. 1976, pp. 134 .

2294. (Women in accounting). NEW YORK TIMES, 9 Ag. 1977, pp. 25, col. 1.

e. Other Business Areas

2295. Bell, Carolyn Shaw. "Report of the Committee on the Status of Women in the Economics Profession." AMERICAN ECONOMIC REVIEW, 64, My. 1974, pp. 519–23.

2296. "Business opportunities for women in real estate." INTELLECT, 103, Ja. 1975, pp. 217–8.

2297. Collins, M., L. K. Waters and C. W. Waters. "Relationships between sex role orientation and attitudes toward women as managers." PSYCHOLOGICAL REPORTS, 45, Dec. 1974, pp. 828–30.

2298. Curd, Edith F. "The changing role of women in the business world." PERSONNEL ADMINISTRATOR, 35, Je. 1972, pp. 29–31.

2299. DeWitt, Karen. "Black women in business: A long tradition of hard work enables them to make the most of gradually opening high-level opportunities." BLACK ENTERPRISE, 5, Ag. 1974, pp. 14–9.

2300. "Foundations discover women: An emerging career field." NATIONAL BUSINESS WOMEN, 54, Oct. 1973, pp. 4–5.

2301. Gelb, Betty D., Garbriel M. Gelb and Ricky W. Griffin. "Women as negotiatiors." BUSINESS HORIZONS, 19, Ap. 1976, pp. 67–8.

2302. Henle, Faye. "New Woman's own investigation of marketing representatives and agents." NEW WOMAN, 1, Sept. 1971, pp. 74–7.

2303. Honomichl, J. J. "Market research good field for women, panel says." ADVERTISING AGE, 13 Oct. 1975, pp. 60+.

2304. "How the top 50 companies see women. (Roles of W pictured in annual reports)." NEW YORK, 28 Nov. 1977, p. 59.

2305. Johnson, B. P. "Women marketers - their aspirations and frustrations." PRODUCT MARKETING, 6, Ja. 1977, pp. 17–22.

2306. Kelly, K. "Women in retailing: How far is up? Room at the top?" STORES, 60, Feb. 1978, pp. 36-8.

2307. Koehn, H. E. "Attitude: The success element for women in business." JOURNAL OF SYSTEMS MANAGEMENT, 27, Mr. 1976, pp. 12-5.

2308. Louviere, V. "Women's growing role in lobbying." NATIONS BUSINESS, 66, Je. 1978, pp. 80-5.

2309. Lyle, J. R. "Empirical study of the occupational standing of women in multinational corporations." LABOR LAW JOURNAL, 24, Ag. 1973, pp. 458–68.

2310. "Men, women and the killer instinct. (Women as likely as men to take big chances in business)." HUMAN BEHAVIOR, 2, Jl. 1973, pp. 49.

2311. Mogensen, J. A. "Women and public pension administration (Editorial)." PENSION WORLD, 14, Ja. 1978, pp. 3+.

2312. Montgomery, Jan. "Including women in formerly all male sales teams." TRAINING AND DEVELOPMENT JOURNAL, 29, Nov. 1975, pp. 22-31.

2313. Rayburn, L. G. "Business careers for women." OFFICE, 75, Ap. 1972, pp. 59+.

2314. Reagan, B. B. "Report of the committee on the status of women in the economics profession." AMERICAN ECONOMIC REVIEW, 67, Feb. 1977, pp. 460-4.

2315. Rhea, J. N. "Status, training, and future of women in business: Critical questions for research in the 1980s." JOURNAL OF BUSINESS EDUCATION, 55, Ap. 1980, pp. 312-4.

2316. Schwartz, Eleanor Brantley. "The sex barrier in business." ATLANTA ECONOMIC REVIEW, 21, Mr.-Je. 1971, pp. 4-9.

2317. Strober, Myra H. "Women economists - career aspirations, education and training." AMERICAN ECONOMIC REVIEW, 65(2), 1975, pp. 92-9.

2318. "Supply and mobility of women economists (Three conference papers)." AMERICAN ECONOMIC REVIEW, 65, My. 1975, pp. 83-107.

2319. Thal, N. L. and P. R. Cateora. "Opportunities for women in international business." BUSINESS HORIZONS, 22, Dec. 1979, pp. 21-7.

2320. Wagel, W. H. "Women: Still outside the corporate main-stream." PERSONNEL JOURNAL, 54, Nov. 1977, pp. 42–3.

2321. Wall, J. A., Jr. and R. Virtue. "Women as negotiators." BUSINESS HORIZONS, 19, Ap. 1976, pp. 67–8.

2322. "Which sex does a better job of selling industrial products? Some electronics and information processing companies say female sales reps outperform their male peers." WALL STREET JOURNAL, 5 Feb. 1981, pp. 23, col. 1.

2323. "Women in a man's world. . .1% of NCUA's examiners are women." NATIONAL CREDIT UNION ADMINISTRATION BULLETIN, 3, Ja. 1972, pp. 8–10.

2324. "Women in estate planning and trust administration: Profiles of success (Panel discussion)." TRUST AND ESTATES, 119, Mr. 1980, pp. 12–14+.

2325. "Women see equal chances in business: First national conference for minority business women produces keen insight." COMMERCE TODAY, 10 Je. 1972, pp. 4–7.

9. Communications

a. Journalism and Advertising

2326. Ahmad, Mufti Jamiluddin. "Ladies of the Fourth Estate." PERSPECTIVE, 5, Nov. 1971, pp. 41–4.

2327. Blumenthal, D. S. "Four women make their mark as sportswriters." EDITOR & PUBLISHER, 28 Jl. 1979, pp. 16–8.

2328. Callan, M. "Women copywriters get better, but male chauvinism in ads rolls on." ADVERTISING AGE, 4 Oct. 1976, pp. 75–6.

2329. Chang, Won H. "Characteristics and self perceptions of women's page editors." JOURNALISM QUARTERLY, 52, Spr. 1975, pp. 61–5.

2330. Crumley, W. and others. "Journalism career patterns of women are changing." JOURNALISM EDUCATOR, 32, Oct. 1977, pp. 50–3+.

2331. "Editors undecided about allowing women in lockers." EDITOR AND PUBLISHER, 4 Feb. 1978, pp. 34.

2332. Finn, C. "Women sports editor does dressing room interviews." EDITOR AND PUBLISHER, 18 Mr. 1978, pp. 20.

2333. Fisher, P. "Job placement service formed for newswomen." EDITOR AND PUBLISHER, 2 Ap. 1977, pp. 12.

2334. Holly, Susan. "Women in management of weeklies." JOURNALISM QUARTERLY, 56, Wint. 1979, pp. 810-15.

2335. Huenergard, C. "Women as newspaper managers: Outnumbered, underpaid and overlooked." EDITOR AND PUBLISHER, 18 Je. 1977, pp. 18.

2336. Kilgore, Margaret. "The female war correspondent in Vietnam." QUILL, 60, My. 1972, pp. 9-12.

2337. Lublin, Joann S. "Discrimination against women in newsrooms: Fact or fancy?" JOURNALISM QUARTERLY, 49, Summ. 1972, pp. 357-60.

2338. Lublin, Joann S. "Women in the newsroom." QUILL, 60, Nov. 1972, pp. 45-7.

2339. McCall, Patricia Ellen. "The current status of newspaperwomen in Wisconsin." 1974. ERIC, 20 pp. ED 095 565.

2340. "The New York Times newspaper and its women employees agreed to a four-year plan that commits the Times to place women in substantially more jobs than they currently fill." WALL STREET JOURNAL, 10 Oct. 1980, pp. 17, col. 2.

2341. "PR: The velvet ghetto of affirmative action." BUSINESS WEEK, 8 My. 1978, pp. 122.

2342. Rupp, C. M. "Our reporter booted out of Broncos' dressing room." EDITOR AND PUBLISHER, 21 Ja. 1978, pp. 9-10.

2343. Rupp, C. M. "Sports editors urged to hire more women." EDITOR AND PUBLISHER, 19 Je. 1976, p. 13.

2344. Rupp, C. M. "Women's progress in communication fields noted by speakers at WICI (annual meeting, 43d, Tulsa Oklahoma)." EDITOR AND PUBLISHER, 18 Oct. 1975, pp. 11+.

2345. Slattery, Karen and Jim Fosdick. "Professionalism in photojournalism: A female/male comparison." JOURNALISM QUARTERLY, 56, Summ. 1979, pp. 243-7.

2346. "Speaker says dailies should hire more women." EDITOR AND PUBLISHER, 9 Je. 1979, pp. 12.

2347. "Survey shows salary levels for press women." EDITOR AND PUBLISHER, 9 Je. 1979, pp. 35.

2348. Taylor, H. "First woman sports editor in Arkansas." EDITOR AND PUBLISHER, 28 Oct. 1978, pp. 54+.

2349. "Ten-point plan developed to advance women in media." EDITOR AND PUBLISHER, 27 Sept. 1975, pp. 11.

2350. Whitlow, S. Scott. "Women in the newsroom: A role theory view." JOURNALISM QUARTERLY, 56, Summ. 1979, pp. 378–82.

2351. "Woman sportswriter sues to open locker room." EDITOR AND PUBLISHER, 14 Ja. 1978, pp. 11.

2352. "Women in advertising get less for same titles, survey reports." ADVERTISING AGE, 3 Oct. 1977, pp. 94.

b. *Broadcasting*

2353. Cantor, Muriel C. "Women and public broadcasting." JOURNAL OF COMMUNICATION, 27, Wint. 1977, pp. 14–9.

2354. "Few minorities and women found in better jobs of cable business." BROADCASTING, 9 Ag. 1976, pp. 45.

2355. Hennessee, Judith. "What progress women at CBS?" PERSONNEL JOURNAL, 52, Jl.-Ag. 1975, pp. 33–44.

2356. Jennings, Ralph M. and others. "Public television station employment practices and the composition of boards of directors: The status of minorities and women." 1973. ERIC, 51 pp. ED 074 742.

2357. "McKee says figures show women are outpointing minorities in finding jobs." BROADCASTING, 12 Ap. 1976, pp. 51–2.

2358. Nash, Abigail Jones and others. "Minorities and women in broadcast news: The national surveys." 1974. ERIC, 23 pp. ED 095 557.

2359. "NOW asks networks to give women more positive role." BROADCASTING, 22 Sept. 1975, pp. 59.

2360. "Report suggests ways for more women, minorities at public stations." BROADCASTING, 30 Ja. 1978, pp. 68–9.

2361. "The world of AWRT: A profile of the membership of American Women in Radio and Television, Inc." 1974. ERIC, 21 pp. ED 102 623.

10. Police Officers and Fire Fighters

2362. Bloch, Peter B. and Deborah Anderson. "Policewomen on patrol." Final report. 1974. ERIC, 76 pp. ED 102 369.

2363. "Finding females to become firefighters ins't easy; after only three of 91 women applicants passed its physical tests, Los

Angeles hired former Olympic gold medal winner Olga Connolly to develop conditioning program for women." WALL STREET JOURNAL, 27 Jl. 1976, pp. 1, col. 5.

2364. Fry, L. W. and S. Greenfeld. "An examination of attitudinal differences between policewomen and policemen." JOURNAL OF APPLIED PSYCHOLOGY, 65, Feb. 1980, pp. 123+.

2365. Garmire, B. L. "Female officers in the department." FBI LAW ENFORCEMENT BULLETIN, 43(6), 1974, pp. 11-3.

2366. Horne, Peter P. "The role of women in law enforcement." POLICE CHIEF, 40 Jl. 1973, pp. 60-3.

2367. Perlstein, Gary R. "Certain characteristics of policewomen." POLICE CHIEF, 16, Ja. 1972, pp. 45-6.

2368. (Police women). NEW YORK TIMES, 3 Mr. 1978, pp. 18, col. 5.

2369. Price, B. R. "A study of leadership strength of female police executives." JOURNAL OF POLICE SCIENCE ADMINISTRATION, 2(2), 1974, pp. 219-26.

2370. Sherman, Lewis J. "A psychological view of women in policing." JOURNAL OF POLICE SCIENCE AND ADMINISTRATION, 1, Dec. 1973, pp. 383-94.

2371. Weldy, William O. "Women in policing: A positive step toward increased police enthusiasm." POLICE CHIEF, 43, Ja. 1976, pp. 46-7.

11. Government Service

a. Federal Government

2372. Bernal, Ledia E. "Status of women at the Department of Health, Education, and Welfare." 1974. ERIC, 88 pp. ED 096 587.

2373. Coughlin, Ellen. "Changing the Peace Corps: Carolyn Payton, Carter's nominee for director, wants to recruit more blacks and women." CHRONICLE OF HIGHER EDUCATION, 11 Oct. 1977, pp. 8.

2374. Markoff, Helene S. "The federal women's program." PUBLIC ADMINISTRATION REVIEW, 32, Mr.-Ap. 1972, pp. 144-9.

2375. Mead, Margaret. "Women in National Service." TEACHERS COLLEGE RECORD, 73(1), 1971, pp. 59-64.

2376. O'Shea, A. "Sexual inequality on the Hill." WORKING

WOMAN, 5, Ja. 1980, pp. 17–20.

2377. "Study of employment of women in the federal government, 1971." 1973. ERIC, 177 pp. ED 079 502.

2378. U.S. Civil Serice Commission. *Expanding opportunities: Women in federal government.* Washington, DC: GPO, 1973.

2379. U.S. Civil Service Commission. *Study of employment of women in the federal government, 1970.* Washington, DC: GPO, 1972.

2380. U.S. Comptroller General "The Federal Bureau of Investigation needs better representation of women and minorities." 1978. ERIC, 54 pp. ED 177 265.

2381. U.S. Congress. Joint Committee on Arrangements for the Commemoration of the Bicentennial. *Women in Congress.* Washington, DC: GPO, 1976.

2382. U.S. Department of Defense. *Utilization of civilian women employees within the department report.* Washington, DC: GPO, 1974.

2383. Vogelgesang, Sandy. "Feminism in Foggy Bottom: Man's world, woman's place?" FOREIGN SERVICE JOURNAL, 49, Ag. 1972, pp. 4+.

2384. "Women hold just three of 32 U.S. Supreme Court clerkships in 1980, the lowest number in this prestigious post since 1976." WALL STREET JOURNAL, 4 Nov. 1980, pp. 1, col. 5.

2385. "Women: The missing half in government (views of S.P. Rockefeller)." U S A TODAY, 108, Je. 1980, pp. 2–3.

b. *State and Local Governments*

2386. Eyde, L. D. "Status of women in state and local government." PUBLIC PERSONNEL MANAGEMENT, 2, My. 1973, pp. 205–111.

2387. Froning, Mary L. "Minorities and women in state and local governments. 1974. Volume II - State Governments." Research report no. 52-2. 1977. ERIC, 405 pp. ED 154 185.

2388. Froning, Mary L. "Minorities and women in state and local governments. 1974. Volume III - County Governments." Research report no. 52-3. 1977. ERIC, 393 pp. ED 154 189.

2389. Kentucky State Commission on Human Rights. "Status of

women in Kentucky, State Agencies." Third report. 23 pp. 1977. (Available from Commission, 828 Capital Plaza Tower, Frankfort, KY 40601.)

2390. Kohler, Vicki. "Women in government: Local and federal." PUBLIC MANAGEMENT, 55, Feb. 1973, pp. 13–4.

2391. Malone, James E. "Minorities, women and young people in local government." PUBLIC MANAGEMENT, 55, My. 1973, pp. 16–7.

2392. Mohr, Judith. "Why not more women city managers." PUBLIC MANAGEMENT, 55, Feb. 1973, pp. 2–5.

2393. Reshad, Rosalind S. "Minorities and women in state and local governments. 1974. Volume 1 - U.S. Summary." Research report no. 52-1. 1977. ERIC, 431 pp. ED 154 187.

2394. Reshad, Rosalind S. "Minorities and women in state and local governments. 1974. Volume V - Township governments." Research report no. 52-5. 1977. ERIC, 370 pp. ED 154 191.

2395. Roxburgh, Richard E. "Women in government: The Burbank experience." PUBLIC MANAGEMENT, 55, Feb. 1973, pp. 10–11.

2396. Skinner, Alice W. "Minorities and women in state and local governments. 1974. Volume IV - Municipal governments." Research report no. 52-4. 1977. ERIC, 396 pp. ED 154 190.

c. Politics

2397. Britton, John H., Jr. "Black women in politics: Do we have a future?" ESSENCE, 5, Mr. 1974, pp. 80+.

2398. Gant, Liz. "Black women organized for action - they collect political IOUs." ESSENCE, 7, Oct. 1976, pp. 46+.

2399. Hawthorne, F. "In the running: Careers in politics." WORKING WOMAN, 5, Feb. 1980, pp. 65+.

2400. "If nominated, she will serve. (Few women are in Congress because few win party's nomination)." HUMAN BE-HAVIOR, 6, Dec. 1977, p. 54+.

2401. Lee, Marcia Manning. "Why few women hold public office: Democracy and sexual roles" POLITICAL SCIENCE QUARTERLY, 91, Summ. 1976, pp. 297–314.

2402. Smith, A. J. "Roads away from power: Women in political campaigns." HIGH SCHOOL JOURNAL, 59, Oct. 1975, pp. 16–26.

d. Military Service

2403. Arbogast, Kate A. "Women in the Armed Forces: A rediscovered resource." MILITARY REVIEW, 59, Nov. 1973, pp. 9–19.

2404. Blumenson, Martin. "The Army's women move out." ARMY, 28, Feb. 1978, pp. 14–25.

2405. Deindorfer, Robert G. "New military careers for women." SEVENTEEN, Mr. 1973, pp. 126+.

2406. Donelan, Frances and others. "Why women in the military?" WIN, 13(4), 1977, pp. 15+.

2407. Dudney, Robert and Jeff Trimble. "Women in combat: Closer than you think; special report." U S NEWS AND WORLD REPORT, 3 Mr. 1980, pp. 30–3.

2408. "Enchancing female participation in the Junior Reserve Officer Training Corps Program." Report of the House of Representatives. U.S. Ninety-third Congress, First Session. 1973. ERIC, 6 pp. ED 092 771.

2409. Fields, Cheryl. "1500 women nominated to three service academies." CHRONICLE OF HIGHER EDUCATION, 9 Feb. 1976, pp. 8+.

2410. Galloway, Judith M. "The impact of the admission of women to the service academies on the role of the women line officer." AMERICAN BEHAVIORAL SCIENTIST, 19, Je. 1976, pp. 647–64.

2411. Goldman, Nancy. "Changing role of women in the Armed Forces." AMERICAN JOURNAL OF SOCIOLOGY, 78(4), 1973, pp. 892–911.

2412. Goldman, Nancy. "The utilization of women in the military." ANNALS OF THE AMERICAN ACADEMY OF POLITICAL AND SOCIAL SCIENCES, 406, Mr. 1973, pp. 107–16.

2413. Jones, Caroline R. "Black women in the army: Where the jobs are." CRISIS, 82(5), 1975, pp. 175–7.

2414. Mahan, Beatrice T. "Career Alternative For Women: ROTC." VOCATIONAL GUIDANCE QUARTERLY, 25, Dec. 1976, pp. 163–9.

2415. Morganthau, T. and E. F. Newhall. "Yes sir, women made the grade (graduates of the three big service academies)." NEWSWEEK, 9 Je. 1980, pp. 43+.

2416. "No 'special stresses' for women in battle: Interview with

Nora Scott Kinzer, military personnel expert." U S NEWS AND WORLD REPORT, 3 Mr. 1980, pp. 34+.

2417. O'Malley, Lillian C. "Marine Corps Reserve (F)." MARINE CORPS GAZETTE, 57, Feb. 1973, pp. 36-8.

2418. Phillips, B. J. "On location with the WACs." MS, 1, Nov. 1972, pp. 53-63.

2419. "Program toward equal opportunity in the army." DOLLARS AND SENSE, 42, Dec. 1978, pp. 17+.

2420. Reilly, T. "Women in the Navy—from typewriters to airplanes." PROFILE, 20(5), 1977, pp. 10+.

2421. Segal, David R. and others. "Military service for female and black youth: A perceived mobility opportunity." YOUTH AND SOCIETY , 10(2), 1978, pp. 127-34.

2422. Shapley, D. "Why not combat?" NEW REPUBLIC, 1 Mr. 1980, pp. 16-7.

2423. Thomas, Patricia J. "The female naval officer: What is her role." 1978. ERIC, 23 pp. ED 173 723.

2424. Thomas, Patricia J. and Kathleen P. Durning. "The young navy woman: Her work and role orientation." YOUTH AND SOCIETY, 10(2), 1978, pp. 135-58.

2425. Turner, Hester. "Women in military services (United States)." DEFENSE MANAGEMENT JOURNAL, 6, Wint. 1970, pp. 12-5.

2426. U.S. Congress. House. Committee on Armed Services. *Hearings on HR 9832 to eliminate discrimination based on sex with respect to the appointment and admissions of persons to the Service Academies, also H.R. 10705, H.R. 11727, H.R. 11268, H.R. 11711, and H.R. 13729.* Washington, DC: GPO, 1975.

2427. U.S. Department of Defense. *Rights and benefits for Navy men, women and their families.* Washington, DC: GPO, 1972.

2428. U.S. Department of Labor. *Final-report on status of minorities and women in Department of Labor, Secretary's EEO Task Force.* Washington, DC: GPO, 1971.

2429. Vitola, Bart M. and others. "Characteristics of women in the Air Force 1970 through 1973." 1974. ERIC, 17 pp. ED 102 345.

2430. Weiss, Laura B. "Woman in the military." CONGRESSIONAL QUARTERLY WEEKLY REPORT, 21 Ap. 1979, pp. 741-3.

2431. (Women in the military). NEW YORK TIMES, 7 Mr. 1978, pp. 34, col. 1.
2432. "Women in the United States Armed Forces." CONGRESSIONAL DIGEST, 59, Ap. 1980, pp. 102+.

12. Technology

a. Science

2433. American College Testing Program. *Women in science and technology: Careers for today and tomorrow.* 16 pp. (Available from Publications Dept. ACT National Office, 2201 N. Dodge Street, P.O. Box 168, Iowa City, IA. 52240.)
2434. Aruitti, Rita. "Women in science: Women drink water while men drink wine." SCIENCE FOR THE PEOPLE, 8, Mr. 1976, pp. 24-6.
2435. Bachtold, Louise M. and Emmy E. Werner. "Personality characteristics of women scientists." PSYCHOLOGICAL REPORTS, 31, Oct. 1972, pp. 391-6.
2436. Cassidy, Marie M. and others. "The extent of participation of women in the sciences." Final report. 1979. ERIC, 401 pp. ED 180 745.
2437. Fields, Cheryl M. "Women in science: Breaking the barriers." CHRONICLE OF HIGHER EDUCATION, 13 Oct. 1977, pp. 7-8.
2438. Hansen, Richard A. and James Neujahr. "Career development of males and females gifted in science." JOURNAL OF EDUCATIONAL RESEARCH, 68, Sept. 1974, pp. 43-5.
2439. Hansen, Richard A. and James L. Neujahr. "A comparison of career development between males and females gifted in science." 1973. ERIC, 9 pp. ED 087 952.
2440. Kashket, Eva Ruth and others. "Status of women microbiologist." SCIENCE, 182, Feb. 1974, pp. 1162-3.
2441. Keeves, John P. and Alison D. Read. "Sex differences in preparing for scientific occupations." 1974. ERIC, 35 pp. ED 110 341.
2442. Lantz, Alma E. and others. "Reentry programs for female scientists." Final report. 1979. ERIC, 333 pp. ED 182 112.
2443. Mattill, J. "Women still on the short end of science." TECHNICAL REVIEW, 82, My 1980, pp. 86+.

2444. "New data show uneven progress for women and minorities in science." SCIENCE, 202, Nov. 1978, pp. 507–8.

2445. Paldy, Lester G. "National and legislative view: The advancement of women in scientific careers." JOURNAL OF COLLEGE SCIENCE TEACHING, 8(1), 1978, pp. 48–50, 53.

2446. Paznik, J. R. "Women seeking to become asset of chemical industry." CHEMICAL MARKETING REPORT, 212, Oct. 1977, pp. 14+.

2447. Randall, J. "Women's place in scientific research, a new look at an old problem." CHANGE, 10, Feb. 1978, pp. 46–7.

2448. "Report on 'The Participation of Women in Scientific Research' (Conference held as part of an AAAS research study project, October 17-20, 1977, in Washington, D.C.; Point/counterpoint (discussion between Philip Handler and Estelle Ramev)." COMMENT, 11, Feb. 1979, pp. 2–3.

2449. *Resources for women in science.* November 1980. 4 pp. (Available from Women in Science Inc., 1346 Connecticut Avenue, NW, Ste 1122, Washington, DC 20036.)

2450. Roark, Anne. "Senate panel would spend $23 million to encourage women to go into science." CHRONICLE OF HIGHER EDUCATION, 5 My. 1980, pp. 15+.

2451. Roark, Anne. "Women in science: Unequal pay, unsold ideas, and sometimes, unhappy marriage." CHRONICLE OF HIGHER EDUCATION, 21 Ap 1980, pp. 3–4.

2452. Roark, Anne. "Women scientists treated equitably, sociologist finds." CHRONICLE OF HIGHER EDUCATION, 5 Nov. 1979, pp. 1+.

2453. Roscher, N.M. "Updating women chemists for active careers." JOURNAL OF COLLEGE SCIENCE TEACHING, 7, Mr. 1978, pp. 220–2.

2454. Ruina, Edith, ed. "Women in science and technology." 1973. ERIC, 43 pp. ED 095 293.

2455. Smith, Walter Scott. "Increasing the participation of women in science careers." 1974. ERIC, 7 pp. ED 098 057.

2456. Strauss, Mary Jo Boehm. "Wanted: More women in science." AMERICAN BIOLOGY TEACHER, 40(3), 1978, pp. 181–5+.

2457. Tomlinson, E. and J. C. DiLeo. "Broadening horizons: Careers for women in science." JOURNAL OF COLLEGE

STUDENT PERSONNEL, 21, Nov. 1980, pp. 570-1.

2458. U.S. Congress. Senate. Subcommittee on Health and Scientific Research. *National Science Foundation Authorization Act for FY 79 and FY 80 and the Women in Science and Technology Equal Oportunity Act.* Washington, DC: GPO, 1978.

2459. White, Martha A. "Psychological and social barriers to women in science." SCIENCE, Oct. 1970, pp. 413-16.

2460. "Women astronomers face obstacles in profession." PHYSICS TODAY, 28(1), 1975, pp. 119+.

2461. "Women chemists (Committee report)." CHEMICAL AND ENGINEERING NEWS, 50, Oct. 1972, pp. 26+.

2462. "Women in the age of science and technology." IMPACT OF SCIENCE ON SOCIETY, 20, Ja.-Mr. 1970, pp. 5-105.

2463. (Women in the hard sciences). NEW YORK TIMES, 20 Nov. 1978, Sec. 4, pp. 11, col. 5.

2464. (Women scientists). NEW YORK TIMES, 10 Ja. 1979, Sec. 4, pp. 15, col. 2.

2465. "Women's toehold on chemistry faculties still just that." CHEMISTRY AND ENGINEERING NEWS, 54, Nov. 1976, pp. 47-8.

2466. Zuckerman, Harriet and Jonathan R. Cole. "Women in American science." MINERVA, 13, Spr. 1975, pp. 82-102.

b. *Engineering*

2467. Adrian, D. "Chauvinism rampant in her profession, an engineer charges (E. Duignan-Wood)." AIR CONDITIONING, HEATING AND REFRIGERATION NEWS, 149, Ja. 1980, pp. 3+.

2468. Alden, John D. "Women and minorities in engineering." ENGINEERING EDUCATION, Ap. 1974, pp. 498-504.

2469. "Anatomy of a female engineer. (Occupational stereotypes of engineers and women in field)." HUMAN BEHAVIOR, 6, Nov. 1977, pp. 72+.

2470. Bugliaro, George and others, eds. "Women in engineering, bridging the gap between society and technology." 1971. ERIC, 112 pp. ED 086 070.

2471. Minor, Barbara. "Enginering—A career for 330 women at Boeing." JOURNAL OF AEROSPACE EDUCATION, 8 Nov. 1974, pp. 10-11.

2472. O'Brien, J. Edwin. "Opportunities and challenges for women engineers in industry." 1974. ERIC, 18 pp. ED 101 117.

2473. Roysdon, Christy. *Women in engineering: A bibliography on their progress and prospects.* 1975. 22 pp. (Available from Council of Planning Librarians, Monticello, IL.)

2474. "Short of men, engineering firms turn to women." NEW SCIENTIST, 77, Mr. 1978, pp. 811+.

c. Other Technology Fields

2475. Bobbitt, Billie M. "Women—technical fields and the time trap." 1974. ERIC, 31 pp. ED 099 712.

2476. Callanen, Glenda G. "Futute space exploration: An equal opportunity employer?" 1975. 8 pp. (Available from Rand Corp., Santa Monica, CA 90406.)

2477. "Computer jobs increasing for women." ELECTRONIC NEWS, 25, Je. 1979, pp. supp. 12S+.

2478. David, Deborah Sarah. "Career patterns and values: A study of men and women in science and engineering." 1971. ERIC, 263 pp. ED 094 933.

2479. Davis, Trenton G., Y. J. Leo, and Richard E. Padgett. "Acceptance of female environmentalists." JOURNAL OF ENVIRONMENTAL HEALTH, 37, Nov.-Dec. 1974, pp. 256–60.

2480. Perrucci, Carolyn Cummings. "Minority status and the pursuit of professional careers: Women in science and engineering (based on conference paper)." SOCIAL FORCES, 47, Dec. 1970, pp. 245–59.

2481. Rose, Clare and Sally Ann Menninger. "Women in computer sciences." 1979. ERIC, 11 pp. ED 180 426.

2482. Trotter, Virginia Y. "The future for women in science and engineering." 1976. ERIC, 11 pp. ED 133 205.

2483. Vetter, Betty M. "Recent changes in opportunities for women in science and engineering." 1976. ERIC, 8 pp. ED 133 222.

2484. Vetter, Betty M. and others. "Labor force participation of women trained in science and engineering and factors affecting their participation." Final technical report. 1979. ERIC, 133 pp. ED 177 016.

2485. U.S. Congress. Senate. *Women in Science and Technology Equal Opportunity Act, 1979.* Washington, DC: GPO, 1979.

2486. U.S. Congress. Senate. Labor and Human Resources Committee. *Women in Science and Technology Equal Opportunity Act, 1980.* Washington, DC: GPO, 1980.
2487. Wexler, H. "Women in mathematics: An overview." AMERICAN EDUCATION, 16, Je. 1980, pp. 38+.
2488. "Women Ph.D's in industry fare poorly (Report from the National Research Council's Commission on Human Resources)." BIOSCIENCE, 30, Ja. 1980, pp. 62+.

13. Social Work, Counseling and Psychology

2489. Astin, Helen S. "Employment and career status of women psychologists." AMERICAN PSYCHOLOGIST, 27, My. 1972, pp. 371–81.
2490. Chafetz, Janet Saltzman. "Women in social work." SOCIAL WORK, 17, Sept. 1972, pp. 12–8.
2491. Denmark, Florence L. "Women in psychology in the United States." 1978. ERIC, 24 pp. ED 171 166.
2492. Kitchener, Karen G. and others. "A study of counseling center hiring practices: What does it take for a woman to be hired?" Student development report volume XII, number 1, 1974-75. 1974. ERIC, 27 pp. ED 106 692.
2493. Nathan, M. M., S. Rouce and B. Lubin. "Career status and satisfaction of women psychologists in medical schools." PROFESSIONAL PSYCHOLOGY, 10 (1), 1979, pp. 104–109.
2494. "Report of the Task Force on the Status of Women in Psychology." AMERICAN Psychologist, 28, Jl. 1973, pp. 611-6.

14. Self-Employment

2495. Adrian, D. "Housewife takes over sheet metal business after husband's death." AIR CONDITIONING, HEATING AND REFRIGERATION NEWS, 149, Ja. 1980, pp. 3+.
2496. "First economic survey available of businesses owned by women." COMMERCE IN AMERICA, 1, Feb. 1976, pp. 18+.
2497. Hurwitt, Anne. "Women business owners: Small but growing number." NEW DIRECTIONS FOR WOMEN, 7, Wint. 1978-9, pp. 11+.
2498. Pearson, J. "Women who farm—a preliminary portrait."

SEX ROLES, 6, Ag. 1980, pp. 561-74.

2499. Pearson, Jessica. "Note on female farmers." RURAL SOCIOLOGY, 44, Spr. 1979, pp. 189-200.

2500. "Presidential task force created to help women become business owners." COMMERCE IN AMERICA, 2, Sept. 1977, pp. 11+.

2501. Scott, G. "Women retailers mean business." BLACK ENTERPRISE, 9, My. 1979, pp. 43-5.

2502. Thomas, Sherry. "58 years a farmer." COUNTRY WOMEN, 31, Nov. 1978, pp. 21+.

2503. U.S. Bureau of Census. Office of Minority Business Enterprise. *Women owned businesses, 1972.* Washington, DC: GPO, 1976.

2504. U.S. Congress. House. Subcommittee on Minority Enterprise and General Oversight. *Women in Business (Hearings).* Washington, DC: GPO, 1977.

2505. U.S. Congress. House. Subcommittee on Minority Enterprise and General Oversight. *Women in Business (Report).* Washington, DC: GPO, 1977.

2506. U.S. Small Business Administration. *Women and the Small Business Administration.* Washington, DC: GPO, 1976.

2507. "Women rise as entrepreneurs." BUSINESS WEEK, 25 Feb. 1980, pp. 85-6+.

2508. Zaleski, Sarah Juniel. "Starting your own business on a shoestring." GRADUATE WOMAN, 73, Sept.-Oct. 1979, pp. 28-31.

15. Entertainment and Professional Sports

2509. Bonham, B. "Women in the graphic arts." GRAPHIC ARTS MONTHLY, 49, Jl. 1977, pp. 51+.

2510. Dyer, K. F. "Social influences on female athletic performance." JOURNAL OF BIOSOCIAL SCIENCE, 8(2), 1976, pp. 123-9.

2511. Epstein, Helen. "All in a day's work. Notes from the orchestra pit (Musicians)." MS, 5, Ap. 1977, pp. 106+.

2512. (Female athletes). NEW YORK TIMES, 24 Jl. 1977, pp. 21, col. 6.

2513. Greendorfer, S. L. "Role of socializing agents in female sport involvement." RESEARCH QUARTERLY, 48, My. 1977, pp. 304-10.

2514. Jepson, B. "You've come a long way: Women in symphony orchestras." MUSIC JOURNAL, 35, Dec. 1977, pp. 12-8.

2515. Jepson, Barbara. "American women in conducting." FEMINIST ART JOURNAL, 4, Wint. 1975-76, pp. 13-8.

2516. Lotner, Larry. 'The return of women models." ART DIRECTION, 25, Sept. 1973, pp. 30-4.

2517. Marks, J. "Changing world of women in sports." TEEN, 24, Ap. 1980, pp. 9+.

2518. Murphy, Johnny. "Climb to fame easing for women in country music; total dedication required." MUSIC SCENE, No. 305, Jan.-Feb. 1979, pp. 10-11.

2519. Neuls-Bates, Carol. *The status of women in college music: Preliminary studies. Proceedings of the Meeting on Women in the Profession, Seventeenth Annual Meeting of the College Music Society, University of Iowa, Iowa City, February 15, 1975.* 1976. 34 pp. (Available for $1.00 from the College Music Society, c/o Dept. of Music, State University of New York, Binghamton, NY 13901.)

2520. Phillips, Karen. "Women musicians offer advice." MUSIC JOURNAL, 31, Mr. 1974, pp. 18-9+.

2521. Schurr, Evelyn L. and Joan A. Philipp. "Women's sports officials." JOURNAL OF HEALTH, PHYSICAL EDUCATION, AND RECREATION, 42, Nov.-Dec. 1971, pp. 71+.

2522. (Sex differences in sports). NEW YORK TIMES, 18 My. 1980, Sec. 6, pp. 30-3+.

2523. Shields, S. "Women musicians: In step with the times." SCHOOL MUSICIAN, 49, Nov. 1977, pp. 64-6.

2524. Stabiner, Karen. "The Belly Room presented comediennes (Women stand-up comediennes)." MOTHER JONES, 4, Jl. 1979, pp. 45-9.

16. Other Occupations

2525. Banner, Lois W. "Why women have not been great chefs." SOUTH ATLANTIC QUARTERLY, 72, Spr. 1973, pp. 198-212.

2526. Barton, Amy E. "Compesinas: Women farmworkers in the California agricultural labor force." Report of a study project by the California Commission on the Status of Women. 1977. ERIC, 77 pp. ED 167 322.

2527. Berkeley, Ellen Perry. "Women in architecture." ARCHI-

TECTURAL FORUM, 137, Sept. 1972, pp. 46–53.

2528. "Final report of the Ad Hoc Committee on the Status of Women in the Historical Profession." 1970. ERIC, 43 pp. ED 065 065.

2529. Flora, Cornelia B. "Woman in rural sociology." RURAL SOCIOLOGY, 37, Sept. 1972, pp. 454–62.

2530. Henry, Alice and Janis Kelly. "Prostitutes convention." OFF OUR BACKS, 6, Jl.-Ag. 1976, pp. 2–3+.

2531. Hernandez, Jose, Jay Strauss and Edwin Driver. "The misplaced emphasis on opportunity for minorities and women in sociology." AMERICAN SOCIOLOGIST, 8, Ag. 1973, pp. 121–4.

2532. Howe, Louise Kapp. "A summer in the life of a beauty parlor. The stories of five women who work there." MS, 5, Mr. 1977, pp. 52–5+.

2533. Johnson, Carolyn R. *Women in architecture: An annotated bibliography and guide to sources of information.* 1974. 25 pp. (Available from Council of Planning Librarians, Monticello, IL)

2534. Kanuk, Leslie. "Women in industrial selling." JOURNAL OF MARKETING, 42, Ja. 1978, pp. 87–91.

2535. Kayem, M. "Women in the hospitality industry." CORNELL HOTEL AND RESTAURANT ADMINISTRATION QUARTERLY, 17, Ag. 1976, pp. 40–9.

2536. Lenorovitz, J. M. "New United pilot hiring plan stresses minorities, females." AVIATION WEEK, 107, Oct. 1977, pp. 30–1.

2537. MacMillian, Jackie. "Prostitution as sexual politics." QUEST, 4, Summ. 1977, pp. 41–50.

2538. Maddox, Brenda. "A woman's place is at the switchboard." NEW SCIENTIST, 69, Mr. 1976, pp. 614–5.

2539. Meredith, Gerald M. and Kathleen M. Bauske. "Gender preference and stereotypes in hiring of licensed beauty operators." PSYCHOLOGICAL REPORTS, 39, Ag. 1976, pp. 46+.

2540. Meredith, Jesse. "Conditions of child care workers neglected." UNION W.A.G.E., No. 60, Jl.-Ag. 1980, pp. 20+.

2541. Moles, Elizabeth R. and Norman L. Friedman. "The airline hostess: Realities of an occupation with a popular culture image." JOURNAL OF POPULAR CULTURE, 7, Fall, 1973, pp. 305–13.

2542. Richardson, Alan and Meryl Stanton. "Role strain among sales girls in a department store." HUMAN RELATIONS, 26, Ag. 1973, pp. 517–36.

2543. Scacco, Anthony M., Jr. "Some observations about women and their role in the field of corrections." AMERICAN JOURNAL OF CORRECTIONS, 34, Mr.-Ap. 1972, pp. 10–2.

2544. Sheehy, Gail. "Caste and class in the hustling trade." NEW YORK, 24 Ap. 1972, pp. 38–44.

2545. Sheehy, Gail. "The economics of prostitution: Who profits, who pays?" MS, 2, Je. 1973, pp. 58–61.

2546. Swan, J. E. and C. M. Futrell. "Men versus women in industrial sales: A performance gap." INDUSTRIAL MARKETING AND MANAGEMENT, 7, Dec. 1978, pp. 369–73.

2547. Taub, Laurie. "Should women be meatcutters? An attitudinal survey." INDUSTRIAL AND LABOR RELATIONS FORUM, 8, My. 1972, pp. 1–33.

2548. Warden, Margaret. "Do women have an advantage in direct selling." SPECIALTY SALEMAN, 61, Ag. 1972, pp. 24+.

2549. White, Joyce. "Women in the ministry: Few serve as pastors." ESSENCE, 7, Nov. 1976, pp. 62+.

2550. Wills, Garry. "The liberated New York nuns." NEW YORK, 28 Ag. 1972, pp. 37–42.

2551. Wise, G. L. and others. "Sex and race discrimination in the new car showroom: A fact or myth?" JOURNAL OF CONSUMER AFFAIRS, 11, Wint. 1977, pp. 107–13.

2552. Wisse, R. R. "Women as conservative rabbis?" COMMENTARY, 68, Oct. 1979, pp. 59–64. Discussion, 69, Feb. 1980, pp. 20–4+.

2553. "Women in political science. Studies and reports of the APSA committee on the status of women in the profession, 1969-71." 1971. ERIC, 143 pp. ED 065 025.

2554. "Women in the railroad industry." QUARTERLY REVIEW, Ap.-Je. 1970, pp. 23–7.

2555. Woods, Susan. "Waitressing: Taking control of our work." QUEST, 5, Summ. 1979, pp. 82–94.

AUTHOR INDEX

Abramowitz, S.L., 594
Acker, Joan, 1549
Adams, A.E., 1834, 1835
Adelman, Irma, 1365
Adkison, J.A., 2046
Adrian, D., 2467, 2495
Aery, S., 1746
Agassi, Judith Buber, 2161
Agin, A.A., 365
Ahmad, Mufti Jamiluddin, 2326
Aiken, Lewis R., Jr., 654
Alberti, J.M., 563
Albrecht, M., 1769
Albrecht, Stan L., 1157
Alden, John D., 2468
Alexander, Karl L., 33, 127
Alexander, Ralph A., 1740
Allen, A. Dale, Jr., 1106
Allen, Deena B., 330
Allen, P., 457
Allen, R.E., 1276
Allen, Robert L., 625
Alliance of Third World
    Students, 1547
Allison, E., 457
Allison, E.K., 1396
Allison, Paul D., 2010
Allwood, Cynthia L., 47
Almquist, Elizabeth M., 399, 482,
    512, 740
Alpander, G.C., 385
Alper, T.G., 106
Altenor, Aidan, 977, 980
Amber, R.B., 1976
American Association of School
    Administrators, 741
American Association of
    University Professors, 35, 204,
    1686
American College Testing
    Program, 2433

American Economic Association
    Committee on the Status of
    Women in the Economics
    Profession, 1158
American Library Association,
    2090
Anderson, Betty R., 1491
Anderson, Deborah, 2362
Anderson, Joan, 2207
Anderson, Julie A., 1397
Anderson, Lisa, 2193
Anderson, Peggy Engelhardt, 1118
Anderson, Ralph E., 742
Anderson, Rosemarie, 153
Andiappan, P., 1555
Andrisani, P.J., 1060
Aneshensel, Carol S., 1277
Angrist, Shirley, 399
Antos, Joseph R., 1652
Anundsen, K., 386
Appelbaum, Alan L., 2143
Apprich, Robert V., 452
Aram, J.D., 1533
Arbogast, Kate A., 2403
Archibald, Kathleen A., 2266
Arlow, Phyllis, 252
Arnold, L., 165
Arter, Margaret Helen, 2047
Aruitti, Rita, 2434
Arvey, Richard D., 1107, 1921
Ash, Philip, 1072
Ashby, Marylee Stull, 483
Association of American Colleges,
    626
Association of American Colleges,
    Project on the Satus and
    Education of Women, 606, 627,
    1006, 1600, 1704
Astin, Helen S., 205, 303, 400,
    1977, 2489
Athanassiades, John C., 2212

SUBJECT INDEX

A.A.U.P. *See* American
Association of University
Professors.
AFDC mothers' employment.
See Welfare mothers'
employment.
AT & T discrimination suit,
1898, 1913, 1917
AWS. *See* Alternative work
schedules.
Absenteeism, 882, 904, 906, 914
Academic achievement. *See*
Educational achievement.

Academic degrees. *See*
Educational achievement.
Academic degrees. *See* Degrees.
Academics. *See* College
teachers.
Accountants, 2286-94
Accounting careers, 2287, 2293
Achievement, Educational. *See*
Educational achievement.
Achievement encouragement
/career aspiration relation-
ship, 478
Achievement motivation, 106,
111, 122, 128, 155, 1066,
1098, 1103

Achievement motivation/career
aspiration relationship, 502
Addison-Wesley discrimination
suit, 1901
Administrative women. *See*
Managerial women.
Admissions, College. *See* Col-
lege admissions.
Adult education, 348, 379. *See
also* Continuing education;
Re-entry students.
Advertising professional women,
2352
Affirmative action, 77, 99, 212,

625, 863, 1487-91, 1493-94,
1496, 1500-01, 1503-12,
1515-21, 1523, 1525-28,
1530, 1532, 1534,
1536-40, 1542, 1545-48,
1689, 1836-37, 1849,
2341, 2536. *See also*
Bakke Case; Minority
recruitment; Weber Case.
Affirmative action in education,
1486, 1492, 1509-10, 1513,
1522, 1524, 1535, 1543-44
1691, 1698, 1970, 2004,
2006, 2028, 2082. *See
also* College minority-
admissions programs.
Affirmative action in
government, 1541, 2419
Affirmative action in libraries,
1499, 2100
Afro-American business-
women, 2299
Afro-American college
administrators, 2073
Afro-American college students,
161
Afro-American college students,
career aspirations, 416, 427,
433, 449-50, 735
Afro-American college teachers,
1996
Afro-American domestic
workers, 1953
Afro-American elementary
school students, 179
Afro-American family income,
1330
Afro-American high school
students, career aspirations,
459
Afro-American managers, 2231.
See also Afro-American
school administrators.

Sexist unemployment insurance, 1464

Sexist wages, 1380, 1385, 1396-1444, 1767, 1986, 1997, 2005-6, 2012-13, 2087, 2137, 2222. *See also* Equal pay for equal work.

Sexist wages/profit relationship, 1398

Sexist work evaluation, 1760-61, 1763-68

Sexist work-study programs, 170

Sexual harassment, 1705, 1707-14, 1716-19

Sexual harassment in education, 1704, 1706

Sexual harassment in government employment, 1715, 1720

Shipbuilders, 2166

Sick leave, 914

Single mothers' education, 700. *See also* Reentry students.

Single working mothers, 1340

Single working women, 889-90, 925, 2170. *See also* Single working mothers.

Sixth-graders, Sexist. *See* Sexist sixth-graders.

Skill/Unemployment relationship, 1480

Skill/wage relationship, 1419

Social classist education. *See* Classist education.

Social Security, 1573, 1586-99

Social status/employment relationship, 1234

Social workers, 2490

Sociologists, 2529, 2531

Soldiers, 2403-19, 2421-22, 2425-26, 2428, 2430-32

Sports officials, 2521

Sports scholarships, 680, 688

Sports, School. *See* School sports.

Sportswriters, 2327, 2332, 2342-43, 2348, 2351

Spouse/employment relationship, 1299

Spouse support/educational choice relationship, 712

Spouse/work status relationship, 1227, 1249

Standardized text sexism. *See* Sexist standardized tests.

Stanford University women teachers, 2017

State education agencies, 611

State government working women, 2386-96

Status attainment. *See* Job success.

Status/blood pressure relationship, 1728

Status/career aspiration relationship, 977, 980

Status/job satisfaction relationship, 1085

Status/retirement relationship, 1579

Status/sex role relationship, 1187

Sterilization, 1722, 1730, 1734, 1739

Stevedores. *See* Longshore workers.

Stress. *See* Job stress.

Striking women, 1693-94, 1702-03

Strong-Campbell Interest Inventory, 531

Strong-Holland Interest Types of Women, 520

Strong Vocational Interest Blank for Women, 512, 514, 519, 524, 528

Student achievement. *See* Educational achievement.

Student aid, 25, 32, 699. *See also* Sports scholarships.

Student loans. *See* Student aid.

Student nurses' work values, 414

Suburban working women, 2188

Success, Fear of. *See* Fear of success.